Forward !

RB Publishing

First published in 2002 by RB Publishing
116, Aldridge Road
Little Aston
Aldridge
WALSALL
WS9 0PF

For

The Boys' Brigade in Birmingham

Charity Registration No: 522846
Centenary House
89-91 Hatchett Street
BIRMINGHAM
B19 3NY

©**Copyright 2002** The Boys' Brigade, Birmingham Battalion & RB Publishing

ISBN 0 - 9521381 - 2 - 3
Design & Layout by **Robin G A Bolton**
Typeset in 10pt Book Antiqua by
RB Publishing, Little Aston, Aldridge, Walsall

Printed and bound in Great Britain by
Warwick Printing Company Limited
Theatre Street, Warwick, CV34 4DR

Also available from RB Publishing:
Badges of the Brigade Volume 1. The Boys' Brigade. ISBN: 0 - 9521381 - 1 - 5
Boys of the Brigade Volume 1. ISBN: 1 - 870708 - 50 - 4 [Originally pubs. by SB Publications]
Boys of the Brigade Volume 2. ISBN: 0 - 9521381 - 0 - 7

The Birmingham Battalion of The Boys' Brigade *1902 -2002*

Forward !

The advancement of Christ's Kingdom among Boys
and the promotion of habits of
Obedience, Reverence, Discipline, Self-respect,
and all that tends towards
a true Christian Manliness.

Paul Arkinstall - Rob Bolton

Congratulations Congratulations Congratulations Congratulations Congratulations

---

From the Bishop of Birmingham:

THE CHURCH OF ENGLAND
DIOCESE OF BIRMINGHAM

I would like to congratulate the Boys' Brigade Birmingham Battalion upon their Centenary this year.

I am particularly grateful for the contribution that the Boys' Brigade has made to the City of Birmingham. The commitment shown to the Christian nurturing and formation of young men has been a great example to us all and I wish the Battalion well in the future.

From the Birmingham County Commissioner:

The Guide Association, Birmingham, has been proud to be associated with the Birmingham Battalion over many years and congratulates them on the occasion of their Centenary. A truly splendid achievement!

Diane Bayley
County Commissioner

From *Joy Mutlow* Clerk of The Religious Society of Friends (Quakers):

Warwickshire Monthly Meeting of the Religious Society of Friends (Quakers), sends greetings and congratulations to the Birmingham Battalion of the Boys' Brigade on reaching their Centenary Year.

Quakers have encouraged and supported the Battalion's work for many years, serving in various ways, in Company activities and serving on Battalion Committees. We wish the Battalion success in the future, working as it does to encourage young people in Birmingham to seek and know God.

BRINGING GOOD NEWS TO YOUNG PEOPLE

From the Brigade President

His Honour Reg. Lockett

I send my heartiest congratulations to the Birmingham Battalion of the Boys' Brigade on your Centenary. This milestone marks 100 years of devotion and service to Boys and their Christian welfare.

Look forward to continuing the advancement of Christ's Kingdom among Boys. May He bless all that has been done and will be done in His Name.

BRINGING GOOD NEWS TO YOUNG PEOPLE

From the Brigade Secretary

Sydney Jones OBE

I extend to the members of the Birmingham Battalion my very best wishes and congratulations as you celebrate your Centenary Year.

In a fast changing society it is, indeed, a matter for congratulation that the Battalion has provided essential support to companies for such a long time and that it is successfully facing the challenge of adapting to meet the needs of present day young people without compromising the values upon which The Boys' Brigade was founded.

I hope the Battalion and the companies within it will continue to bring the good news of Jesus to boys and young men for many years to come.

THE GIRLS' BRIGADE

BIRMINGHAM DISTRICT

The Girls' Brigade, Birmingham District, wish to congratulate the Boys' Brigade Birmingham Battalion in this their Centenary Year. We are happy to be associated with your celebrations and wish you well for the future and long may you continue to bring the boys of Birmingham to be followers of our Lord Jesus Christ.

Dorothy Tomkinson
District Commissioner

'No one will ever know the full extent of the positive contribution BB has made to the life of our community over the last century. Men from all walks of life have found their moral and spiritual bearings through the work of the Brigade, not least among our Baptist Churches in the West Midlands. I count it a privilege to greet the Battalion at this special time in its history.'

Revd Brian Nicholls
Regional Minister (Team Leader)
Heart of England Baptist Association

scouts
be prepared . . .

The Scout Association County of Birmingham wish to congratulate the Birmingham Battalion of The Boys' Brigade in this their centenary year.

We have many happy memories of the co-operation between our two Movements and the friendships which have been formed over the years. We hope that the Battalion has a wonderful year of celebration that will be remembered with joy for many years to come. All good wishes to your members and Leaders.

Gordon Higginson
County Commissioner

SIR CLIFF RICHARD

To the Boys Brigade, Birmingham Battalion. Congratulations on your Centenary! Best wishes — God Bless Cliff

We thank God for all the boys who have been members of the Birmingham Battalion of the BB over the past 100 years, and for all they have received: for the fun and enjoyment; for everything they have been taught; and for the seeds of faith that have been sown. We pray that this excellent work will both continue and grow.

Revd. Kevin Jones.
United Reformed Church
Birmingham District

It gives me great pleasure to be able to offer greetings, on behalf of the Birmingham Methodist District, to the Birmingham Battalion of The Boys' Brigade on your 100th Anniversary.

In many of our churches The Boys' Brigade has been a significant part of our work with young people throughout the last century, and has been consistent in trying to offer a balance of physical, mental and spiritual challenge. Many of those in leadership in the church today can testify to the grounding in the Christian faith that they were given through their membership of the Brigade.

We thank God for all that has been done over the past 100 years and pray for God's continued blessing and guidance as the Brigade responds to the challenges of 21st century.

With best wishes,

Rev. John Hellyer (Deputy Chair)
The Methodist Church
Birmingham District

Foreword

Dr Carl Chinn MBE Community Historian, University of Birmingham

Sundays used to be a day when you didn't know what to do as youngsters. Normally you would visit family, listen to Family Favourites, have your dinner and wonder what else you could do on a day when you weren't allowed to run the streets loudly and play raucously. But there was one thing that you knew would enliven Sundays - and that was the Boys' Brigade Band. Do you remember how you and your pals would be standing around, fearful of disturbing the Sunday quiet? Then you would hear it. The faint strains of bugles and the distant thumping of drums. And slowly, the music of the band would get nearer and nearer, and you would start to half run up and down the street because you couldn't work out from which direction the sounds were a-coming. Suddenly, you cottoned on to which direction the Boys' Brigade were coming and you'd rush to that end of the street. Almost immediately they were there and you'd be half dancing and half walking beside them. And as quick as they'd appeared they'd gone and the music would drift off into the distance.

Whether or not you were in The Boys' Brigade, they made a big impression on you. That big impression later became stronger as you came to know the importance of The Boys' Brigade through the passing on of its virtues - respect, discipline, honour and Christian ethics. It is fitting that all those who have taken on board those virtues should be brought to mind in this a most significant history of the Birmingham Battalion of The Boys' Brigade.

Forward is its title and Forward shall go the Birmingham Battalion of The Boys' Brigade.

Carl Chinn

A Message from the Battalion President Tony Wakeman

Forward! has been produced to mark the Centenary of the Birmingham Battalion and highlights in pictures and narrative some of the personalities, stories, events and activities from the founding of the first company to the present day.

I hope the book will bring back many memories to former members and provide inspiration to today's leaders and boys. The BB has continually tried to keep up with changing times, new activities have been introduced and uniforms have changed, but the founding objective of the movement has remained, "The advancement of Christ's Kingdom among boys...".

I trust that readers will find these pages not only informative but interesting and perhaps fascinating and that they will provide an insight into our great movement. I pray that The Boys' Brigade will continue to flourish in the City of Birmingham, for there is still much work to be done.

A. R. Wakeman Battalion President.

The Lord Mayor's Parlour

On behalf of the City of Birmingham I am delighted to send congratulations and best wishes to the officers and members of the Birmingham Battalion of The Boys' Brigade. The Boy's Brigade has been represented in Birmingham since 1889 and since the formation of your Battalion, in May 1902, relationships between the City and the Brigade have always been most cordial and mutually beneficial. Your service to the youth of the City has been exemplary. The fact that a number of my predecessors have been either lifelong Boys' Brigade members or had been members 'in the ranks' is testimony to the benefit gained through years of service in the Brigade. I wish you every success in the future.

Councillor Jim Whorwood
Lord Mayor of Birmingham

Special Centenary Events 2002

Orienteering Event
Civic Reception Council House
Children In Need Fund-Raising
Carol Service at the Cathedral
Birmingham Quiz Company HQ's
Pop Quiz Centenary House
Praise Party Evening 2nd Sutton Coldfield HQ
Zoo Clean & Feed Birmingham Nature Centre
Golf Range Event Three Venues
Dr Carl Chinn Evening Carrs Lane Church
Camp Weekend Felden Lodge
Celebration Service Symphony Hall

Participation at:
 Lord Mayor's Show Birmingham
 Cosford Air Show RAF Cosford
 Bournville Festival Bournville

Party In The Field Aston
Brigade Council Meeting Aston University

The Authors

Rob Bolton

Paul Arkinstall

Robin joined the 57th Birmingham (Pheasey) Life Boy Team in 1957 and served in the company as boy and officer until 1983.

As an active officer, Rob was probably best known for his work with bands being Bandmaster of the Battalion's top band for many years, founding both the BB West Midland District and the National Contest. He was also involved in the production of the Battalion's 'Showtime 70' and organiser of the Centenary Bonfire on Barr Beacon. Throughout his time as an officer he was involved in a wide range of activities, always working to make the company an active part of the church.

Today, as an 'Associate Member' of the Brigade, Rob is a member of the National Archive Support Team and recently he was a Questionmaster for the National 'Masterteam' competition. A member of the Stedfast Association and the BB Collectors' Club he is the author of three 'Brigade' books before this one. Listeners to the 'Carl Chinn Show' on BBC Radio WM may have heard Rob on more than one occasion being interviewed about his books and Brigade memories.

Paul joined the 95th Birmingham (Pype Hayes) company shortly after it started in 1963. Although the 95th was a small company, it had its own band and attended Annual Summer Camp and Paul had a great time. He gained his Queen's Badge in 1968 and became a Staff Sergeant in 1970. Unfortunately the Company Section of the 95th closed in 1972 and he transferred to the 2nd Sutton Coldfield. An officer in the 2nd Sutton, he took over the Captaincy in 1992. Between 1989 and 1997 he was the North East Divisional Commandant. He has been a member of the Battalion 2002 Planning Group.

Always having an interest in history, Paul's hobby became focused during the Brigade's 1983 Centenary Celebrations when he joined the BB Badge Collectors' Club, now called the BB Collectors' Club. For some years he has been the Battalion's Archivist. It was Paul's idea to produce a book to record the Centenary of the Battalion, and work began some two years ago, firstly with the help of Carl Steadman and then in partnership with Robin Bolton.

CONTENTS

Preliminary Pages:

(iv)   Centenary Messages
(v)   Foreword - Dr Carl Chinn MBE & Message from the Battalion President.
(vi)   Lord Mayor's Message/ Centenary Events/Authors
(vii)   Contents
(viii)   Acknowledgements & Sources
(ix)   Preface
(x)   About the Boys' Brigade
(xi)   Introduction
(xii)   Boys' Uniforms 1902 - 2002

The Boys' Brigade in Birmingham 1889 - 2002

The First Company in Birmingham 1
The Aston Lads' Brigade .... 1 - 2
The Boys' Life Brigade .... 2 - 3
The Battalion is Formed 1902 .... 3 - 4
Birmingham's Boost 1908 4
Growth & Union 1909 - 1914 .... 4 - 5
The War 1914 - 1918 5
'With Which is United...' 1920s .... 5 - 7
Birmingham Looks Forward 1930s .... 7 - 8
The Darkest Hour 1940s .... 8 - 10
Tonics a plenty 1950s .... 10 - 11
Facing the Situation 1960s .... 11 - 12
The New Order 1970s .... 12 - 13
Two Centenaries 1980s .... 13 - 14
A 'Happening' Time 1990s 14
New Millennium 2000 and beyond 14

List of Birmingham Companies

1st - 12th 15
13th - 26th 16
27th - 47th 17
48th - 65th 18
66th - 91st 19
92nd - 96th 20
The Aston Manor Companies 20
The Sutton Coldfield Companies 20
Other Locally Designated Companies 20
The Boys' Life Brigade Companies 21

Location Map of Birmingham Companies 2002 22
Portrait of the Battalion in 2002 .... 23 - 27
The way we were 50 - 60 yrs ago 28
Battalion Presidents .... 29 - 30
Battalion Secretaries 31
Battalion Organisation. Office Bearers 2002 32

Battalion Headquarters

No Fixed Abode 33
Whittall Street 33
Wrottesley Street 34
'Temporary Accommodation' 1941 - 1963 35
Hatchett Street .... 35 - 36

Church Parades .... 37 - 42
Ambulance-First Aid .... 43 - 46

Follow the Band

The Early Years .... 47 - 48
Aston Bands Rule .... 48 - 49

Torchlight Tattoo .... 49 - 50
The Trumpet Call Obey 50
'Mad' Mulingani 50
FDF National Band 51
A Proud Record 51
Rudford & Felden 51
L/Cpl Alton Douglas 51
Soggy Jamboree 52
Strange but true 52
The 60s & 70s 52
Salute to the Queen .... 52 - 53

Brum Bits 'did yer know?' 54

Sports

Athletics .... 55 - 57
Cricket .... 57 - 58
Cross - Country Running .... 58 - 59
Football .... 59 - 62
PT & PE .... 62 - 65
Swimming .... 65 - 67
Table - Tennis .... 67 - 68
5 - a - Side Football 68
Other Sports 68
Sports Fields: Stechford & Pembroke 69

Civic Service 70

The Joys of Camp

The First Camp 71
Scouting 71
Camp 1914 72
Wartime Camping .... 72 - 73
More Group Camps .... 75 - 76
International & National Camps .... 76 - 79
The Future of Camping 79
Camp 1932 aboard the Implacable 80
Battalion Camp Criccieth 1929 81

Cadbury Bournville .... 82 - 83
The King George V Silver Jubilee Run 84

Young Brother

The Boy Reserves .... 85 - 86
The Lifeboys .... 86 - 87
The Life Boys .... 87 - 90
Outings .... 90 - 91
Displays, Pageants & Festivals .... 90 - 92
The Junior Section .... 90 - 92
Sportagama's .... 92 - 93
Annual Services 93
Just Like Big Brother .... 93 - 94
The Anchor Boys .... 95 - 96

Brummie BB Heroes .... 97 - 99
The Battalion Colours .... 100 - 101
Perrycroft .... 102 - 103
The BB Centenary 1983 104
Amicus/Charity 105
The Visit of Her Most Gracious Majesty Queen Victoria 1989 106
BUMP 107
Trophies .... 108 - 114
Statistics .... 115 - 116

Acknowledgements and Sources

The authors are grateful to the following for the help given:

Clive Andrews R.O. Former Battalion Vice President & Activities Convenor
Debbie Arkinstall BA(Hons) 2nd Sutton Coldfield Coy.
Archives Dept. Central Library, Birmingham
David Aubrey Q.C. Vice President, Wales District BB.

Fred. Barker 59th Coy. Ex. Battalion President
Don Bastin Ex. 46th Coy.
Paul Battarbee 51st Coy.
Peter Beale 29th Coy.
David Bevan 3rd Sutton Coldfield Coy.
Mr G. R. Bolton
Canon Roy Brookstein
Ralph Kilner Brown OBE MA, Ex. Capt. 29th Coy, Ex. Battalion President
Ken Brown Ex. 60th Coy.
Trevor Burgess Capt. 22nd Coy.

Paul Casswell 72nd Coy.
Janet Chamberlain (The late G. Oakton's Grandaughter)
David Chant, 2nd Sutton Coldfield Coy.
Dr Carl Chinn MBE Birmingham University/Radio WM
Rob. Clarke Capt 1st A Coy.
Paul Coley George Dixon G.M. School, Edgbaston
Ian Crockford 80th Coy.

Duncan Daniels 6th Coy.
Brenda Davies Ex. 62nd Coy. Ex. Junior Section Sec.
Alton Douglas Ex. 12th Coy.

Pat Finney Ex. 67th Coy. J/S Officer
J. B. Fletcher Ex. 25th Coy.

Trevor Gibbs 51st Coy., Ex. Capt 40th Coy., Ex. West Mids Field Officer. West Midland District Secretary
W. E. Glascott Esq. Ex. 10thA Coy.
Phil Goon Capt. 1st Water Orton. Coy.
Roger Gough Capt. 19th Coy.
David Gough 19th Coy.
Roger Green Battalion Secretary. 35th Coy.
Les Green Ex. 63rd & 64th Coys. Ex. Battalion Band Staff

Jim Hale Capt. 3rd Sutton Coldfield Coy.
R. Hotchkiss Capt. 7th Coy.
Les Howie MA (Hons) Dip Ed. Ex. Edinburgh BB. Proof Reading

Allan Jones Capt. 83rd Coy.

Albert Lakins Ex. Capt 10th Coy. Battalion Treasurer. Hon. Battalion VP

Lord Mayors Office Council House, Birmingham
John Mendus MBE 73rd Coy, Battalion Bandmaster
Don Mulingani Ex. Capt 72nd Coy.

Barbara Nash Ex. 40th Coy. Ex. JS Chairman Hon. Battalion V.P.

Roy Pagett 59th Coy.
Graham Powell (Photographer)
Rev. Ken Powell Bishop, Free Church of England. Ex. Capt. 52nd Coy.
John Pritchard 2nd Sutton Coldfield Coy.

Sir Cliff Richard Brigade Hon. Vice President
Dennis Riley Ex. Batt Sec./Administator Hon Battalion V.P.
John Russell Stedfast Association. (London)

Alf Smith R.O. Former Battalion Bandmaster, Ex. 32nd Coy.
Pat Stansbie Ex. 4th Sutton Coldfield Coy.
Paul Stansbie Ex. 4th Sutton Coldfield Coy.
Brian Stansbie Ex. 4th Sutton Coldfield Coy.
Carl Steadman 1st Alford Coy. Ex. 1st Castle Bromwich Coy.
Tony Summers Ex. Capt 55th/16th Coy.

Chris Taylor Capt 73rd Coy.
Pat Thomas Ex. Capt 4th S/C Coy. Battalion Hon VP
Geoff Tomkinson 8th Coy.

A. R. (Tony) Wakeman 73rd Coy. Battalion President.
Wesley Owen Books & Music, Birmingham.
John Weston Ex. Capt. 8th Coy.
Peter White 29th Coy.
Gill White Ex. Capt. 29th Coy. Chair of 2002 Battalion Steering Group
John Wilson 11th Coy.
Dave Wingate Capt. 57th Coy.
Olive Woolass 85th Coy.

Thanks to all the Company Captains & Staff who have allowed us to take the photographs for our 'portrait' pages and of course to all the members of the Battalion for their excellent co-operation.

SOURCES

Battalion Annual Reports 1906 - 1982 (Photocopies or originals in the Battalion Archive. Missing Reports: 1905-06, 1911-12, 1925-26, 1928-29, 1929-30.)

BB Gazette 1902 - Present. Collections belonging to John Russell, David Aubrey & the Authors.

Battalion Bulletin: Mainly 1990s - 2000s
Battalion Archive & Authors.
Postcard/Photo Collection. R. Bolton.

Collection of Display Programmes/Church Parade Service Orders/Camp Handbooks etc. Battalion Archive.

Photograph Albums, Battalion (DGB-1935-45), (DGB Photo Montage 1935 - 54) (Council 1949), 3rd Coy (1923-29) (1919 - 25) (Batt Camps 1920 -24), 9th Coy (c1915), 33rd Coy (1934-37) (1935-38), 8th Coy, 1st Coy, 10th A Coy, 32nd Coy, 55th/16th Coy, 57th Coy, 67th Coy (J/S & Lifeboys).

Album of Press Cuttings 1955 - 1975 Battalion Archive.

Folders of loose Photographs, 1stA Coy, 1st Coy, 10th Coy, 29th Coy, 32nd Coy. 57th Coy. 95th Coy, 2nd S/C.

Battalion Minute Books etc.: Ambulance Committee 1909 - 1912, Boy Reserves 1921-23. Life Boy Training Register 1937 -38 (& some 1958), Life Boy & Junior Section training Register 1961 - 1983. Life Boy Council Minutes 1927 -

1965, Life Boy Executive Minutes 1953 - 1966. Junior Section Council Minutes 1971 - 1973 (& Correspondence), Life Boy and Junior Section Committee Minutes 1965 - 1979.

Diaries: Alf Smith Ex. 32nd Coy 1933.

Company Histories/Publications: 1st Coy Aston (1891 - 1929) & (9th May 1945), 1stA Coy, 6th, 8th, (Anniversary Booklets, 25yrs, 50 yrs 75 yrs) 10th (1929),33rd (1994) 55th/16th , 57th (1973), 64th, 2nd S/C (1998).

Company Histories other documents
7th, 53rd, 60th, 72nd, 80th, 83rd.

Shields, Cups & other Trophies with records of Competitions. (Where available).

Interviews, personal recollections. (See Acknowledgements above)
Tape Recorded Interview with George Oakton BEM (1990) R. Bolton.
Tape Recorded Interview with Barbara Nash & Brenda Davies (2002) R. Bolton.

Boys' Life Brigade Publications/Letters. (Collection of the Late Sir Donald Finnemore)

Correspondence: The BB Centenary (1983) Folder.

Books: Sure & Stedfast. Spinghall et.al. 1983 ISBN 0 00 434280 1. Badges of the Brigade Vol 1. The Boys' Brigade. Bolton et. al. 2000 ISBN 0 9521381 1 5

Preface

Our title, of course, originates with the City's motto, but was first used in connection with the BB in Birmingham in 1927 shortly after union with the BLB. In the Boys' Brigade Gazette of 1st Jan 1927 at the end of a report on union celebrations the author finishes by saying, 'And now Birmingham - Forward !'

The Birmingham Battalion of The Boys' Brigade is in reality no more than the group of Boys' Brigade Companies within the Birmingham area. So is the whole group greater than the sum of all its parts? We could, in this volume, focus entirely upon individual companies, since on a weekly basis; this is the reality of the Battalion. Many of the pictures and stories in this volume originate at Company level, and rightly so. We have included as a special section, and as far as we know for the first time in a Battalion History, a photograph of virtually every boy in the Battalion in this Centenary year; not in a mass picture, but in his respective company. This is of course, one way to involve each member in what is, after all, his centenary. The Battalion, like the Church, is the people in it and not some building or set of rules. BB boys have, since the formation of the movement in 1883, been taught that 'their' company is always the best. As a kind of extended family it is both the focus of and vehicle for 'esprit de corps' - loyalty, friendship and , of course, guidance, both religious and secular. In Birmingham there has, for a hundred years, been a larger, wider extended family. This family has given support by providing exemplars of good practice, keen competition, training, publicity, proficiency testing and a great fellowship of inspiration, motivation, and dedication. Often numbering many thousands, led by people with firm commitment, far-sighted vision and deep Christian faith. This is the Birmingham Battalion, often referred to today as 'The BB in Birmingham'

Of course there are those who say, 'why go over the past, its gone and that's it.' We should know from experience that decisions made in the past affect everything we do today. We are products of our past. Not that we can't change direction, of course, or even strive for something better; our City's motto and the title of this book - complete with the addition of the exclamation mark - suggests that we can, and indeed we should, look forward. But how difficult is it to see where you are going if you don't know where you are coming from. The first thing we need to know when we give directions is 'from where are you starting?' and its not sufficient to say 'if I were you I wouldn't start from here!'. Our history describes the roots of the Battalion. A gardener who does not respect the roots of a plant is more likely to witness its premature demise.

There has been some misunderstanding about which 'Centenary' we celebrate this year. If it is the 'BB in Birmingham' then we are, unfortunately, thirteen years too late for it was in 1889 that the movement came to the city. If it is the 'Birmingham Battalion' then we are quite correct, that title having been used since May 1st 1902. We need have no 'hang-ups' about the word 'Battalion', as it has served us well for a hundred years and this service is the very raison d'être of this publication. If we, from this year, refer to 'The BB in Birmingham' when we mean an organisation to which all the companies within the area belong, then so be it. Strictly speaking we should be considering the fact that some are not in Birmingham at all, and what we are doing even calling them 'companies' if they are not part of a Battalion? Evolution, rather than revolution, is perhaps a healthier and more sustainable goal. Messing about with names could be problematical. Would Cadbury's sell more chocolate if they stopped calling it Cadbury's?

In writing this history we have, perhaps needless to say, encountered many difficulties. However, when viewed as challenges they have not seemed so bad. What we thought would be a brief passing shower of information turned into a prolonged deluge. We were told that bombing had destroyed the archives, we were told that people are not interested in the past, that folks would want to hold on to their own company memories and not share them with others, that it was more important to look forward than back, etc.. Some people admittedly were cautious but we have encountered nothing but enthusiasm for the project from all with whom we have been in contact, past and present members, friends and supporters. Selection of, rather than searching for material for the book has been perhaps, the single most perplexing aspect of the compilation process. The Boys' Life Brigade was never part of the Battalion, its members being united with the BB in October 1926, yet the influence of this organisation in Birmingham has been so great that we felt it could not be overlooked. A book of this size could be written about the Birmingham Battalion of the 1930s, the War Years, the 1950s or indeed any decade. Particularly impressive and tempting has been the wealth of available material from the 1932 - 1952 period when the numbers built to a peak of over five thousand; every event was then a 'Great' event. We have tried to maintain a balance in terms of the decades. We have attempted to use material from a wide range of companies to portray a wealth of activities. Unfortunately the 'best' photographs do not always appear with this politically correct bias. We can only apologise if we have failed to focus on a particular event or company. There have been nearly 300 companies over the years, so even one picture from each would cause problems with space. The most difficult job by far, has been in the 'selection' of people who are photographed and or named. Battalion Presidents and Secretaries are featured as are serving Hon. Vice - Presidents. Former Vice-Presidents, where possible, have been included in the General Text and appear named in photographs. It has been simply impossible to name all those dedicated men and women who have served the boys of the Battalion so well over the century.

Our brief was neither to produce an academic history nor one which was light and trivial. We have, hopefully, avoided the safe and often used ploy of writing a history of the BB 'as viewed from' Birmingham. The 'Acknowledgements and Sources' page lists much of the material which has been made available to us and by whom.

Our aim was to provide a readable, illustrated and accurate account of England's largest Boys' Brigade Battalion in a format which would captivate and enthral current members, former members and anyone else interested in uniformed Christian youthwork in this great City of Birmingham and beyond. We trust that we have been successful in our endeavours.

Rob. Bolton. Paul Arkinstall. May 2002

About the Boys' Brigade

Patron: H. M. The Queen

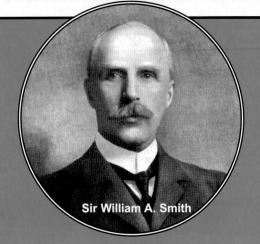

Sir William A. Smith

The original Boys' Brigade emblem, the anchor, with its motto of 'Sure & Stedfast' taken from Hebrews 6 v 19.

The Boys' Brigade object:
'The advancement of Christ's Kingdom among boys and the promotion of habits of Obedience, Reverence, Discipline, Self-respect and all that tends towards a true Christian Manliness.'

Brief History

The Boys' Brigade was founded at the North Woodside Mission in Glasgow on the 4th October 1883 by William Alexander Smith
(Knighted in 1909 for his Brigade work).

Smith was a committed Sunday School teacher who wanted to maintain discipline and retain for the church the teenage boys in his class. In those days boys started work at the age of thirteen and after being 'involved' in Sunday School for as long as they could remember, wanted something different. What they wanted was to mimic the world of the soldier. Soldiers, and their manly exploits, were very much the heroes of the day in the 1880s. Smith was a part-time soldier and able to give the boys a taste of that military life, but one which was anchored within the Christian caring framework of the Church. He demonstrated that there was such a thing as 'Christian Manliness'. After about eighteen months and the adoption of a simple 'uniform', Smith's 'Boys' Brigade method' had been copied many times over.
It soon became necessary to form a national organisation.Within a decade it had spread throughout the world.

The Boys' Brigade was influential in the formation of many similar organisations. 'The Brigade Movement' which followed included The Church Lads' Brigade, The Girls' Life Brigade, The Jewish Lads' Brigade, The Catholic Boys' Brigade & The Boys' Life Brigade. It was also responsible for much of the initiation of The Scout Movement and the Youth Service.

The present Boys' Brigade emblem is the old BB anchor with the words 'Sure & Steadfast', (Note the updated spelling) behind which is the red cross of The Boys' Life Brigade.

The Boys' Life Brigade

Dr. J. B. Paton

The BLB emblem with the red cross at its centre and the motto 'To Save Life'.

The Boys' Brigade - Structure:
The BB is Interdenominational with individual units (Companies) in virtually all of the Christian Churches. Over the years the lower age limit has reduced, initially with the growth of Junior organisations more recently integrated as Sections within the Brigade. Today, the structure is: Anchor Boys [5 - 9 yrs], Juniors [8-12 yrs], Company [11-16 yrs], Seniors [15-18 yrs]. There are also 'Amicus' groups in some areas with young people aged 15 - 22 yrs. There are some 90,000 members in the UK

Founded in 1899 by Dr John Brown Paton under the auspices of the National Sunday School Union, the Boys' Life Brigade took root amongst those churches which disliked the so-called 'militarist' tendency of The Boys' Brigade. Paton was an influential Congregational Minister who liked the BB method but knew that his church and other similar churches such as the Baptists and Quakers would not stand for military drill with 'rifles'- even if the rifles were only dummies! The BLB emphasised Life-Saving from fire and water as a substitute for military drill. In many places, such as Birmingham, the BB and BLB worked well together, but the affiliation of some BB companies to the Cadet Force in 1917 kept the organisations apart. Only in 1926, after the BB's abandonment of dummy rifles and all Cadet Affiliation, did the two organisations unite.

Introduction

The Boys' Brigade is a Christian Youth Movement. It was founded upon the 'twin pillars' of Religion and Discipline. If you really know the Boys' Brigade, however, you will not, for much of the time witness or experience 'overt' Religion, or indeed in 2002 even less outward discipline in the form of marching and uniforms. It's not that the BB has abandoned its great object or that it has changed direction, in fact it remains 'Stedfast', (well, 'Steadfast') today.

It was said of the founder of the BB, Sir William Alexander Smith, that he seldom talked Religion - he just practised it. This is the tenet which underpins the Boys' Brigade. Practical Christianity as part of the local Church interpreted through the BB 'family' - the Company. Officers lead by example, and are role models and mentors for their boys. Young people are challenged and taught to work and play together in a framework of informal education, care and understanding.

One function of a Battalion is to co-ordinate the activities of a group of companies in a particular area, to provide greater motivation and challenge than could be obtained in an individual company by organising competitions. Battalions also organise Training, highlight and encourage good practise and regulate the award of badges and other attainments. Publicity and extension are areas also entrusted to the Battalion, a slogan in the 1930s stated that BB companies were 'Centres producing the Better Boy in Birmingham' and that the city was better for it.

The BB has been in the City of Birmingham for as long as it has been a city. For a hundred years the Birmingham Battalion has been furthering the object of the Brigade... the Advancement of Christ's Kingdom ... and with this aim it continues like the great city itself, to go forward!

BB Boys of the 1970s

Boys' Uniforms worn in Birmingham Battalion 1902 - 2002

Including BLB Uniform

1. 1902 - c.1930 BB Pill - Box Cap, Belt & Haversack over normal clothing.
2. 1919 - 1927 BLB 'Full Uniform'. Before c.1919 similar to BB as per No.1.
3. 1927 - c1980s 'Full Uniform' Favoured by the former BLB Companies
4. 1927 - Field-Service Cap, Belt & Haversack over normal clothing.
   New - Style Field Service Cap worn after 1970 (Discontinued after 2006)
5. 1963 - Full Uniform. Worn with New Hat after 1970.
   (Discontinued after 2006)
6. 1999 - New Formal Uniform, no Haversack. Hat optional.
7. 1999 - New Informal Uniform an optional alternative.

The Boys' Brigade in Birmingham
1889 - 2002

The first BB company in Birmingham was connected with Camp Hill Presbyterian Church and formed in 1889. A Programme of a Display by the Coy, in 1890, showed that Sir John Barnsley was Inspecting Officer. His son, D. Gordon Barnsley, was destined to play a vitally important part in the development of the Battalion over the ensuing years.

Mr Henry H. Mason, a former Col. Sgt. from the 1st Birmingham and described as 'Birmingham's oldest BB 'Boy', was quoted in 1949 as saying that it required no small measure of pluck to belong to the BB in the early years.

'Gangs of street ruffians used to lie in wait for members proceeding to and from the Company Drill meeting each week - caps were bravely worn with the rest of the simple uniform'

The 2nd Birmingham Coy. was formed at St. Thomas' Church, Bath Row in 1891, and in the following year a third Coy. took shape at Christ Church, Sparkbrook. The 2nd was closed in 1893. Other Companies opened at

The Aston Lads' Brigade

Meanwhile, in the neighbouring Borough of Aston Manor in 1889, an organisation called the 'Aston Lads' Brigade' was started by one of Canon Eliot's sons and associated with Aston Parish Church and its numerous Missions. The Aston Lads' Brigade had a Brass Band and a headquarters at Hoadley's Bedstead Works, Aston Lane. The Captain was Rev. Arthur Pritchard. In October 1891, the Aston Lads Brigade was enrolled as the 1st Aston Manor Coy. BB. We can, perhaps, presume that what would eventually become the 2nd and 3rd Aston Manor Coys. were also taken under the same umbrella organisation perhaps operating as platoons, no doubt because their age was below that required for full BB membership. By September 1893 the 'Company' was 're-organised' by Capt. Doogood - a fitting name! A photograph exists, a copy of which is printed in a booklet published in 1929 captioned as 'the earliest company photograph of 1st Aston Manor Coy 1894'. However, all the boys have No's '2' or '3' on their caps an indication that

1st Aston Manor Company c.1894. The First Company Photograph

Left to right, T. Hill, R.E. Doogood (Capt), C.A. MacGuire, Rev. C.E. Cope, late Vicar of Christ s Church Stone, Staffs. Picture taken by Mr T. Hill.

The problem is that the boys have only No s 2 & 3 on their caps ! The uniforms, particularly the soft top pill box caps would indicate a date pre. 1896 as would the wearing of peaked caps by the officers. Mr Hill is wearing a cap badge which has a crown above, probably the badge of the Aston Lads Brigade. This badge has been identified on other early photographs being worn in the caps of the younger Boys.

Broad St Presbyterian Church (4th Coy. 1894), Edgbaston Congregational (5th Coy. 1895), Heath Green Road Sunday School (6th Coy. 1895) and Islington Wesleyan (7th Coy. 1896). Many of these early Companies did not survive beyond the first decade of the 20th century. The 2nd Company was re-started at St. Clements, Nechells as early as 1898. Generally it could be called a somewhat 'shaky' start.

they may have been in fact members of 'platoons'. Membership of the 1st was, in 1893, supposedly limited to boys of Vicarage Road Sunday School and the HQ.was at Alfred Street School. Capt. Buckley was appointed in July 1895 and by September of the same year the HQ was transferred to the newly built Dyson Hall. 1896 saw the official formation of the 2nd Aston Manor Coy. under the captaincy of Mr Doogood.

1st Aston Manor Coy. c.1896 Bromsgrove.
The 'non-BB' uniforms of the younger boys can be clearly seen.
These may have been the 'Aston Lads' Brigade' uniforms

It was also in 1896 that Cannon Sutton wrote:

'Dyson Hall favours the Boys' Brigade. The Company is known as the "1st Aston Manor" (the second is stationed at St. James' rooms)....'

Capt. MacGuire, the most famous of all BB Captains in Birmingham in the early years of the century, who appears on the '1894' photo was appointed Captain of the 1st Aston Manor Coy. in May 1901. The first canvas camp was held at Habberley Valley in August 1901. In 1904, the 3rd Aston Manor came into being as a separate Company. In February 1910, the title of the 1st Aston Manor was changed to '1st Birmingham (Aston) Coy.' as the Borough of Aston Manor was included within the City and the 3rd Aston Manor became the 17th Birmingham Company. We can find no references to the fate of the 2nd Aston Manor Company.

The Boys' Life Brigade

The Boys' Life Brigade came to Birmingham in 1901, just two years after the organisation was founded. There is an unsubstantiated newspaper report from the 1930s which states that the 1st BLB Company in Birmingham was at 'Mount Zion Chapel'. There is plenty of evidence, however that a '1st Birmingham BLB Company' was started at the Friends Institute Moseley Road on 21st March 1901, the Captain being Mr Herbert Darling. This was a Quaker Company, the Company President being Mr Barrow Cadbury from the famous chocolate manufacturing family. Sometime between 1901 and 1907 a 2nd Coy was formed of which we have no record. In 1907, six new Companies appeared; the 3rd (Moseley Road. Congregational), the 4th, (?) 5th, (?) 6th, (?) and 7th (Kings Norton Congregational). The 1st Kings Heath (Kings Heath Baptist) was formed in 1906. Another 2nd Coy was re-formed in 1912 at Stratford Road Baptist Church. In 1912, the 1st Birmingham BLB embraced 'Peace Scouting' relinquishing its BLB title. The 1st was re-formed by Donald Finnemore in November 1913 at the People's Chapel (Baptist) in Hockley. We dont know when the

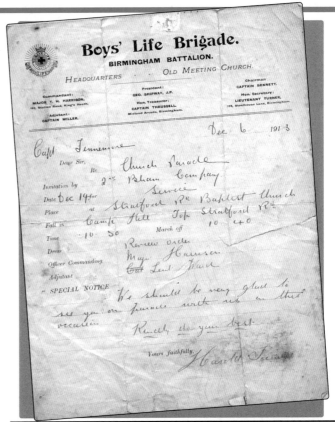

The letter inviting the newly re-formed 1st Birmingham Coy. BLB to take part in a Church Parade with 2nd Birmingham Coy. on 14th December 1913.

Capt. Donald Finnemore leads the 1st Birmingham BLB (People's Chapel - Baptist) c. 1915.

Birmingham BLB Battalion was formed, but it existed by 1913 with Headquarters at the Old Meeting Church. The President was Geo. Shipway J.P. the Commandant being Major T. H. Harrison from 1st Kings Heath Coy. The problems with 'defections' to the Peace Scouts paled to insignificance compared to the effect of the Great War. The Birmingham BLB Battalion found itself by Spring 1919 with a total of just three companies and 60 boys. Fortunately the effects of the war were temporary and within a year the number of companies rose to 14 and the boy-strength to 600. 1920 found the Battalion actively recruiting to reach a total of 1,000 boys. The year 1920 was a good one for the BLB Battalion with Church Parades, a Town Hall Display, Shield Competitions for Drill and Ambulance, Summer Rally and Sports and last, but not least, a United Sea-side Camp of over 300 a feature of which was that the Officers and Warrant Officers agreed to forego smoking and a smokeless camp was the result. In 1920 the Battalion President was 'The Rt. Hon. The Lord Mayor', Commandant A. Thrussell (Major, BLB), Adjutant & Hon. Sec. D. L. Finnemore MA (Capt., BLB). Two years later, when a party of members of the Danish BB The FDF (Frivilligt Drenge Forbund), visted the Battalion, the Battalion President was Hugh Morton Esq, J.P.

The Battalion is Formed - 1st May 1902

Under the terms of the Brigade's Constitution in 1902, six or more Coys could form into a Battalion, the main purpose and object being co-operation and competition. In the BB, the Battalion is not a 'tier of government' from National Headquarters, unlike outwardly similar organisations such as the CL&CGB. Each BB company is independently run by the church of which it is a part. On May 1st 1902, upon the formation of the Birmingham Battalion there were nine companies with a total membership of 541. Mr C. J. Cooke, Captain of the 6th Company and the founder of the Battalion was appointed the first Battalion

Ernie Glascott's CLB Membership Card 1896

President. From the outset the Battalion consisted of many denominations from most wings of the Christian community - Anglican to Methodist. The system of using a Battalion structure to enhance the work of each company had been proved beyond doubt in many other parts of the

UK where Battalions had been formed many years before. Growth was not rapid; two years after the formation of the Battalion, in the 'BB Gazette of 1st February 1904. Vol 11 p. 85, it stated:

'No report from the Birmingham Battalion has yet come to hand, but the annual returns show 8 companies on the strength, of which all but one, the largest-have sent in their contributions, averaging 11/-.'

According to a later Annual Report, the Battalion was 're-organised' in 1904 , but it does not say what was changed; presumably it was to introduce a more efficient system of returns! In Birmingham there had been informal co-operation between companies for years, including links with the Aston companies which would not be part of the Battalion for another five years.

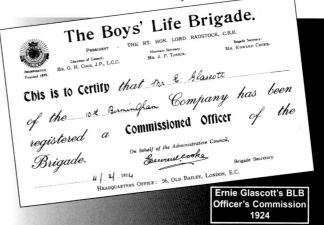

Ernie Glascott's BLB Officer's Commission 1924

Example and influence from Aston had even resulted in the formation of four Church Lads' Brigade Companies in the city: All Saints, Witton, St. Silas and Lozells.

Typical of this interaction between the organisations is the story of one lad who joined the St. Silas CLB in 1896 - Ernie Glascott. He went on to be a Quaker and founder of the 10th Birmingham Boys' Life Brigade (Friends Hall, Farm Street) in 1924, which then became the 10thA Boys' Brigade in 1927 after union with the BB. Ernie was involved with young people in his 'Day Job' working in Remand Homes and in the mid 1930s being in charge of the Copley Hill Hostel in Erdington a kind of 'halfway house' for ex-offenders. He was certainly respected in the 10thA. His nephew Eric who was in the company as a lad says that he was often known as 'Big Ernie'. Mr Glascott can be seen on the 1949 photo as one of the Battalion's senior hosts for Brigade Council, having responsibility for liaison with the University where the Council meeting was being held.

The new Battalion which had struggled at first to function due to financial worries, shortage of leaders and boys was, by 1907, at its lowest ebb. The Annual Report of 1907 - 1908 stated that *'we should examine ...where we have failed'*.

Heading from Boys' Herald 1908

A Stirring Story of Boy Life in Birmingham, of Particular Interest to all Brigade Boys.

Failure is not usually a word used in Annual Reports, but the Battalion had not increased. In fact, thirty boys were lost. There was, however, some light at the end of the tunnel. The 1st Battalion Display had been held in the Town Hall in 1907, and there had been '...*a great deal of foreboding lest we should be more heavily in debt than we were before.*' Fortunately, these fears were proved to be groundless and the Annual Report says '...*the public supported us in loyal fashion and we were able to hand over a substantial balance of £9.*' Besides the boys doing the entertaining, the Battalion was able to arrange some entertainments for the boys in the 1906 - 1907 Session, as the Annual Report points out: '*We also wish to thank Mr. Waller Jeffs for so kindly inviting the Battalion to his Display of Animated Pictures again this year. A most enjoyable afternoon was spent at the Curzon Hall, some 400 officers and boys being present.*'

Birmingham's Boost 1908

What a difference a year can make. 1908 turned out to be the year the Battalion really did move forward, with four new companies being formed and an increase of 182 boys. Why 1908? Well, there were in fact many reasons for this upturn in fortune. It was a special year for The Boys' Brigade - its Semi-Jubilee, accompanied by large-scale national publicity. The King and Queen visited the city and the Battalion were asked to line the part of their route inside the University Campus - a high profile spot. The Scout movement was advancing rapidly and scouting activities were being taken - up eagerly by the companies in the Battalion. By 1909, there would be an official 'BB Scout' uniform and badge. The city too was expanding, taking in the areas of Aston and Handsworth. A local author, Ernest Protheroe, wrote a story for the weekly boys paper 'The Boys Herald' all based on the exciting doings of Birmingham BB Boys. It was launched using the whole front page of the paper. Started in September 1908, 'Boys of the Brigade' was serialised and eventually turned

into a successful book. Being in the Brigade was becoming 'the thing'. By 1909, the Battalion Executive was arranging for the national Brigade Council meeting to be held in the city as well as contemplating a central Battalion Headquarters.

Two of the new companies formed in 1908, the 4th and the 10th would become pillars of the Battalion, both providing much respected BB Captains who went on to become eminent long-serving Battalion Presidents.

Growth and Union 1909 - 1914

1909 turned out to be the first of two significant 'union' years for the Birmingham BB Battalion. The two Aston Manor Companies joined - up, just as the City itself was taking the Aston area within its boundary. Two companies may not seem like much to make a fuss about, but one of them, the 1st Aston Manor under the captaincy of Mr. C. Macguire, was no ordinary company. The 1st was a large, progressive and efficient force, well led and highly motivated. It was just what the struggling Battalion needed. It was also opportune that the old 1st Coy. had folded because here was a brand new ready made 'first' which would lead from the front for the next twenty years and contribute enormously to the success of the Battalion throughout virtually all of the next ninety three years.

The years 1910 - 1914 were full of confidence for the future of the Battalion. However, the negotiations with the Army Council in 1910, concerning the possible entry of the Brigade in Birmingham into the Cadet Force, had been rather unsettling. Under the guidance of President Mr Alfred H. Angus B.Sc. and Secretary Charles L. Beckett, both anti-affiliation, the Battalion firmly rejected the advances of the military. Unlike the Church Lads' Brigade and Jewish Lads' Brigade, there would be no 'BB Cadets' in Birmingham, now or later. There was considerable progress in the following years encouraged by a series of significant events. The Fifth Annual Demonstration in March 1911 at the Town Hall was attended by Sir William A. Smith, Captain of the 1st Glasgow Company and Founder of The Boys' Brigade.

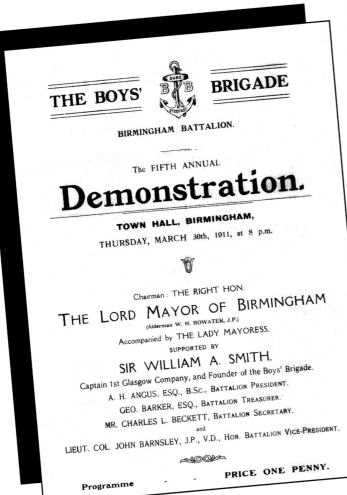

The Mayor was indisposed for the Demonstration so the chair was taken by Mr Angus. The Mayoress was presented with a bouquet of flowers by William Smith... Private William Smith the smallest boy in the Battalion! The event was a great success except for the view of the arena which was considered to be unsatisfactory for some of the audience. The Central Hall was chosen for the Demonstration in 1912 because of the *'clear view of the floor area from every seat in the hall'*. William Smith (that is the Founder not the Private) was given a reception at the Council House and took the opportunity of attending a number of Battalion Committee meetings whilst in Birmingham. A year later he returned to attend the Sixth Annual Demonstration at the Central Hall.

1912 was the year The Boys' Brigade Council met in Birmingham for the first time. The Council meeting at the Central Hall was chaired by Lord Guthrie with 200 members of council and many other officers in attendance.

There were representatives present from the Danish F.D.F. and the United Boys' Brigades of America. At last, after ten years Birmingham Battalion was 'coming of age'. Battalion reports in the period leading up to the 1st World War mention much co-operation with other uniformed groups within the city. For instance, the CLB was invited to provide judges for Drill competitions, and there was a Battalion representation at the Scout Rally in Perry Hall Park in July 1913 comprising members of the 1st Birmingham Coy. which ran a 'BB Scout' Troop.

The War 1914 - 18

At the start of the Great War the Battalion was soon involved in helping with the War effort on the home front. One project was assisting with street collections for the Prince of Wales' War Relief Fund and the Belgian Refugees Fund when nearly £200 was collected at some 15 stations throughout the city staffed by the BB. The Battalion was hampered by loss of Officers who had answered the call of King and Country. The Annual Camp in 1914, scheduled to be the first of many, was not repeated throughout the war years. In many ways the aim was to keep the activities of the Battalion going. Most events, such as the Swimming Gala and Annual Demonstration continued. Most companies remained 'open for business'. The Battalion Secretary who at this time convened the Executive Committee was looking forward to a time after the war when a *'central office for the Battalion'* would be required. The Battalion President since 1913, Lt. Col. D. Gordon Barnsley, Capt. 8th Coy. was on active service so Charles MacGuire, Capt. of 1st Coy. took on the responsibility. In 1918 a full-time paid Secretary was taken on in the light of increased work due to greater co-operation with other agencies in the city and the establishment of a Labour Bureau. The Brigade Council, due to meet in Nottingham in 1918, had the meetings switched to Birmingham at the last minute. The Council meetings were very successful and a tribute to Birmingham Battalion's competence and standing within the Brigade.

'With which is United...' The 1920s

After the war, with Gordon Barnsley back at the helm following distinguished war service and the award of M.C., the development and expansion of the Battalion continued. With greater size it became an increasingly significant part of City life. On January 14th 1920, by invitation of the Lord Mayor, a BB Guard of honour formed from 100 boys, including the Brass Band of the 1st Coy, was formed up outside the Town Hall. The occasion was the visit of H.R.H. Prince Henry (standing-in for H.R.H. Prince Arthur of Connaught). Battalion Trophies were being keenly competed - for and more were donated. The

Battalion Camp was revived, the first since 1914 being held in 1920. By 1921 there were 17 companies, 73 officers and 820 boys. Increasing membership and greater competition meant that in 1922 there was in addition to the Executive Committee, the usual Committees for Bible Class, Drill, Ambulance, Recreation and Band, but all with larger numbers and far more work. Many of the boys, it seems, were not that busy, there being much unemployment. The Annual Report was quick to state that the BB was the *'simplest and the least expensive'* organisation for boys. Gordon Barnsley resigned as President in 1924, due to work committments with the family building firm and was followed by Mr J. H. Donald Hurst, a Barrister.

The most famous 'Union' in the BB came about on 1st October 1926 when The Boys Brigade united with The Boys' Life Brigade. Donald Hurst, Barrister, and Donald Finnemore, Barrister, both relinquished their positions as President of the Birmingham BB and BLB respectively. With the two Donalds as Vice - Presidents Mr Hugh Morton became the first President of the new united Battalion. Left to Birmingham folk the two organisations would probably have joined forces years before. At Easter 1924, for instance, Alfred Angus, former President of Birmingham BB, now a college Principal, called a special national conference of the BB and BLB at Westhill College Bournville, to discuss union. However, he found that the type of relationships and degree of understanding between the two Brigades outside of Birmingham was not good. Many in the BB regarded the BLB as newcomers on the Brigade scene with little to offer. Many of those in The Boys' Brigade who were in favour of union wanted a simple 'take-over' of the BLB; this didn't happen.

In 1926, there were 20 BB Coys in Birmingham with a total membership of 749, and 17 BLB Coys with a membership of 567. The BLB had grown up within those churches in the city which adopted a 'pacifist' standpoint with regard to Brigade membership of the Government 'Cadet Force' and the use of dummy rifles for drill, both abandoned in the BB by 1926. Generally, the BLB strength lay within the Baptist, Congregational and Quaker denominations, all strong within a Birmingham proud of its liberal traditions. The BLB had an enviable influential presence in the City with high profile supporters such as the Quaker, Barrow Cadbury from the famous chocolate-making family. BLB Battalion Treasurer was Norman (later Lord) Birkett. Donald Finnemore had been a national prime mover for union following his Birmingham experience of how well the brigades could work together. It was wholly appropriate therefore, that the first Brigade Council meeting of the new Brigade, in 1927, would be staged in Birmingham, surely the finest testimony to friendly co-operation.

In Birmingham at the time of union, where two compa

The front of the Programme for the 1927 Annual Council meeting of The Boys' Brigade. Held in Birmingham, it was the first since union of the BB & BLB.

nies were found to have the same distinctive number, the senior in each case was allowed to retain it and the junior had the option of changing to another number or of adding the letter 'A' to the number. The only trace of this which remains in 2002 is in the designation of the 1stA (People's Chapel), originally the 1st Birmingham Coy. BLB, re-formed in 1913. Upon Union the `Pill Box' Hats worn by the BB in Birmingham were given up in favour of the Field-Service type similar to those worn by the BLB. The Autumn Church Parade on 16th Nov. 1930 at the Central Hall had 1,200 Officers and Boys present. The BB Gazette summed up the scene:

'The Parade was memorable as the first since Union in which the whole Battalion was in the same type of cap, all Officers and Boys wearing the new pattern. The gain in appearance was striking.'

The session 1927 - 1928 had been designated 'A Year of Crusade' by the Battalion, two more new companies were formed taking the total to 56, with the total membership rising to over 2000. The first Battalion Headquarters, so eagerly anticipated for many years, was officially opened in Whittall Street in early 1929, a great boost to the work of Administration, Committees, Training and Equipment supplies. More than 1,500 Boys paraded in Cannon Hill Park on Saturday, the 13th July 1929 , for the first Battalion review and display since Union. The inspecting Officer was Major A.H.S.Waters V.C., who was accompanied by Mr Edward Cooke, Southern BB Secretary, and the Battalion President, Mr Hugh Morton, was in command. The displays included fire drill, gymnastics, transport-wagon drill, tent-pitching, and first-aid.

Birmingham Looks Forward! - The 1930s

A turning point in the leadership of the Battalion came in 1930. Mr Hugh Morton's sudden and premature death and the retirement of Mr Donald Hurst brought Mr Donald Finnemore back into the Presidency with the Honorary President being Mr Barrow Cadbury. Mr Charles Lockwood Beckett's 25 yrs as Hon. Battalion Sec. were acknowledged. The Alexandra Theatre provided the venue for a 'staged' Battalion Display. The Annual Battalion Report in 1931-32, now running to sixteen pages and numerous photographs provides us with a helpful summary of what the Battalion was all about thirty years into its life: *'The Battalion does for the companies what they cannot do for themselves, thus enlarging their scope and usefulness. It has its central Office and Equipment and Publications Department. It has spacious Playing Fields at Stechford and organises Football and Cricket Leagues. It arranges systematic Swimming at most of the Corporation Baths. It has its combined Church Parades, Displays and a Seaside Camp in August. It organises inter-company competitions and examinations...'* During that session it had also appointed a permanent Secretary, Mr P. A. Lawrence a

man of many years' BB experience in the City. There is no mention of Mr Lawrence in the 1932-33 Report.

The 1932 - 33 Session brought with it a great sense of anticipation. 1933 was Brigade Jubilee Year and it was to

be a great excuse for celebration. The Birmingham festivities must have been amongst the first to start in the UK with the great Garden Party at Cadbury's in June 1932. (See page 82). Normal Battalion events were given the 'Jubilee' tag, but everything in 1933 was to be done in style. The Jubilee Demonstration at the Central Hall, the NCO's Jubilee Dinner at the Cobden Hotel, excursion to the Great Jubilee Display at Wembley, The Annual Sports moved to the Alexander Stadium and the Battalion Parade boosted by a special contingent of 'Old Boys' of the BB and BLB. Even the Summer Camps were dubbed 'Jubilee Camps' and of course one of those was the Great Camp at Dechmont on the Brigade Council weekend, September 8th - 11th. Thirty Officers and 60 boys of Birmingham were amongst 30,000 plus reviewed in Glasgow by Prince George in Glasgow that weekend. Back in Birmingham, there was the Jubilee Swimming Gala and the Jubilee Commemoration and Thanksgiving Service at the Central Hall. The pride of Birmingham, however, was the ambitious Pageant; 'Boys!' The Story of Boyhood through the Ages, performed over two days, 23rd and 24th October 1933. The event, which featured 400 members of the Battalion, was held at the Town Hall. A 24-page Souvenir programme was produced which expounded the way in which The Boys' Brigade by producing the Better Boy in its 61 companies and 40 Life Boy Teams, has made a better Birmingham. Boys! was described as *'a triumph of patience, skill, training, faith and enterprise.'* On a page in the programme under the heading 'BIRMINGHAM NOW LOOKS FORWARD!' Mr Gilbert Southall, Hon. Treasurer, appealed for cash to meet the balance for the purchase of the New HQ. The Whittall Street lease was due to expire and freehold premises in Wrottesley Street had been secured. Typically, profits from the Pageant were donated to a charity, the Birmingham Hospital Saturday Fund.

Mr Harry Anderson, Captain of the 4th Coy became President in 1933 starting a presidency lasting fourteen years, a period of continuous office never surpassed, and only equalled once since. There were to be many challenges facing the Battalion in the 1930s but the one regarded as most pressing in 1934 was to provide BB companies to operate on the new rapidly growing housing estates on the fringes of the city. The Annual report didn't mince words: *'Many thousands are living remote from any religious association at all, and unless much greater provision is made for the spiritual and moral training of youth in the new suburbs, there is a danger of a new generation becoming practically a pagan people.'* Clearly, the establishment of new BB companies was the answer. Typical, of such estates was the massive Kingstanding development to the North of the City and it wasn't long before new companies were established. In Kingstanding, the re-allocated 29th Coy, which met at the Methodist House of Friendship, was started by Mr R. K. Brown and the 57th Coy., run by the Society of

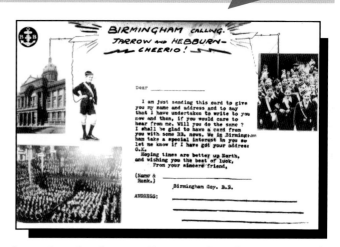

Friends in Sutton Coldfield, met at the Peckham Road Schools and the Kingstanding Community Hall. It is said that the 29th, a particularly strong company in the 1930s would march from Kingstanding into central Birmingham for the Battalion Parade and then back again afterwards. They must have been the fittest company in the Battalion! In August 1934 the 1stA Coy made a visit to Germany for their '21st Birthday Camp'. They were welcomed by a party of officers from the Hitler Youth from Godesberg on the Rhine. The party was hosted by schoolmaster Herr Koch for twelve days of rambles, bathing, games, receptions and visits. The BB Gazette carried a report from the 1stA Capt. - Donald Finnemore describing a dinner given by the Burgomeister:

'…we were joined by a party of German youths, and who will ever forget that wonderful night…above all the easy and natural fraternisation of the Boys. Language was no barrier, for they found in the exchange of badges and uniform a method of expressing their feelings….Boys are much the same all the world over, and therein, perhaps lies the hope of the future. Certainly Anglo-German peace and friendship would be safe in the keeping of those Boys who so quickly and joyously made friends.'

The 1stA with their German Hosts, August 1934. The HJ (Hitler Youth) Officer can be seen second from the right at rear.

Unfortunately, Anglo-German peace and friendship was not on the agenda of Herr Hitler. The next time Capt. Finnemore was in Germany he was part of the British Legal team at the War-Crimes Tribunal in Nuremberg.

The New Battalion Headquarters in Wrottesley St. off Smallbrook St. and *'a stones throw from New St. Station'*, according to the Annual Report, came into use in 1935. A new part-time paid 'General Secretary' was appointed; none other than Mr D. Gordon Barnsley MC, BA, former Battalion President. Mr C. L. Beckett remained as 'Hon. Secretary' for a further two years. He probably expected to be Secretary again within twelve months of the appointment, as had happened on two previous occasions! This was certainly not the case as Gordon Barnsley was to remain in the job for twenty years. Spring 1935 was

a busy time for the new Secretary, less than two months after the HQ opening there was the Silver Jubilee Celebrations of H.M. King George V. (See page 84)

In response to a request from Brigade Headquarters, the Birmingham Battalion 'adopted' the Jarrow and Hebburn Battalion. With over 60% unemployment in that distressed part of Britain the need was obvious. Boots and clothing were collected parcelled and sent north. A pen-pal sheme was initiated between Jarrow and Birmingham boys. Throughout the years of the great depression, Birmingham with its diversity of manufacturing and service industry, was better positioned to 'ride out the storm'.

1935 was the year that the Battalion's most eminent Hon. Treasurer, Major (later Sir) Arnold Waters, V.C., D.S.O., M.C. started upon his thirty seven years of devoted service to the Battalion in that capacity. He was eventually made an Honorary Vice-President of the Battalion in appreciation of his contribution. One of the most pressing financial priorities of the mid to late 1930s was to clear the debt on BB House. Mr Barrow Cadbury made a wireless broadcast on the BBC in January 1937 and in 1936 and 1937 'Cornflower Days' were held when the Battalion was given the privilege of holding a street collection. The debt was cleared. The Annual Display in Coronation Year, 1937, took the form of a Pageant called 'The Torch' performed by 300 boys at the Alexandra Theatre.

The Darkest Hour - The 1940s

The war dealt a severe blow to the Birmingham Battalion. In its first year Gordon Barnsley vacated his position as Secretary, just as he had his Presidency in the previous conflict; to serve in the military. Mr R. G. Williams was to take his place for most of the war years followed by C. Eric Skinner working in conditions very much less than satisfactory. The loss of a Secretary, whilst significant, was to be the least of the Battalion's worries. Many officers were called-up, boys were evacuated, and many halls used for regular BB meetings were initially not available due to inadequate blackout. Although the Battalion

Display and Annual Church Parade were both cancelled, most other activites continued. In 1940, even with the Battalion strength falling, three new companies were enrolled. Special wartime activities were undertaken, such as the Emergency Hospital Messenger Service detailed elsewhere in this volume. The Blitz of early 1941 exacted a heavy toll upon the Battalion. The Wrottesley St. HQ. was bombed as was the Pavilion at Stechford. The two greatest physical assets of the Battalion were wiped out within days of each other. The real asset of the Battalion of course, was in its members and they were not to be cowed by this seemingly devastating 'double wham-mie'. The Annual Report of 1940-1941 summed up the spirit :

'Looking back over the past winter, with the intensive air-raids on our City, we have much to be thankful for that so many of our Companies have been able to continue. It has been a severe test, but the importance of our work, and the devotion of the Officers engaged in it, has triumphed over the difficulties. Our own Headquarters, BB House in Wrottesley Street were damaged, and are unfit for use; the Pavilion at our Playing Fields was burnt out, and 14 of our Companies have lost their headquarters and are temporariliy suspended, but despite all this, 47 of our Companies are carrying on, and never was our work for the welfare of the boys more necessary than it is to-day.'

Temporary accommodation was found for the Battalion HQ at the Headquarters of the 8th Coy. Islington Methodist Institute in St. Martin's Street. Typical of the way in which adversity was faced is the story of the 2nd Coy. as reported in the Boys' Brigade Gazette of June 1942:

'A fine example of triumph over adversity is provided by the 2nd Birmingham Company... It is an old Company, started nearly thirty years ago (under BLB auspices) by Mr P.A. Lawrence. Twice has the Company had to face the fiery ordeal of a great war, and twice it has triumphed. Early in the present conflict it lost its hall, commandeered by the military authorities. Later it was restored, only for the Company to lose it again for a second spell, and a second time to regain it. Then came the air attack of 1940-41. The 2nd were in one of Birmingham's

Boys evacuated from Birmingham Companies who formed a provisional Company at Cheltenham

most blitzed quarters; the hall suffered from the bombardment; for a time drill was suspended, but the Bible Class went on under all conditions. At the end of last session only twenty Boys could be returned as on the strength. Today the Company numbers are stronger than at any time in the past twenty years. Many of the Boys are busy on war emergency duties. The NCO's run the Life Boy Team, and constitute the male staff of the Sunday school. Eight of the Boys have recently joined the fellowship of the Church.'

After the war, the Battalion was quick to regain morale and numbers. No fewer than five new companies being opened in 1944-45. By 1946-47 there were two more new companies and seven which were re-opened.

Flt.-Lt. Dennis Haycock DFC
Photograph taken whilst in training

The Distinguished Flying Cross

During the years 1943 - 45 the Battalion was honoured by two of its stalwart BB men occupying the position of Lord Mayor of the city in successive years. Alderman L. G. H. Alldridge, O.B.E., J.P., followed by W. T. Wiggins-Davies. It was also clear, in 1945 that a great number of Birmingham ex-BB boys had distinguished themselves whilst serving in the forces. Typical of these, but unfortunately awarded posthumously, was the award of the Distinguished Flying Cross to the late Flight-Lt. Dennis Haycock, R.A.F. an Old Boy of the 10th Birmingham. The 10th at Moseley Road Methodist, was one of the company HQ's which suffered war damage. Built in 1872, it was destroyed by enemy action in 1940, but rebuilt in prefabricated form in ten weeks in 1944. In 1950, a Foundation Stone for a New Church was laid by Cpl. Kenneth Stormont a member of the company. The Stone was Dedicated by the Rev. C.V. Corner, Minister of the Church and Coy. Chaplain. Presumably it was always regarded as one of the `Corner' Stones!

The Battalion Colours, originally dedicated to the fallen officers and old boys of the Battalion in the Great War, were re-dedicated in memory for those 92 who had lost their lives in the 2nd World War. (See page 101) One was Kingsman George Arthur Tucker of the 32nd who had proudly carried the message to the King in 1935. These colours were paraded in a number of special parades, notably the 'V. E. Day' and 'Victory' parades.

In 1946 Mr Harry Anderson (4th Coy.) the Battalion President stepped down as one of the two West Midland representatives on the Brigade Council to be replaced by Mr Charles Taylor Battalion Vice President and Capt. of the 55th Coy. The Battalion Signalling Committee arranged two very successful outdoor exercises at the Lickeys and Sutton Park. The premature death of Mr Anderson in February 1947 brought Mr Ralph K Brown (Capt. 29th Coy.) into the position. At this time the Battalion strength was 3002 of which a third were 15 yrs or older. In addition the Life Boy membership was 1385.

A visitor to Battalion HQ in 1947 was Mr S. E. Barnes, Brigade Headquarters Secretary for Training and Extension. Mr Barnes was a former Captain of the 8th Birmingham Coy. and the BB Officer who negotiated the Brigade's purchase of the National Training Centre `Felden Lodge' in Hertfordshire, now in 2002, the Brigade National H.Q, . The decade of the 1940s which had begun

Festival Run 1951

10th Coy Bearer & Escort handing over the Message to H.M. The King at the 'Wheatsheaf' Coventry Rd. Sheldon. Midnight, Tuesday May 8th 1951

thing was carried out made a very fine impression indeed on all the visiting Officers, who formed the highest opinion of the Birmingham Battalion.'

Brigade Council Meeting 1949 Birmingham University

so disastrously for the Battalion was to be finished in confident style with the 60th Annual Meeting of Brigade Council held at Birmingham University in September 1949. This mammoth event was attended by over 700 officers and was a resounding success as a letter received by the Battalion Sec. from Mr G. Stanley Smith, Brigade Secretary pointed out:

'I am directed by the Brigade Executive to ask you to convey to evey Officer and Boy in the Birmingham Battalion the grateful thanks of the Brigade Council for the splendid work they all did during the Council week-end. The meetings were a triumphant success and in many ways the finest Brigade Council week-end we have had for many years. This was due to the devoted labours of a great many of your Officers and Boys, and I can assure you that the efficient and smooth way in which every

Tonics a plenty - The 1950s

The Festival of Britain, in 1951, was designed as a `tonic for the nation'. The Battalion took part in a special `Festival of Britain Run' which finished on the 10th May at Buckingham Palace where the King, as patron of the Brigade, received loyal greetings from the 166,283 Brigade members in the UK. The format used was identical to that of the great 1935 King George V Jubilee run. There were 50 boys from Birmingham amongst the 2190 taking part. 1952, was of course 'Jubilee Year' for the Birmingham Battalion. The Brigade President the Rt. Hon. Lord Maclay, K.B.E., sent the following message to the Officers and Boys of the Battalion:

'On the occasion of your Jubilee Celebrations I send greetings and most sibcere congratulations. Nowhere is there a finer record of BB effort and achievement than in the history of the Birmingham Battalion, and it is from such strongholds that the whole Brigade gains strength and character. May your faith and enthusiasm contribute likewise to the present and the future.'
Signed

MACLAY
Brigade President

In Battalion Jubilee year there was a record membership of 3312 Boys' Brigade all ranks plus 1754 Life Boys and staff. A special 'Jubilee Week' 6th - 12th July was organised which opened with the Annual church Parade. There was an exhibition at Messrs Lewis's Store and displays all round the city. The Athletic Sports held at the new City Sports Arena, Salford Sports Stadium, concluded the week.

The year of Coronation, 1953 saw continued expansion of

Floral Bed in Ward End Park 1954

companies, four more being enrolled, but boy numbers remained steady. Fourteen boys from the Battalion, chosen by ballot, were in attendance on the Coronation route in central London on 2nd June. 1954 was a special year for the BB worldwide, 'Founder's Centenary Year' to celebrate the birth of William Smith in 1854. On a more local level, the Battalion NCO's Association under the chairmanship of Vice-President Mr Harold Burnett, held its third Annual Dinner, Mr E. R. Staniford Editor of the New BB Boys Magazine 'Stedfast' was also in attendance. The greatest National BB event was undeniably the International Camp held at Eton (described elsewhere).

A floral bed in Ward End Park representing the BB Crest with the words 'Founder's Centenary' was admired by all. It contained over 30,000 plants and took two gardeners more than 10 days to lay out. Their labours were well rewarded because it won the City of Birmingham Cup for the best Floral Bed in the City Parks during 1954. A landmark in Battalion History came in August 1954 when Mr D. Gordon Barnsley retired from his position as Secretary.

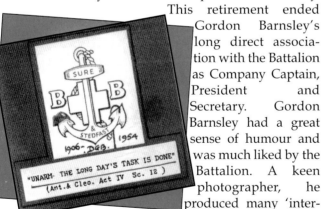

This retirement ended Gordon Barnsley's long direct association with the Battalion as Company Captain, President and Secretary. Gordon Barnsley had a great sense of humour and was much liked by the Battalion. A keen photographer, he produced many 'interesting' photo-montages during his years as Secretary. Always witty but sometimes slightly disrespectful of authority and even a little saucy. He distributed this final picture in 1954 showing his cap and stick hung up on the anchor flukes, accompanied by a quote from Shakespeare.

A great Founder's Centenary event 'The Festival of Boyhood' was held at Wembley and a 'Special' was laid on by British Railways to take the Birmingham contingent.

1955 was a year of `All Change' in the Battalion. In February 1955, Mr. W. Gordon Innes, late of 32nd Coy., took over as Secretary after a brief period of temporary Secretaryship by Mr Reg. Webb an officer in the same company. Mr R. K. Brown retired as Battalion President and Sir Donald Finnemore agreed to his third term of Presidency with Mr Harold Burnett, Capt 10th Coy. acting as Chairman of the Executive. 1958 was the 75th Anniversary of the Boys' Brigade with a number of special events being organised. The Caribbean camp attended by four Birmingham boys and the Battalion Secretary,

Another Floral Bed... in Cannon Hill Park 1958

and the '750' Training Camp, attended by 35 Birmingham boys, being two such ventures. The loss of Mr Barrow Cadbury at the great age of 95 was keenly felt. The Duke of Edinburgh's Award which was passing through its experimental stage had its first Birmingham 'Gold' recipient L/Cpl Victor Harding of 73rd Birmingham Coy.. A special Battalion Committee was formed to deal with the award. Another Floral bed was constructed to celebrate the 75th Anniversary, this time in Cannon Hill Park.

Facing the Situation - The 1960s

As the 50s decade finished and the 60s began the Battalion remained strong, numbering nearly 5000 all ranks.

Interest in the Duke of Edinburgh's Award scheme was growing. A party of Russian Youth Leaders whilst visiting the city were taken to visit the 55th Coy.. They were impressed, but puzzled at the wide variety of Youth provision in the UK. The 1960s brought H.Q. worries to the fore. Nationally cash was required to find a new Brigade HQ and another 'Run' was organised in 1961 with messages being carried to the Lord Mayor of London in The Mansion House. Birmingham boys were again involved as one of the messages passed through fourteen stages across the city. Nearer to home, in fact the Battalion's own home the current HQ in Union St, was in line for redevelopment and new premises would soon be required. High rents seemed to be ruling out a central site. Redevelopment was not just threatening the HQ, all round the inner ring the CDAs (Comprehensive Development Areas) were being established, old properties and complete communities were being bulldozed into oblivion. The Inner City area had been one of the strongholds of the Battalion, a tour on the No.8 bus would have taken you past the H.Q.'s of the most famous Birmingham companies. As the Annual Report stated: *'...the changing situation must be faced faily and squarely.'*

One 'situation' faced by the Battalion in the 60s was to re-establish companies within the redeveloped areas. Companies would now need to take on board the implications of serving the new immigrant communities from the West Indies and Indian Sub-continent. One such company the 41st, was established at City Road Baptist Church.

Battalion stand at the Boys' & Girls' Exhibition 1963

In 1963 history repeated itself. A new Battalion Headquarters complete with a new Battalion Secretary, a situation which had happened nearly thirty years before.

This time it was Mr R. H. Webb who took up duties as full-time Battalion Training Officer and Secretary. The new HQ was situated in Hatchett St. (See pages 35 - 6). The strength of the Battalion at this time was actually increasing when the trend in other organisations and even the Brigade nationally was quite the opposite. One reason was perhaps - publicity, for two years the Battalion had a stall at the Boys' and Girls' Exhibition in Bingley Hall. (That is the old Bingley Hall off Broad St).

The Haynes Report, published in 1964, has been described as a 'wind of change' which swept The Boys' Brigade. In an era of National Reports this was not one to be left on the shelf. The report's proposals which were recommended by the Brigade Executive were eventually accepted. There would be a three tier programme with the Life Boys becoming the Junior Section of the BB, the Company Section and the extended Senior Section. In Birmingham publicity was still regarded as being a priority with a Recruiting Drive taking place in September 1964, one event being Birmingham's very own 'Run', messages being brought to the Lord Mayor from outlying parts of the City and from neighbouring Boroughs such as Solihull Smethwick and Sutton Coldfield. In 1965, Sir Donald Finnemore resigned as President and was unanimously elected as Hon. President. Mr Harold Burnett, Capt 10th Coy., who had been Deputy President since 1963, was elected in his place. The Brigade Council Meeting was held in Birmingham in September 1967 by invitation of the West Midland District, whilst strictly speaking the Battalion was not the host, as part of the West Midland District the Battalion was fully involved in the proceedings. The venue was again the Great Hall of the University and a Civic Reception and Ball was hosted by the Lord Mayor. The Church Parade involved the use of the St Martin's Church, Central Hall and the Town Hall. The meeting was particularly important in that the Report of the Brigade Training and Activities Committee included an outline of the proposed new scheme for programme and awards in the Company Section. An interesting diversion was made on the Saturday of the Council meetings when the 94th Coy (St. Chad's Erdington) as the current Battalion Drill champions, demonstrated the new 'Drill in Threes'. The company went on to win the Battalion Drill Competition many times thereafter. The Lord Mayor of Birmingham in 1967 was an Old Boy of the 4th Coy., who was followed into office in 1968 by an Old Boy of the 10th Coy.. The strength of the Battalion was 80 companies.

The New Order - The 1970s

During the Autum of 1970 the Battalion Stage Show `Showtime 70' was produced at Cadbury's Theatre over three nights, a new venture involving hundreds of boys of all sections. The Battalion's Country House `Perrycroft'

Birmingham Battalion Boys at a Duke of Edinburgh's Award Exhibition 1970.

Photo: Post & Mail

was opened on 1st May 1971. (See pages 102 - 3) In 1971 Mr Dennis Riley was appointed 'Assistant to The Battalion Secretary', taking up the post of 'Assistant Secretary' in 1973. During the 1972-73 Session the first five 'Queensmen' of the Battalion attained the award under the new, much more demanding conditions. In the following session three distinguished Officers of the Battalion died. Irene Bartlett gave wonderful service to the Life Boys and as a member of the Uniform Committee was one of those responsible for the Junior Section Boys' and Lady Officers' uniform. Allan Carlyle had given 40 years service to the Battalion as one of the Financial Secretaries Sir Donald Finnemore had served the Brigade for more than sixty years and his contibution can only be described as 'incalculable'. On 15th October 1976 Mr Reg Webb retired as Secretary and Mr Dennis Riley took up the reins. 1976-77 was the seventy fifth session of the Battalion and many meassages of congratulation were received. The Battalion strength was 3694 all ranks in 71 companies. In 1977 the Brigade officially recognised the 'Pre Junior Section' for the 6 - 8 Yr olds and the name adopted for them in Birmingham was 'Anchor Boys', which eventually became the name adopted by the whole Brigade. On the 1st June 1979, Mr Stanley H. Gilbert succeeded Mr Harold Burnett as President. Harold Burnett, now awarded the MBE for his services to the BB, remained as Hon. Treasurer and was made Hon. President.

Two Centenaries - The 1980s

The 1980s like the 1970s proved to be a challenge for the Battalion. However, there were a great many uplifting events and much good work produced. In 1983, the celebration of the Brigade's Centenary was taken - up with determination and enterprise. Many companies made an extra effort with publicity and the Battalion organised

special events. (See page 104) The year started with a chain of Beacons accross the country. One of the largest, lit on the stroke of midnight on New Years Eve 1982 - 1983 by BB boys in uniform, was on Barr Beacon to the North of the City. This massive fire was managed by the N.E. Division of the Battalion and attracted thousands of spectators as well as live Radio coverage. A Gala Day was held at the National Children's Home, Princess Alice Drive New Oscott. A special centenary float accompanied by runners in relays, bearing messages from H.M. The Queen, The Prime Minister and The Brigade President, made its way from the Council House via Perry Barr to the Gala Day event, escorted back and front by police. A special Battalion cloth Blazer badge was produced. The Brigade's national Centenary buttonhole Badge was made in Birmingham, the Battalion President being presented with the very first one. Many companies met in uniform on the exact day at the precise hour of the Centenary. One new company, the '83rd Birmingham', was formed at that exact time. There was a Centenary Civic Reception at the Council House on the Saturday nearest the 4th October (the 8th). This was followed by a Thanksgiving Service in the Town Hall on Sunday 9th. The Centenary Display, the last of its type in Birmingham, took place over three days in December at the Central Hall.

The National 'Brigade Council Meeting' was again hosted by the Battalion in 1985. The location was the University of Aston with the actual meeting being held in the nearby Central Hall. The meeting was the first to be chaired by the new Brigade President The Rt. Hon. Viscount Thurso of Ulbster. Lord Thurso, who turned out to be a wonderful Brigade President was very much the `new kid on the block' and was not at all versed in BB culture. He was given the luxury of being driven around in a Range Rover specially loaned by Land Rover in Solihull. One of his first trips was to buy a pair of brown leather gloves to complete his BB uniform! A major topic of concern was the new Anchor Boy section with discussions on leadership and a report on uniform. The Saturday evening entertainment called 'Brum Beat', also staged in the Central Hall, was billed as 'An Entertainment by Birmingham Battalion and Friends'. Bands from the Battalion Beat Retreat in Victoria Square. In 1987, the Battalion sold its beloved Hatchett St. H.Q., but fortunately stayed-on to occupy part of the premises.(See page 35) In 1989, to celebrate the centenary of City status, a visit by 'Queen Victoria' to

Birmingham, was staged on the evening of Friday January 13th. Over 300 members of the Battalion turned out in `costume' and made a splendid contribution to proceedings. (See page 106).

A 'Happening' time - The 1990s

On 12th June 1991, members of the Battalion turned out in uniform for the visit of H. M. The Queen to Birmingham. They lined Her Majesty's route across Centenary Square, and in the words of the City Council's representative: *'looked very impressive and greatly added to the colour and splendour of the occasion'*. On the 30th April 1994 a large contingent of `Queensmen' from the Battalion took part in a Royal Review at Windsor Castle. Her Majesty the Queen reviewed over 1000 senior members of the Brigade on what was a glorious occasion. Her Majesty personally presented Queen's Badges to one Queensman from each District in the Brigade. S/Sgt. Richard West, a member of 31st B'ham. Coy., represented the West Midlands. Lord Thurso, very much the 'new boy' back in 1985 but now with nearly ten years service, officially handed over the presidency of the Brigade to Lord Strathmore at the Review.

Whilst large events were to be a feature of the 1990s, innovation in a relatively small, but quite significant way was

Picnics at the 'Big Event'

The BIG Event!
Saturday, 8th July 1995

Open Air
Live Concert
Featuring:

Remission Gospel Choir   Simon Foster
The Jim Bailey Band   The Leon Evans Worship Band
Paul Poulton   Jeff Lucas

at
Moor Lane Sports Ground
off College Road, Kingstanding, Birmingham B6

Admission £2   For further information call: (0121) 236 2997 or (0121) 359 1866   from 7.00 p.m.

also taking place. The first `Amicus' group in the world was meeting at the headquarters of the 6th Coy. in Kings Heath. (See page 105). The big event of 1995 was, `The Big Event' on July 8th . Organised by Rev. David Woodfield the Battalion Chaplain, in conjunction with the BB & Girls' Brigade in Birmingham, an afternoon `Fun Time' for the 5 - 11 yr olds, and a Picnic and `Praise Party' was followed in the evening by a live open air concert. Moor Lane Sports Ground was the venue for what turned out to be a great success, in glorious sunshine with over 2000 turning up. The Big Event was repeated in 1996, `Big Event 2' following a similar format to it's progenitor with an 'Afternoon Happening' and an evening concert. As in

1995, although organised by the BB and GB, the event was open to everyone. July 1996 heralded the arrival of new Battalion Secretary Roger Green upon Dennis Riley's retirement after twenty-five years working for the Battalion, twenty of them as full - time Secretary, and certainly a `hard act to follow'. In 1997, there was another `happening', this time to highlight the plight of Street Children in Durban South Africa. `The Alive Kids', a

group of 32 young people from the Kwa Mashu township, brought their song dance and drama show to Sutton Coldfield Baptist Church (H.Q. 4th S/C Coy.) on Saturday 8th November. The whole UK tour was part of The Boys' Brigade International Teams `Streetwise' campaign. The Alive Kids had been on BBC 's 'Blue Peter' the previous Wednesday and appeared on ITV's 'Sunday Live' the day after. `The Alive Kids' stayed at `Perrycroft' whilst appearing in the midlands.

To promote the BB and raise funds for charity a unique event was organised over one day in 1998. The 'Chaplains Challenge' actually took place on Friday night 24th and all day on Saturday 25th April. The two Battalion Chaplains, `Tom & Clifford' (Rev. Tom Duncanson and Rev. Clifford Grimason) challenged themselves to visit as many companies in the Battalion as possible. They managed a 'Whistle-Stop' visit of ten minutes to twenty companies to participate in a charity event being organised by each company; this being the company's part of the challenge. They were driven 150 miles by Battalion Secretary Roger Green stopping to take part in events as varied as 'shoe - shines', coffee mornings (a real strain!) and whacky wheelbarrow races.

New Millennium 2000 and beyond

In the Summer of 2001 the Birmingham Uniformed Members Party, or 'BUMP' for short, held at Blackwell Court, was enjoyed by all. (See page 107). The Birmingham of 2002 is a very different one from that of 1902 and so is the Boys' Brigade in Birmingham. Smaller companies, but more of them, many more younger members, a new uniform and very different challenges from those of a century ago. As the last Brigade Council of its type comes to Birmingham in September 2002 we could ask the question; where do we go from here? We have our answer, it's on every membership card: *'So remember your Creator while you are still young. Remember the Lord in everything you do, and He will show you the right way.'*
Ecclesiastes Ch. 12, Verse1 & Proverbs Ch. 3, Verse 6.

BIRMINGHAM COMPANIES - The Complete List

Company Designation	Church Connection	Active Dates	Notes
1st Birmingham	Camp Hill Presbyterian	1889 - 1909	
1st Birmingham (Aston)	Aston Parish Church	1909 - 1930	Formerly 1st Aston Manor Coy.
1st Birmingham (Aston)	Aston Parish Church	1932 -	Dyson Hall
1stA Birmingham	People's Chapel (Bapt) Great King St. Hockley	1926 -	Formerly 1st Birmingham BLB
2nd Birmingham	St. Thomas Sunday School	1891 - 1893	
2nd Birmingham	St. Clement's Church, Nechells	1898 - 1931	
2nd A Birmingham	Stratford Road Baptist Church	1926 - 1932	Formerly 2nd Birmingham BLB
2nd Birmingham	Stratford Road Baptist Church	1932 - 1985	Became 2nd when St Clements closed.
3rd Birmingham	Christ church, Sparkbrook	1892 - ?	Closed by 1900
3rd Birmingham	Central Hall Wesleyan Mission	1900 - 1914	
3rd Birmingham	Wesleyan Church, Sandon Rd Edgbaston	1919 - 1926	Company designation changed to 33rd
3rd Birmingham	Congregational Church, Moseley Rd	1926 - c1944	Formerly 3rd Birmingham BLB
3rd Birmingham	Newbridge Baptist Church	1947 - 1986	
4th Birmingham	Presbyterian Church, Broad St.	1894 - c1907	
4th Birmingham	Church of the Redeemer (Baptist) Hagley Rd	1908 - 1960	
4thA Birmingham	Ebenezer Congregational Church, Steelhouse Lane	1926 - 1931	Formerly 4th Birmingham BLB
4thA Birmingham	Carrs Lane Congregational	1931 - 1935	Change of Church connection
4th Birmingham	Phoenix Hall Bordesley Village (Baptist)	1999 - 2000	
5th Birmingham	Edgbaston Congregational Church	1895 - c1900	
5th Birmingham	Highbury Chapel	1901 - c1904	
5th Birmingham	Carrs Lane Mission, Cattell Rd. Small Heath	1906 - c1914	
5th Birmingham	Monument Rd. Morning School.	1921 - 1944	
5th Birmingham	Stirling Rd. Methodist	1944 - 1969	Change of Church connection
5th Birmingham	West Smethwick Church	1987 - 1989	
6th Birmingham	Heath Green Rd. Sunday School	1895 - 1902	
6th Birmingham	Christ Church Summerfield	1902 - 1911	Change of Church connection
6th Birmingham	Christ Church Summerfield	1913 - c1918	Re-started Coy.
6th Birmingham	Brookfields Baptist Mission, Ellen St.	1921 - 1926	Company designation changed to 36th
6th Birmingham	Kings Heath Baptist Church	1926 -	Formerly 6th Birmingham BLB
7th Birmingham	Islington Wesleyan Chapel	1896 - c1899	
7th Birmingham	Newtown Row Wesleyan, N. Birmingham Mission	1900 - 1915	
7th Birmingham	Aston Parish Church (Alfred St. Schools)	1918 - 1926	Company designation changed to 37th
7th Birmingham	Kings Norton Congregational	1926 - 1915	Formerly 7th Birmingham BLB
7th Birmingham	Kings Norton Congregational	1919 - 1986	Re-started after WWI
7th Birmingham	Cotteridge United Reformed	1986 -	Change of Church connection
8th Birmingham	St Barnabas Church, Ladywood	1901 - c1905	
8th Birmingham	Islington Wesleyan Church, St. Martin's St.	1906 - c1915	
8th Birmingham	Islington Wesleyan Church, St. Martin's St.	1919 - 1939	Re-started after WWi
8th Birmingham	Islington Wesleyan Church, St. Martin's St.	c1941 - 1960	Re-started after WWII
8th Birmingham	Ladywood Methodist Church	1961 - 1962	Change of Church connection
8th Birmingham	Summer Hill Methodist Church	1963 - 1976	Change of Church connection
8th Birmingham	St. Boniface Quinton	1976 -	Change of Church connection
9th Birmingham	Carrs Lane Mission, Moseley St.	1902 - 1908	
9th Birmingham	Central Hall Wesleyan Mission Belmont Row	1909 - 1932	Change of Church connection
9th Birmingham	Central Hall Methodist	1932 - 1963	Amalgamated with 36th.
9th Birmingham	Central Hall Methodist	1974 - 1986	J/S Coy formed 1973
9th Birmingham	Lichfield Rd. Methodist Church, Aston	1986 - 1992	Change of Church connection
10th Birmingham	Mount Zion Baptist Church	1902 - c1906	
10th Birmingham	Moseley Rd. Wesleyan Church	1908 - 1991	
10thA Birmingham	Friends Hall, Farm St. Hockley	1926 - 1960	Formerly 10th Birmingham BLB
11th Birmingham	Nelson St. Early Morning Adult Sunday School	1902 - 1911	
11th Birmingham	Summer Hill Wesleyan Church Monument Rd	1911 - 1913	Change of Church connection
11th Birmingham	St. Marks Church, King Edwards Rd. Ladywood.	1918 - c1921	
11th Birmingham	Baptist Mission, Cross Street Smethwick	1923 - 1925	
11th Birmingham	Franchise St. (Westminster) Congregational Mission	1925 - 1926	Company designation changed to 41st
11th Birmingham	Newtown Row Wesleyan	1926 - 1939	Formerly 11th Birmingham BLB
11th Birmingham	St. Hilda's Church, Warley Woods	1947 - 1958	
11th Birmingham	John Bunyan Baptist Church	1961 - 1993	Formerly platoon of 1stA
11th Birmingham	Kingsland Rd School	1993 -	Change of Church connection
12th Birmingham	London Rd. Wesleyan Chapel	1903 - c1906	
12th Birmingham	St. Matthews Church Smethwick	1908 - 1911	
12th Birmingham	St. Cuthbert's Church of England, Winson Green	1912 - 1940	
12th Birmingham	St. Cuthbert's Church of England, Winson Green	1947 - 1947	Re-started after WWII
12thA Birmingham	Theodore St. Mission Hall, Hockley	1926 - 1931	Formerly 12th Birmingham BLB
12th Birmingham	Small Heath Methodist Church, Yardley Green Rd.	1952 - 1986	

BIRMINGHAM COMPANIES CONTINUED

13th Birmingham	Congregational Church, Coventry Rd., Small Heath	1903 - 1910	
13thBirmingham	Ladypool Rd, Congregational Church	1926 - 1943	Formerly 13th Birmingham BLB
13th Birmingham	Bethel, Baptist Church, Ward End	1949 - 1951	
14th Birmingham	Lodge Rd. Institute & Mission (Congregational)	1905 - 1951	
14th Birmingham	Nineveh Methodist Church, Soho	1951 - 1959	Change of Church connection
14th Birmingham	Villa Rd Methodist Church	1959 - 1963	Change of Church connection
14th A Birmingham	Raddlebarn Road Mission	1926 - 1927	Formerly 14th Birmingham BLB
15th Birmingham	Bolton Rd.Wesleyan Mission	1909 - 1911	
15th Birmingham	Primitive Methodist Church, Stratford Rd, Sparkhill	1913 - 1914	
15th Birmingham	St. Mary's Parish Church, Bearwood	1924 - 1931	
15th Birmingham	Washwood Heath U. Methodist Church	1932 - 1941	
15th Birmingham	Washwood Heath Methodist Church	1947 - 1951	Re-started after WWII
15th Birmingham	Regent St. Baptist Church, Smethwick	1953 - 1973	
16th Birmingham	Astbury Memorial Wesleyan Church Handsworth	1909 - 1912	
16th Birmingham	St. Catherine's Church Nechells	1914 - 1918	
16th Birmingham	Wesleyan Mission, Buck Street	1924 - 1925	
16th Birmingham	Wycliffe Baptist Church, Bristol St	1926 - 1929	Formerly 16th Birmingham BLB
16th Birmingham	Acocks Green Wesleyan Church	1929 - c1931	
16th Birmingham	Rookery Rd. Methodist Church	1933 - 1941	
16th Birmingham	South Yardley Methodist Church	1948 - 1961	Company designation changed to 55th/16th
17th Birmingham	Holy Trinity Mission Church (Aston)	1909 - 1911	
17th Birmingham	St. James' Church Ashted	1914 - 1916	
17th Birmingham	Asbury Memorial Wesleyan Church, Soho Rd	1924 - 1941	
17th Birmingham	Asbury Memorial Wesleyan Church, Soho Rd	1947 - 1966	Re-started after WWII
18th Birmingham	Aston Park Congregational Church	1909 - 1945	
18th Birmingham	Aston Park Congregational Church	1947 - 1955	Re-started after WWII
18thA Birmingham	Stockland Green Wesleyan Church	1926 - 1930	Formerly 18th Birmingham BLB
18th Birmingham	Washwood Heath Methodist Church	1964 - 1975	
18th Birmingham	Ward End Methodist Church Centre	1975 - 2000	Change of Church connection
19th Birmingham	St. John the Baptist, Parish Church, Harborne	1911 - 1921	
19th Birmingham	Yates St. Baptist Church	1925 - 1926	Company designation changed to34th
19th Birmingham	Friends' Institute Moseley Rd	1926 - 1983	Formerly 19th Birmingham BLB
19th Birmingham	Friends Meeting House Colmore Rd K. Heath	1983 -	Change of Church connection
20th Birmingham	Icknield Square Wesleyan Methodist Mission	1911 - 1915	
20th Birmingham	Icknield Square Wesleyan Methodist Mission	1918 - 1933	Re-started after WWI
20th Birmingham	St. Catherine's Church, Nechells	1935 - 1950	
20th Birmingham	St. Matthews Duddeston	1950 - 1954	Change of Church connection.
20th Birmingham	New Testament Church of God, Brookfield Estate	1986 - 1989	
21st Birmingham	Lozells Hall, Wesleyan Mission, Lozells St.	1911 - 1913	
21st Birmingham	Wattville St. Protestant Evangelical Chapel	1915 - 1917	
21st Birmingham	Holliday St. Wesleyan Mission	1925 - 1926	
21st Birmingham	Guildford St. Baptist Chapel	1926 - 1937	Formerly 21st Birmingham BLB
21st Birmingham	Methodist Church, Chapel St., Handsworth	1938 - 1943	
21st Birmingham	Methodist Church, Chapel St., Handsworth	1945 - 1947	Re-started after WWII
21st Birmingham	Banners gate Congregational Church	1947 - 1953	Company designation changed to 1st S/Coldfield.
21st Birmingham	Harborne Baptist Church	1954 - 1961	
22nd Birmingham	Bearwood Baptist Church	1912 - 1918	
22nd Birmingham	Bearwood Baptist Church	1919 - 1940	Re-started after WWI
22nd Birmingham	Bearwood Baptist Church	1945 -	Re-started after WWII
23rd Birmingham	Carrs Lane Chapel (Congregational)	1913 -1914	Company designation changed to 24th
23rd Birmingham	Hall Green Wesleyan Chapel	1925 - 1926	Company designation changed to 43rd
23rd Birmingham	Society of Friends, Bull Street.	1926 - 1927	Formerly 23rd Birmingham BLB
23rd Birmingham	St. Cyprians with St. Chads Hay Mills	1930 - 1983	
24th Birmingham	Digbeth Institute (Congregational)	1913 - 1921	
24th Birmingham	Sparkhill Wesleyan Sunday School, Warwick Rd.	1926 - 1940	
24th Birmingham	Sparkhill Wesleyan Sunday School, Warwick Rd.	1945 - 1976	Re-started after WWII
25th Birmingham	St. Peter's Mission, Deykin Avenue, Witton (Aston)	1913 - 1953	
25th Birmingham	Rookery Rd. Methodist Church	1956 - 1964	
26th Birmingham	Holliday St. Wesleyan Mission	1913 - 1917	
26th Birmingham	Holliday St. Wesleyan Mission	c1921 - 1925	Company designation changed to 21st
26th Birmingham	Acocks Green Wesleyan Church	1929 - 1976	

BIRMINGHAM COMPANIES CONTINUED

27th Birmingham	Ladywood United Methodist Church, Monument Rd.	1926 - 1935	Formerly 27th Birmingham BLB
27th Birmingham	Ladywood United Methodist Church, Monument Rd.	1936 - 1937	
27th Birmingham	Parish Church of St. Mark, Stockland Green, Erdington	1937 - 1946	
27th Birmingham	Glebe Farm Baptist Chapel	1948 - 1953	
27th Birmingham	Glebe Farm Baptist Chapel	1956 - 1981	
28th Birmingham	Springfield Primitive Methodist Church	1927 - 1965	
29th Birmingham	West Smethwick Congregational Church	1926 - 1932	Formerly 29th Birmingham BLB
29th Birmingham	Kingstanding Methodist Church	1933 -	
30th Birmingham	Christ Church Baptist, Six Ways Aston	1926 - 1982	
31st Birmingham	Tyseley Primitive Methodist Church	1926 - 1934	Formerly 31st Birmingham BLB
31st Birmingham	Digbeth Branch Institute (Yardley) Congregational	1937 -	
32nd Birmingham	Cannon Street Memorial Baptist	1926 - 1953	Formerly 32nd Birmingham BLB
32nd Birmingham	Kingswood Meeting House, Unitarian.	1978 -	
33rd Birmingham	Sandon Road Wesleyan	1926 -	Formerly 3rd Birmingham BB
34th Birmingham	Aston Baptist Church.	1925 - 1928	Formerly 19th Birmingham BB
34th Birmingham	Witton Baptist Church.	1930 - 1948	
34th Birmingham	Brays Rd. Methodist Church, Sheldon	1954 - 1972	
34th Birmingham	St. Giles Church of England, Sheldon	1978 - 1991	
35th Birmingham	Digbeth Institute	1926 - 1938	Formerly 35th Birmingham BLB
35th Birmingham	Shirley Methodist Church	1943 -	
36th Birmingham	Summer Hill Methodist Church	1921 - c1924	
36th Birmingham	Ellen St. Baptist Mission	1926 - 1942	Formerly 6th Birmingham BB
36th Birmingham	Springhill Baptist Church	1942 - 1950	
36th Birmingham	Summer Hill Methodist	1950 - 1963	
36th/9th Birmingham	Summer Hill Methodist	1963 - 1968	New Company designation
36th Birmingham	Birmingham Central Mission (Cent. Hall)	1968 - 1970	
37th Birmingham	Aston Parish Church, Holy Trinity Mission, Alfred St.	1926 - 1962	Formerly 7th Birmingham BB
38th Birmingham	All Saints Church, Kings Heath	1926 - 1940	
38th Birmingham	St. Paul's Church, Bordesley Green	1945 - 1946	
38th Birmingham	Villa Rd. Methodist Church	1948 - 1951	
38th Birmingham	Longbridge Baptist Church	1955 -	
39th Birmingham	Wylde Green Congregational Church	1926 - 1927	
39th Birmingham	Winson Green Congregational Church	1930 - 1998	Change of Church connection
39th Birmingham	Bishop Latimer Church, Winson Green	1998 -	Change of Church connection
40th Birmingham	Billesley Wesleyan Methodist Church	1927 - 1997	
41st Birmingham	Franchise St., Mission (Congregational)	1926 - c1928	Formerly 11th Birmingham BB
41st Birmingham	City Rd. Baptist Church Sunday School	1930 - 1941	
41st Birmingham	City Rd. Baptist Church Sunday School	1946 - 1949	Re-started after WWII
41st Birmingham	City Rd. Baptist Church	1963 - 1980	
42nd Birmingham	Bromford Wesleyan Church	1927 - 1934	
42nd Birmingham	Aston Parish Church Mission (Ellen Knox Memorial)	1935 - 1969	
42nd Birmingham	St. Peter and St. Paul Church of England, Aston	1973 - 1979	Company designation changed to 1st
43rd Birmingham	Hall Green Methodist Church	1926 - 1937	Formerly 23rd Birmingham BB
43rd Birmingham	Hall Green Methodist Church	1940 - 1996	
44th Birmingham	Hay Mills Congregational Church	1927 - 1935	
44th Birmingham	Rocky Lane Methodist Church	1936 - 1945	
44th Birmingham	Nechells Hall Methodist Church	1945 - 1963	
44th Birmingham	Grenfell Baptist Church	1975 - 1995	
45th Birmingham	St. Pauls Church, Hamstead	1927 - 1927	
45th Birmingham	Great Barr Wesleyan Chapel	1928 - 1929	Change of Church connection
45th Birmingham	Sparkhill Primitive Methodist Church	1931 - 1938	
45th Birmingham	Yardley Wood Baptist Sunday School	1942 -	
46th Birmingham	St. Martins Mission Church, Perry Common	1928 - 1968	
46th Birmingham	St. Martins Parish Church, Perry Common	1974 - 1976	Re-started as J/S Coy.
46th Birmingham	St. Martin's Church of England Perry Common	1976 - 1984	
47th Birmingham	Watery Lane Central Mission (Congregational)	1928 - 1941	
47th Birmingham	Watery Lane Central Mission (Congregational)	1948 - 1951	Re-started after WWII
47th Birmingham	Watery Lane Congregational Church	1954 - 1956	
47th Birmingham	Small Heath Congregational Church, Coventry Rd.	1956 - 1967	
47th Birmingham	New Testament Church of God, Chelmsley Wood	1979 - 1980	

BIRMINGHAM COMPANIES CONTINUED

48th Birmingham	Wesleyan Methodist Central Hall, Corporation St	1928 - 1932	Company designation changed to 9th
48th Birmingham	Lord St. Primitive Methodist Church	1932 - 1941	
48th Birmingham	Castle Bromwich Methodist Church	1943 - 1988	
49th Birmingham	Rubery Congregational Church	1928 - 1932	
49th Birmingham	St. Basil's Church, Heath Mill Lane, Deritend	1932 - 1934	
49th Birmingham	Little Bromwich Hall (Society of Friends)	1936 - c1937	
49th Birmingham	St. Pauls Church, Bordersley Green	1938 - 1945	Change of Church connection
49th Birmingham	St. Pauls Church, Bordersley Green	1946 - 1946	Company designation changed to 38th
49th Birmingham	Sparkhill Congregational Church	1948 - 1969	
49th Birmingham	Elim Pentecostal Church, Selly Oak	1973 - 1974	
49th Birmingham	Cheswick Green Family Church	1982 -	J/S Coy formed 1981
50th Birmingham	Selly Park Baptist Church	1927 - c1940	
50th Birmingham	Selly Park Baptist Church	1943 - c1975	Re-started after WWII
51st Birmingham	Undenominational Church, Alton Rd. Bournbrook	1928 - 1930	
51st Birmingham	Northfield Baptist Church	1932 -	
52nd Birmingham	Emmanuel Church, Alum Rock	1929 - 1989	
52nd Birmingham	St. Philip and St. James Church of England, Hodge Hill	1995 -	
53rd Birmingham	United Methodist Church, Baldwin St., Smethwick	1929 - 1933	
53rd Birmingham	St. Hugh's Church, Stirchley	1935 - 1937	
53rd Birmingham	Kings Norton Methodist Church, Cotteridge	1944 - 1985	Company designation changed to 7th
54th Birmingham	Ward End Primitive Methodist Church	1929 - 1933	
54th Birmingham	Birmingham Parish Church, (St, Martins)	1936 - 1941	
54th Birmingham	Parish Church, St. Martin's, Birmingham	1947 - 1980	Re-started after WWII
55th Birmingham	Coventry Rd. Wesleyan Church	1929 - 1960	Company designation changed to 55th/16th
55th/16th Birmingham	South Yardley Methodist	1960 -	
56th Birmingham	St. Margaret's Church, Ladywood	1932 - 1935	
56th Birmingham	St. John's Church, Sparkhill	1936 - 1937	
56th Birmingham	St. Bede's Church, Greet	1942 - 1955	
56th Birmingham	Hawkesley Anglican/ Methodist Church	1977 -	
57th Birmingham	Society of Friends, Sutton Coldfield	1932 - 1940	
57th Birmingham	Pheasey Methodist Church	1948 - 1995	
57th Birmingham	The Beacon Church (Anglican/Methodist)	1995 -	Change of Church connection
58th Birmingham	St. Saviour's Church, Villa St. Hockley.	1932 - 1941	
58th Birmingham	Walmley Parish Church, Sutton Coldfield	1949 - 1953	Company designation changed to 2nd S/C
58th Birmingham	St. Chad's Parish Church, Erdington	1953 - 1954	
58th Birmingham	Yardley Baptist Church	1957 - 1992	
59th Birmingham	Edward Rd. Baptist Church	1933 - 1937	
59th Birmingham	Greet Methodist Church	1937 - 1941	
59th Birmingham	Tyseley Methodist Church	1941 - 1945	Change of Church connection
59th Birmingham	College Rd. Methodist Church, Quinton	1949 -	
60th Birmingham	Balfour St. Methodist Church, Balsall Heath	1933 - 1935	
60th Birmingham	St. Christopher's Church, Springfield	1938 - 1957	
60th Birmingham	St. Christopher's Church, Springfield	1965 - 1986	
61st Birmingham	Franchise St. Congregational Mission	1933 - 1935	
61st Birmingham	Wharf Rd. Baptist Church, King's Norton	1938 - 1939	
61st Birmingham	Wharf Rd. Baptist Church, King's Norton	1941 - 1944	
61st Birmingham	Erdington Baptist Church	1951 - 1986	
61st Birmingham	Erdington Baptist Church	1990 -	
62nd Birmingham	Lodge Rd. Baptist Church	1934 - 1935	
62nd Birmingham	Lozells Congregational Church, Wheeler St.	1938 - 1973	
62nd Birmingham	South Aston United Reformed Church	1973 - 1985	Change of Church connection
63rd Birmingham	Harborne Baptist Church	1934 - 1937	
63rd Birmingham	Weoley Hill Presbyterian Church	1937 - 1940	
63rd Birmingham	Weoley Hill Presbyterian Church	1946 - 1955	Re-started after WWII
63rd Birmingham	St. Gabriel's Church, Weoley Castle	1960 - 1970	
64th Birmingham	St. John's Church, Harborne	1934 - 1996	
65th Birmingham	St. Pauls Church (City) Church	1935 - 1945	
65th Birmingham	Nechells Hall Methodist Church	1945 - 1945	Company designation changed to 44th
65th Birmingham	St. Boniface's , Worlds End	1952 - 1963	
65thBirmingham	New Testament Church of God, Muntz St.	1976 - 1980	
65thBirmingham	New Testament Church of God, (Small Heath)	1982 - 1988	

BIRMINGHAM COMPANIES CONTINUED

66th Birmingham	Methodist Church, Brasshouse/Halfords Lane, Smethwick	1938 - 1939
66th Birmingham	Small Heath Baptist Church, Coventry Rd.	1946 - 1995
67th Birmingham	Methodist Church, California	1938 - 1948
67th Birmingham	St. Mary's Church, Selly Oak	1952 -
68th Birmingham	Perry Beeches Baptist Church	1938 - 1994
69th Birmingham	Saltley Congregational Church	1939 - 1941
69th Birmingham	St. Pauls Church Lozells	1943 - 1952
69th Birmingham	Edward Rd. Baptist Church	1968 - 1969
69th Birmingham	First United Church of Jesus Christ (Apostolic)	1970 - 1978
70th Birmingham	Hay Mills Congregational Church	1939 - 1961
70th Birmingham	George Rd. Baptist Church	1969 -
71st Birmingham	St Nicolas with St. Edwards	1943 - 1948
71st Birmingham	Chester Rd. Baptist Church, Sutton Coldfield	1952 - 1953 Company designation changed to 3rd S/C.
71st Birmingham	Union Row Congregational Church, Handsworth	1955 - 1968
71st Birmingham	Nechells Methodist Church	1979 - J/S Coy formed 1978
72nd Birmingham	Shirley Baptist Church	1946 -
73rd Birmingham	Sheldon/ Lyndon Methodist Church	1940 -
74th Birmingham	Westley Rd. Mission	1944 - 1948
74th Birmingham	Gospel Lane Methodist Church, Acocks Green	1948 - 1967 Change of Church connection
74th Birmingham	St. Michael's Anglican Methodist, Hall Green	2000 -
75th Birmingham	Old Oscott Evangelical Church	1944 - 1948
75th Birmingham	Marston Green Free Church	1950 - 1953
75th Birmingham	Stechford Baptist Church	1955 - 1963
75th Birmingham	St. Peter's Church, Tile Cross	1964 -
76th Birmingham	Stechford Methodist Church	1944 - 1989
77th Birmingham	Gospel Lane Methodist Church, Hall Green	1943 - 1946 Company designation changed to 26th
77th Birmingham	Londonderry Baptist Church, Smethwick	1950 - 1954
77th Birmingham	Hope St. Baptist Church	1964 - 1968
78th Birmingham	Mafeking Rd. Mission, Smethwick	1945 -
79th Birmingham	Methodist Mission, Lozells St.	1953 - 1956
79th Birmingham	Parish Church of St, Paul Lozells	1968 - 1973
79th Birmingham	St Silas, Lozells	1973 - 1999
80th Birmingham	Parish Church of St. John and St. Basil	1955 - 1959 Company designation changed to 54th
80th Birmingham	The Parish Church of St. Peter Hall Green	1968 -
81st Birmingham	Mansfield Rd. Methodist Church	1956 - 1972
81st Birmingham	Lozells Hall Methodist Church	1972 - 1974 Change of Church connection
81st Birmingham	Villa Rd. Methodist Church	1974 - 1984 Change of Church connection
82nd Birmingham	St. Matthew's Church Perry Beeches	1956 - 1960
82nd Birmingham	Cannon St. Memorial Baptist Church	1979 - 1988
83rd Birmingham	Ridgacre Methodist Church	1959 - 1966
83rd Birmingham	St. Stephen Church of England, Elmdon	1984 - J/S Coy. formed 1983
84th Birmingham	Kingshurst Methodist Church	1958 - 1982
85th Birmingham	Perry Barr Methodist Church	1958 -
86th Birmingham	Westminster Rd. Congregational Church	1958 - 1974
86th Birmingham	Wilton Road United Reformed Church	1974 - 1999 Change of Church connection
87th Birmingham	St. Agnes' Church, The Cotteridge	1958 - 1976
87th Birmingham	St. Johns Methodist Church	1983 - 1986
88th Birmingham	The Maypole Methodist Church	1959 - 2000
89th Birmingham	Kingstanding Congregational Church	1960 - 1973
89th Birmingham	George Rd. Baptist Church	1973 - 1990 Change of Church connection
90th Birmingham	Perry Beeches Methodist Church	1960 - 1966
91st Birmingham	Spurgeon Baptist Church, Castle Bromwich	1960 - 1971

BIRMINGHAM COMPANIES CONTINUED

92nd Birmingham	Spring Hill Baptist Church	1960 - 1981
93rd Birmingham	Wattville Rd. Evangelical Protestant Church	1962 - 1986
94th Birmingham	St. Chad's Parish Church, Erdington	1963 - 1992
95th Birmingham	Pype Hayes Congregational Church	1963 - 1973
96th Birmingham	St. Cuthbert's Church of England , Castle Vale	1967 - 1985

THE ASTON MANOR COMPANIES

(Originally formed as the **'Aston Lads' Brigade'** in 1889)

No.1 Aston Lads' Brigade	Aston Parish Church (HQ Hoadley's Bed Works)	1889 - 1891	Joined The Boys' Brigade
1st Aston Manor	Aston Parish Church (HQ Alfred Street School)	1891 - 1895	
1st Aston Manor	Aston Parish Church (HQ Dyson Hall)	1895 - 1909	Company designation changed to 1st Birmingham (Aston) BB
No.2 Aston Lads' Brigade	St. James' Mission (HQ Hoadley's Bed Works)	c.1889 - 1896	Joined The Boys' Brigade
2nd Aston Manor	St. James' Mission (HQ St. James' Rooms)	1896 - 1909	
No.3 Aston Lads' Brigade	Holy Trinity Mission ?	c.1889 - c.1895	
3rd Aston Manor	Holy Trinity Mission	1904 - 1909	Company designation changed to 17th Birmingham BB

THE SUTTON COLDFIELD COMPANIES

(From 1953 - 1968 affiliated to the Battalion. From 1968 - part of Battalion.)

1st Sutton Coldfield	Hill Parish Church	1899 - 1903	
1st Sutton Coldfield	Four Oaks Boys Christian Association	1903 - ?	Change of Church connection
1st Sutton Coldfield	Bannersgate Congregational Church	1953 - 1976	Formerly 21st Birmingham
2nd Sutton Coldfield	Walmley Parish Church	1953 -	Formerly 58th Birmingham
3rd Sutton Coldfield	Chester Rd. Baptist Church	1953 -	Formerly 71st Birmingham
4th Sutton Coldfield	Sutton Coldfield Baptist Church	1962 -	

OTHER LOCALLY DESIGNATED COMPANIES

* = affiliated

1st Quinton	Carter Lane Baptist	1930 - c.1933	
1st Quinton		? -1948	Company designation changed to 2nd South Staffs.
1st Solihull	Methodist Church, Solihull.	1930 - ?	
1st Solihull	St Francis of Assisi, Solihull	1951 - 1954	
1st Solihull	Hobs Moat Congregational Church	1960 - 1986	
1st Solihull	Hobs Moat Congregational Church	1990 - 1994	
1st Chelmsley Wood	St. Andrew's Anglican/Methodist Church	1969 - 1972	
1st Marston Green	Marston Green Free Church	1970 - 1974	
1st Marston Green	Marston Green Free Church	1993 - 1995	
1st Castle Bromwich	St. Clement of Alexandria Anglican	1974 -	J/S Coy formed 1972
1st Water Orton	Water Orton Methodist Church	1984 -	
1st Walsall Wood*	Walsall Wood/Ebenezer Methodist Church	1949 - 1968	Joined S. Staffs Batt.
1st Knowle	Knowle Congregational Church	1954 - 1958	

THE BOYS' LIFE BRIGADE COMPANIES

1st Birmingham BLB	Friends Institute Moseley Rd.	1901 - 1913	Became Peace Scouts
1st Birmingham BLB	People's Chapel (Baptist) Great King St. Hockley	1913 - 1926	Company designation changed to 1stA BB
2nd Birmingham BLB	Stratford Rd. Baptist Church	1912 - 1926	Company designation changed to 2ndA BB
3rd Birmingham BLB	Moseley Rd Congregational Church	1907 - 1926	Company designation changed to 3rd BB
4th Birmingham BLB	Ebenezer Congregational, Steelhouse Lane	1924 -1926	Company designation changed to 4thA BB
5th Birmingham BLB	No record		
1st Kings Heath BLB	Kings Heath Baptist Church	1906 - 1922	Company designation changed to 6th BLB
6th Birmingham BLB	Kings Heath Baptist Church	1922 - 1926	Company designation changed to 6th BB
1st Kings Norton BLB	Kings Norton Congregational Watford Road	1907 - 1909	
7th Birmingham BLB	Kings Norton Congregational Watford Road	1909 - 1926	Company designation changed to 7th BB
8th Birmingham BLB	No record		
9th Birmingham BLB	No record		
10th Birmingham BLB	Friends Hall, Farm St. Hockley	1924 - 1926	Company designation changed to 10thA BB
11th Birmingham BLB	NewTown Row Wesleyan Methodist Mission	? - c1914	
		1924 - 1926	Company designation changed to 11th BB
12th Birmingham BLB	Theodore St. Mission Hall, Hockley	1920 - 1926	Company designation changed to 12thA BB
13th Birmingham BLB	Ladypool Rd, Congregational Church	1920 - 1926	Company designation changed to 13th BB
14th Birmingham BLB	Raddlebarn Rd Mission	? - 1926	Company designation changed to 14thA BB
15th Birmingham BLB	No record		
16th Birmingham BLB	Wycliffe Baptist, Bristol Street	? - 1926	Company designation changed to 16th BB
17th Birmingham BLB	No record		
18th Birmingham BLB	Stockland Green Wesleyan Church	1924 - 1926	Company designation changed to 18thA BB
19th Birmingham BLB	Friends' Institute Moseley Road.	1922 - 1926	Company designation changed to 19th BB
20th Birmingham BLB	No record		
21st Birmingham BLB	Guildford St. Baptist Chapel	1921 - 1926	Company designation changed to 21st BB
22nd Birmingham BLB	No record		
23rd Birmingham BLB	Society of Friends - Bull St.	? - 1926	Company designation changed to 23rd BB
24th Birmingham BLB	No record		
25th Birmingham BLB	No record		
26th Birmingham BLB	No record		
27th Birmingham BLB	Monument Rd. United Methodist	1923 - 1926	Company designation changed to 27th BB
28th Birmingham BLB	No record		
29th Birmingham BLB	West Smethwick Congregational Church	1924 - 1926	Company designation changed to 29th BB
30th Birmingham BLB	No record		
31st Birmingham BLB	Tyseley Primitive Methodist Church	1925 - 1926	Company designation changed to 31st BB
32nd Birmingham BLB	Cannon St. Memorial Baptist Church, Soho Rd, Handsworth	1926 - 1926	Company designation changed to 32nd BB
33rd Birmingham BLB	No record		
34th Birmingham BLB	No record		
35th Birmingham BLB	Digbeth Institute	1922 - 1926	Company designation changed to 35th BB

Location of Birmingham BB Companies 2002

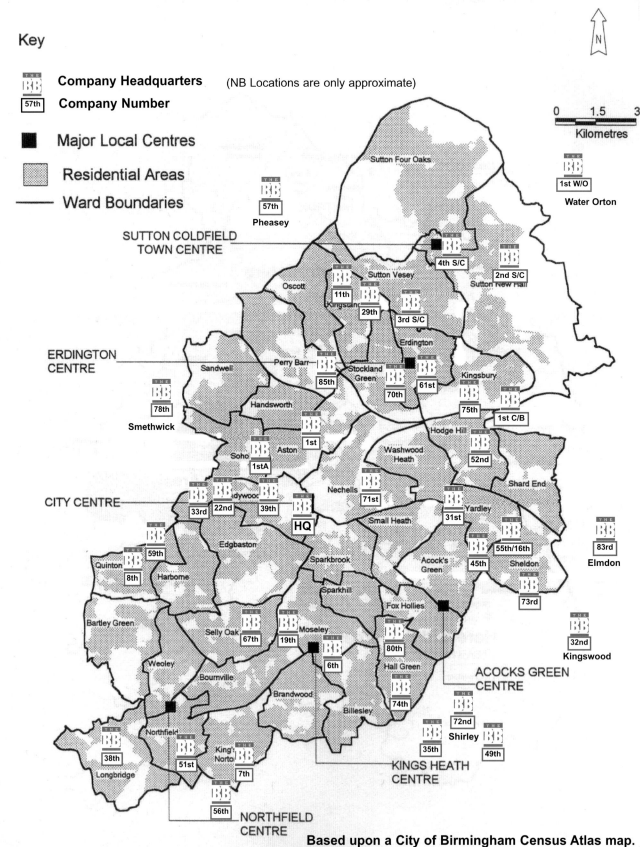

Key

🅱🅱 **Company Headquarters**   (NB Locations are only approximate)

57th **Company Number**

■ **Major Local Centres**

▦ **Residential Areas**

— **Ward Boundaries**

Based upon a City of Birmingham Census Atlas map.

Produced By The Information Team, Dept of Planning & Architecture

Portrait of the Battalion in 2002

1st Birmingham

1stA Birmingham

6th Birmingham

7th Birmingham

8th Birmingham

11th Birmingham

19th Birmingham

22nd Birmingham

Portrait of the Battalion in 2002

29th Birmingham

31st Birmingham

32nd Birmingham

33rd Birmingham

35th Birmingham

38th Birmingham

39th Birmingham

45th Birmingham

Portrait of the Battalion in 2002

49th Birmingham

51st Birmingham

52nd Birmingham

55th/16th Birmingham

56th Birmingham

57th Birmingham

59th Birmingham

61st Birmingham

67th Birmingham

Portrait of the Battalion in 2002

70th Birmingham

71st Birmingham

72nd Birmingham

74th Birmingham

73rd Birmingham

73rd Birmingham

75th Birmingham

78th Birmingham

Portrait of the Battalion in 2002

80th Birmingham

83rd Birmingham

85th Birmingham

2nd Sutton Coldfield

3rd Sutton Coldfield

4th Sutton Coldfield

1st Castle Bromwich

1st Water Orton

The way we were... 50-60 Years Ago

55th Birmingham 1944

10th Birmingham 1954

1stA Birmingham 1955

Battalion Presidents

C. J. Cooke 1902 - 1910

The Founder of the Birmingham Battalion. Captain of the original 6th Company at Christ Church Summerfield. He died in office. His sons took on the job of running the 6th.

Alfred Henry Angus B.Sc. 1911 - 1913

Headmaster of George Dixon School Edgbaston. (1906 - 1913). In 1913 he seems to have moved from B'ham relinquishing his Presidency. He became a College Principal and was a co-opted member of Brigade Exec. until 1921. After 1921 he became Brigade Hon. Vice President a position he held until his death in 1959. He convened a meeting between the BB & BLB at Westhill College in 1924 to discuss union.

D. Gordon Barnsley MC BA 1913 - 1924

The Son of Sir John Barnsley, Battalion Hon. Vice President and first Inspecting Officer of the BB in Birmingham in 1889. He Formed the 8th Coy. at Islington Row Wesleyan Methodist Mission in 1906, with his brother Eric. A Territorial soldier with the Warwick's before the Great War, he served with distinction in the Gloucestershire Regt. during the conflict, becoming Lt. Colonel. He formed the 3rd Birmingham, at Sandon Rd. before leaving to work in London. He was for a while Capt. of 1st Wychwood Coy. before taking up the position as Battalion Secretary in 1935. In 1936, he formed the 54th Coy. at Batt. HQ and part of St. Martin's Church. He spent his time in WWII running a military camp in Southern England. He was for many years Associated with the Wesleyan Assurance Society becoming Deputy Chairman after retiring from his position as Battalion Sec. in 1954. He served two periods as Hon. Battalion Vice-President.

Charles MacGuire (Acting) 1915 - 1918

Captain of 1st (Aston) Coy. 1901 - 1929 & 1932 - 35 a large and very efficient company. In the early years of the 20th Century he was a regular correspondent with the Founder Sir William Smith. He acted as President during D. Gordon Barnsley's War Service.

His Hon. Sir Donald Hurst MA. 1924 - 1927

Stepped-down through pressure of work as a Judge shortly after union with BLB. Was for 1926 - 27 'Joint President' with Donald Finnemore. Remained as Hon. Vice President until his death in 1980.

The Hon. Sir Donald Finnemore M.A. LLD. 1926 - 1927 (Joint President with Donald Hurst). 1931 - 1933, & 1955 - 1965.

County Court Judge 1940 -1947. Judge of High Court (Queen's Bench Division) 1948 - 1964
Vice- President, The Boys' Brigade 1947 - 1974, Member of Brigade Executive. Life Governor of Birmingham University. Founder, in 1913, of the re-formed 1st Birmingham Coy. Boys' Life Brigade which upon union in 1926 became the 1st `A' Birmingham Coy. He also formed the 11th Coy. in 1962 originally a platoon of the 1st`A'. Commandant of the great International `Founder's Camp' on the playing fields of Eton in 1954. President of the Baptist Union of Great Britain & Ireland a post he held between c.1961 - 1967.

Hugh Morton MA, JP. 1927 - 1930

Former President of Birmingham BLB. Brought in upon the BB/BLB union so as not to favour either of the two existing Presidents. Died in office.

Harry Anderson 1933 - 1947

Thirty-Nine years Capt. 4th Birmingham Coy, Hagley Road. Member of Brigade Executive for many years.

In 1st World War served with a City Battalion of the Royal Warwickshire Regiment in France, becoming Adjutant of his Battalion.

In WWII he commanded the 30th Staffordshire Battalion of the Home Guard. Died whilst in office.

The Hon. Sir Ralph Kilner Brown. 1947 - 1955

Founder and first Captain of 29th Birmingham Company 1931 - 1939. Brigadier at Field-Marshal Montgomery's Headquarters, mentioned in Despatches. British Amateur Athletic Champion, 440 Yards Hurdles. Judge of the High Court.

Harold S. Burnett MBE ABSI 1965 - 1979

Capt 10th Birmingham Coy. From 1941 - 1988 Hon. Battalion President 1979 - 1990 Hon. Vice - President of The Boys' Brigade 1981 - 1990

For many years Chairman of the N.C.O.'s Association.

Battalion 'Chairman of Executive' 1955 - 1963, and `Deputy President' 1961 - 65.

Stan Gilbert. 1979 - 1988

1945 Appointed as West Midland District Organiser, position he held until 1967. Ex. Capt. 53rd Coy. Kings Norton Methodist Church. Shared offices at 24 Union St. alongside D. Gordon Barnsley & W. Gordon Innes.

Fred Barker 1988 - 1998

59th Coy. Since 1998 serving as 'Honorary President' in recognition of his work for the Battalion. Brigade training Officer.

Anthony Wakeman 1998 -

73rd Coy. Captain of Company 1969 - 1996. Former Chairman of Coy. Section Committee. Vice President 1980 - 1984

Chairman of the Battalion Trustees.

Battalion Office-Bearers 2002

Albert Lakins Hon. Battalion Treasurer Hon. Vice-President Trustee	**Barbara Nash** Hon. Vice-President	**George Scott** Hon. Vice-President Trustee	**Dennis Riley** Hon. Vice-President	**Pat Thomas** Ex 4th S/C Coy Vice-President & Hon. Vice-President

Paul Battarbee 51st Coy. Vice-President	**Kevin Collins** Capt. 8th Coy. Vice-President	**Malcolm Sorby** Capt. 67th Coy. Vice-President	**Gill White** Ex. 29th Coy Vice-President

Battalion Secretaries & Staff 1902 - 2002

Charles Beckett

Mr. Charles L. Beckett. Hon. Sec. 1906 - 1934
Mr. Frederick C. Pullen, Full Time Secretary 1919 - 1920 (Resigned)
Mr P. A. Lawrence 'Permanent' Full Time Secretary 1931 - 32 (Resigned)
Mr Ernest Willatt Hon. Assistant Secretary - 1933.

Mr. D. Gordon Barnsley M.C. B.A. Part-Time Secretary 1935 - 1940
Mr. R. G. Williams Acting Hon. Sec. 1940 - 1942
(Whilst D.G.B on Military Service)
Mr. C. Eric Skinner, Hon Sec. 1943 - 1945
(D.G.B. termed `General Secretary')
D.G.B. Part Time Secretary 1945 - 1954
Mr. Horace Caney & Miss. J. Gibbs in office.
Mr. Reg. H. Webb Acting Hon. Sec. 1954 - 1955

Gordon Barnsley

Mr. W. Gordon Innes
Part Time Secretary, 01/02/1955 - 30/04/1964

Mr. Reg. H. Webb Full Time Secretary 01/05/1964 - 16/10/1976
Mr. John White Full Time Assistant to Sec. 1970 - 1971
Miss Robina Hewlett & Miss Christine Ball, Full Time Secretaries,
Mr. Bob Pacey Part Time Supplies Salesperson. Cleaner.

Gordon Innes

Mr. Dennis Riley Assistant to Sec. then Full Time Assistant Secretary 1972 - 1976
Mr. Dennis Riley Full Time Secretary 16/10/76 - 30/06/96
Mrs Sandra Willson Full Time Assistant to Secretary.
(? until 31/07/1980)
Mr. Les Dimbylow Part Time Office Assistant. Mrs. Val Morton Full Time Assistant to Secretary 08/09/1980 - 6/11/86
(Cleaner, Part - time)

Reg Webb

Mrs. Pat Stansbie Part Time Assistant to Sec./Admin Officer. 27/04/87 - 31/12/95

Mr. Roger Green
Full Time Secretary 01/12/1995 -
Mrs. Sue Jones, Assistant 11/03/02 -

Dennis Riley

Roger Green

BRIGADE COUNCIL 1949 - RECEPTION COMMITTEE
A 'who's who' of the first half century of Birmingham Battalion office-bearers!

Back Row (Left to Right)
A. H. Thorn (Adjutant) George W. Oakton (Carey Hall), Frank Lock (Stewards), Reg Webb (Transport) Stan Gilbert (West Mid District), Ron A. Smith (Arden)

Middle Row
Rupert Wastell (Imperial), Jack Mulingani (Bands), Ernie Glascott (University), Charles L. Beckett (Cobden), George F. A. Scott (Cobden), Miss J. Gibbs (H.Q. Office) Horace Caney (H.Q. Office)

Front Row
Charles Taylor (Publicity), Alan Carlyle (Finance), W. Gordon Innes (Arden), D. Gordon Barnsley (Secretary), Ralph Kilner Brown (Battalion President), Lionel G Alldridge (Civics), C. Eric Skinner (Imperial), E. "Man" Roberts (Saltley Col.), Harold S. Burnett (Finance).

Hon. Presidents

1902? - 1911	The Right Honorable The Earl of Warwick.
1914 - 1925	The Lord Mayor of Birmingham
1930 - 1958	Barrow Cadbury J.P.
1965 - 1974	The Hon Sir Donald Finnemore
1979 - 1990	Harold Burnett MBE
1998 -	F. A. Barker

Hon. Vice-Presidents
Over the years a great number of men & women have served the Battalion well, as Vice Presidents. Many have subsequently been given the title 'Hon. Vice-President'. There are too-many names to list separately.

Battalion Chaplains 2002

Rev. Peter Bates

Rev. Steve Fellows

Rev. Ken Hawkings

Mr. Brian Morris

Rev. Richard Taylor

Battalion Trustees

The Trustees of the Birmingham Battalion have responsibility for admininstering two main funds:

1. **The Stechford Trust Fund**, money invested from sale of land in Stechford and from 'Perrycroft'.
2. **The proceeds from the sale of the former Battalion HQ** at Hatchett St.

The income from these funds is distributed for the benefit of the boys of the Birmingham Battalion as agreed annually by the Battalion Council.

The following Trustees have served the Battalion since 1965:

Sir Donald Finnemore	1965 - 1974
Harold Burnett	1965 - 1990
Charles Taylor	1965 - 1986
Allan Carlyle	1965 - 1973
John Chaplin	1965 - 1970
Tom Richards	1971 - 1986
Arthur Riley	1971 - 1989
George Scott	1974 -
Ken Bushell	1975 - 1989
Stanley Gilbert	1986 - 1990
Albert Lakins	1986 -
David Piearce	1986 - 2000
Fred Barker	1989 - 1993
Anthony Wakeman (Chairman)	1989 -
Mel. Inman	1993 -
Roger Gough	1993 -
Kevin Jones	2000 -
Ian Stott	2001 -

The Anatomy of the Battalion

In many ways a Battalion is a living changing organism, reflecting the needs of the companies of which it is composed. In the early years in Birmingham companies were slow to form and change was gradual. There was only a small group of officers to run things, generally company captains. Conveners of Committees made up the Battalion Executive with a few specialists called in to assist. The Treasurer and Secretary were Ex-Officio members of all Committees. Mr Charles Beckett, the first Hon. Secretary carried the burden of day to day administration. For the first thirty years or so Mr Beckett was very much `Mr Birmingham BB'. Committees with new ideas would tentatively ask 'What do you think Mr Beckett will say about it?'

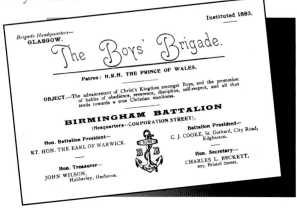

In its first decade companies came and went quite quickly, and a policy, which was to last out the century, of numbers being re-allocated when a Coy folded or was dormant for twelve months, became established. In 1909 the two Aston Manor companies joined as Aston Merged with Birmingham politically, as the original 1st Coy had closed the 1st Aston Manor took over as 'No 1'.

The Union with the BLB in 1926 virtually doubled the size of the Battalion, so to make it easier to administer some 50 Coys in those days before mass car and telephone ownership, four 'Groups' were created. The 1927 Battalion Rules stated:

'The Battalion shall be divided into four Groups, NE, NW, SE & SW, comprising all companies situated within the areas divided by the following boundaries:- NE & NW Corporation Street, Lancaster Street, Newtown Row, Birchfield Road and the Walsall Road. NW & SW New Street, Congreve Street, Summer Row, Spring Hill, Dudley Road. SW & SE Pershore Street, Sherlock Street and Pershore Road. SE & NE. LMS Railway, New Street Station to Stechford.'

Group Councils arranged competitions for Drill and Efficiency, First Aid, Physical Training and Swimming. (Rules were set by Battalion, exactly the same for each Group). Councils also arranged for badgework examiners.

In the session 1935-1936 five 'Divisions' were introduced in place of the Groups, each Division having a `Commandant' in charge. Commandants and Divisions were terms inherited from the BLB. The Divisions were:
Central: St Paul's, St. Mary's, Duddeston & Nechells, Ladywood, Market Hall, St Martin's & St. Bart's. (14 Coys)
North West: Sandwell, Soho, Handsworth, Lozells, All Saints & Rotton Park. (10 Coys)
North East: Perry Barr, Erdington, Gravelly Hill, Aston, Bromford, Washwood Heath & Saltley. (11 Coys)
South East: Stechford, Yardley, Small Heath, Sparkbrook, Sparkhill, Acocks Green, Hall Green, Moseley & Kings Heath, Balsall Heath. (17 Coys)
South West: Edgbaston, Harborne, Selly Oak, King's Norton, Northfield, & Borough of Smethwick. (10 Coys)

The Second World War created havoc with Battalion organisation. Some 14 Companies lost their H.Q.s as well as the Battalion H.Q. being destroyed. The Inner City, much of the old `Central' Division, was most seriously affected. After the war the Battalion reverted to Four Divisions, doing away with the old 'Central' grouping. Nevertheless, improvements came rapidly. In 1949, the 1st Walsall Wood Company was allowed to 'affiliate'. It took part in many competitions and displays until 1968. Three Sutton Coldfield Coys. were designated in 1953 (Ex. B'ham No's 21st, 58th & 71st) they too now became 'affiliated'. At this time authorisation came from Brigade HQ to allow the Battalion to enlarge its boundaries to include Smethwick, Solihull and Aldridge UDC's. However, this had already been done some years earlier, but at least, now it was 'legal'!

Divisions ran many competitions such as Band and Drill, and also held their own Founder's Day Parade Services. After 1966 Junior Section events, and Anchor Boy events from 1978, gave the Divisions an enhanced role as a 'local' provider. By 1967, the highest numbered company in the Battalion, the 96th Birmingham Coy. at St. Cuthbert's Castle Vale, had started. Sadly, the many companies started since that date have had a 'previously used' number. In 1968, the Sutton Coldfield companies became part of the Battalion, six years before the Town became subsumed by the City. A Study Group examined the Battalion structure in 1987 but made no changes to the four Divisions.

In 2002, the Battalion has an Officers Council and an elected Executive Committee, headed by a President. There are also 'Honorary' positions. Before 1993, there was a 'Committee' structure based upon the age groups within the Battalion. Today the 'Activitiy Forum' is the main policy-making and steering group for all ages.

Welcome to...
Battalion Headquarters

Before 1928, the Battalion 'HQ' was generally regarded as being where the Secretary was based. Between 1906 and 1928 Batt. Hon.Sec.Charles Beckett operated from home, which he moved at least four times, and from his Tailoring Business in Pinfold St. However, between 1907 and 1910 the Headquarters was given on Battalion Notepaper as the office of the Hon. Treasurer, George Barker, probably because it was convenient for Mr Beckett. After the 1st World War the Battalion took on a full-time Secretary who worked at the office of the Hon. Treasurer. The appointment was, however, short-lived. Charles Beckett who had remained 'Hon.' Sec. simply took up his position again. Below is a summary of the premises from which the Battalion was run:

No Fixed Abode...

Batt. Hon. Sec. Charles Beckett:
1906 - 1907 - **207 Bristol Street & Corporation Street.**
1908 - 1912 - **153, City Road Edgbaston.**
1907 -1910 - **'Battalion Headquarters' 77 Colmore Row** (Business Address of Hon. Treasurer)
Batt. Hon. Sec. Charles Beckett:
1912 -1916 - **40, Selwyn Road, Edgbaston.**
1917 - 1918 - **Avenue Road Dorridge**.
Batt. Sec. (Full-Time) Fredk. C. Pullen:
1918 - 1919 - **'Battalion Headquarters' 45a International Exchange**, Edmund Street.
(Business Address of Hon. Treasurer) [F.C. Pullen resigned on medical orders]
Batt. Hon.Sec. Charles Beckett,
1919 - 1920 - **35, Pinfold St.**
1920 - 1922 - **Avenue Road Dorridge**
1922 - 1928 - **35, Pinfold St.**

St. Mary's Hall **Whittall Street** Opened Wednesday 9th January 1929.

1928 - 1935

Whittall Street

Report from the Birmingham Gazette, Thursday 10th January 1929.

Birmingham Boys' Brigade.
Lord Mayor Opens New Headquarters.
'Admirable use has been made of the church hall formerly attached to St. Mary's Church, Whittall street, Birmingham, for it has become the headquarters of the Birmingham Battalion of the Boys' Brigade.
The battalion's headquarters, which will be used for administrative purposes, were opened last night by the Lord Mayor, (Alderman W. Byng Kenrick).
In introducing the Lord Mayor, Mr Hugh Morton (battalion president) stated that at the present time there were 54 companies associated with the Brigade in the city, with a membership of 2,000. For many years they had lacked central administration headquarters, and they believed the acquisition of St. Mary's Hall would give a great stimulus to their work.
In declaring the hall open, the Lord Mayor commended the work of the Brigade to all his fellow citizens, and referred to the urgent need of additional voluntary assistance in carrying out its activities. He congratulated them upon securing so well-adapted a building. There was still an enormous field in the city for such work among boys, and the more clubs there were opened the greater would be hope for the future of the city.
In proposing a vote of thanks to the lord mayor, Mr Gilbert Southall (hon. treasurer) referred to the valuable voluntary work done by the officers of the battalion. To a large extent they had been responsible for the furnishing and equipping of the hall.
This was seconded by Mr Donald Hurst, who paid a tribute to Mr. G. Southall's efforts in securing the building for the battalion. Its acquisition would be amply justified if it resulted, as he believed it would, in greater activity in the movement.
Mr. D. L. Finnemore (vice-president) was unable to attend, as he was out of town on a professional engagement.'

The hall had a large room for conferences and training classes, a committee room and an office accommodating a part-time lady clerk. It was rented from a Miss S. J. Turner.
Cost of refurbishment etc. was £245.12.9p Most raised from donations. (£75 subsidy from general account)

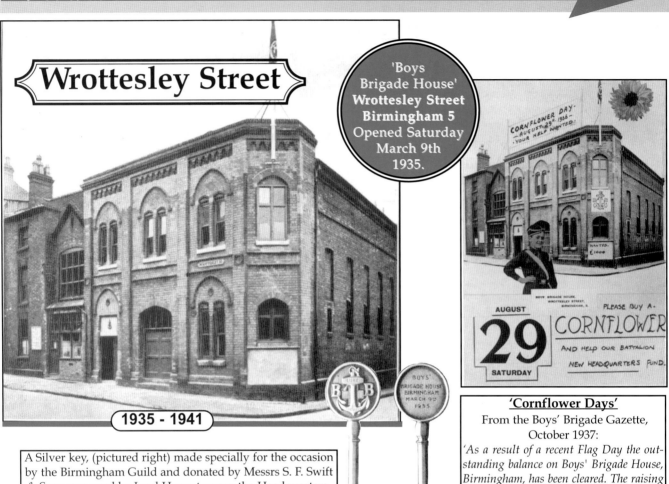

Wrottesley Street

'Boys Brigade House' **Wrottesley Street Birmingham 5** Opened Saturday March 9th 1935.

1935 - 1941

A Silver key, (pictured right) made specially for the occasion by the Birmingham Guild and donated by Messrs S. F. Swift & Sons was used by Lord Home to open the Headquarters. The key was presented to Lord Home.

'Cornflower Days'
From the Boys' Brigade Gazette, October 1937:
'As a result of a recent Flag Day the outstanding balance on Boys' Brigade House, Birmingham, has been cleared. The raising of the £5,000 has been made possible by the efforts of our Officers and Boys and the generosity of the citizens, two flag days and a broadcast appeal by the Battalion Hon. President, Mr Barrow Cadbury, who from the first has been one of the most generous supporters of the scheme.'

Opening of Birmingham's New Headquarters by Earl of Home,
It was the coldest week-end of the winter according to Battalion Sec. Gordon Barnsley who wrote in the Boys' Brigade Gazette:

'…Lord Home, after inspecting a well turned out, but very frozen, guard of honour, unlocked the doors with a silver key... The premises, centrally situated-almost within stone-throw of New Street Station-will meet a long felt need. They comprise a large, well lighted hall for meetings, Officers' and N.C.O.s' training classes, and Old Boy activities, together with administrative offices, committee rooms,canteen, store rooms and equipment department.'

The premises were formerly occupied by the Hebrew Community. Reconstruction work was carried out by Messrs. S. F. Swift and Sons to the designs of Mr. W. J. Green.

Lord Home inspects the 'frozen Guard of Honour' at the opening ceremony, accompanied by Mr Harry Anderson Batt. President. (on the left)

Wrottesley Street HQ was, sadly, destroyed by enemy action in 1941.

'Temporary accommodation' 1941 - 1963

Between 1941-1945 a temporary HQ was set up at **Islington Methodist Institute**, the HQ of the 8th Company, in **St. Martin's Street,** Birmingham 15.

1945 - 1963 HQ **24, Union Street,** Birmingham 2.
The HQ, which shared premises with the West Midland District Office, was on the third storey and was somewhat utilitarian, particularly as it was approched - as Gordon Innes stated in his final Annual Report assembled in Union St...
'Despite its rather dismal and fitness -testing approach, 24 Union St. has made a grand contribution to the welfare of the Birmingham Battalion.'
In the 1961 - 62 Annual Report the Secretary observed that *'With all the surrounding property being re-built it is obvious that eviction hangs, like the sword of Damocles, continuously over our heads.'* The Battalion eventually had to move out because the building was due for demolition; another permanent HQ would need to be found in double quick time.

1963 HQ Colmore Chambers, 1, **Newhall Street** Birmingham 3.
Colmore Chambers was always going to be temporary; the Battalion moved in on August 1st 1963. The offices were on the fourth storey, and there was a lift (which did not not operate between 1-2 p.m.). It was described as being *'...well amongst the starlings'*. The rooms were smaller but brighter than at Union St.. There was no room for Stan Gilbert and the District office, which was now located at 218c Monument Rd.. Finances, according to the Annual Report, it seems were *'strained to the utmost'*, but help was just round the corner...well not far away.

Hatchett Street

1962

**'BB House'
Hatchett Street
Birmingham 19.
Opened Saturday
5th December
1963**

1963 - 1989

1989 -

BB House in the 1960s. Little changed from its days as 'Havergal House'. The New Town Row Wesleyan Methodist Mission originally stood to the right of the building, its site being used here as a makeshift car - park. Despite the large expanse of wall the somewhat unpretentious 'Boys Brigade House' sign can be clearly seen - if you look hard enough!

Centenary House today. The extensive alterations and additions can be clearly seen and the Scout Fleur-de-Lys emblem is prominent. Whilst the original Havergal House could never have been described as attractive, the somewhat utilitarian appendage fails to do it justice.

The 'Hatchett St.' Story

Opened on Nov. 21st 1934, 'The New Havergal House' designed by Mr. A. L. Snow, A.R.I.B.A. was a purpose-built project organised by the New Town Row Methodist Mission. It was a replacement for the 'Havergal House Girls' Club for Working Girls' established in 1890 and named after the famous hymn-writer Frances Ridley Havergal a personal friend of the minister Rev. J. G. Mantle. Initially meeting in the school room of the New Town Row Mission, the club moved out to premises in New Town Row, near the Mission, but behind and over the shops of Messrs George Masons and the Shoe Warehouse. New Town Row had become one of the poorest most overcrowded districts of the city as wealthier residents moved out to the new suburbs of Handsworth and Perry Barr. The site of the new hostel was next door to the 'Barnsley Hall' also part of the New Town

Hatchett Street In 1905
The Street has many back to back houses along with courts and tenements. The corner of New Town Row and Hatchett St. is dominated by the Wesleyan Mission, Sunday School and Barnsley Hall.

Row Mission and spacious home since the early years of the century, to the 11th B'ham. Coy. BLB which became the 11th B'ham. Coy. BB in 1926. Barnsley Hall, built in 1895, was dedicated to the memory of Harold Barnsley the son of Thomas Barnsley Esq. J.P., a well-known local builder, who provided the £1000 needed for its construction.

Many classes took place in the new building including a Girls' Life Brigade Company. Boxes of flowers on the roof-garden were tended by the girls and the bathrooms, a rarity in the area, were much used. The Wesleyan Mission, opened in 1837, occupied the corner site of Hatchett St. and New Town Row next to Barnsley Hall and a caretaker's house. On the night of the last Sunday in August 1940 a delayed-action bomb fell on the Minister's vestry and exploded later, demolishing both the church and Barnsley Hall. Havergal House, which had miraculously escaped with only broken windows, was registered and adapted for worship. However, due to the depopulation of the New Town area, and the need for road widening of New Town Row, the Chapel was not rebuilt and so Havergal House continued to house the Church. By 1963, the Methodist Church in Birmingham no longer had a use for the building, offering it for sale to The Boys' Brigade. The original Barnsley Hall and Mission site is the area now occupied by the car park and a widened New Town Row.

Havergal House became 'BB House' in 1963 an altogether satisfactory arrangement. Firstly, because the Battalion needed a home in the central area of the city. Secondly, because the site had been the

HQ of the 11th Coy. BLB/BB. And last, but not least, the 'Barnsley' family was, of course, the same one which had produced a Battalion Hon. Vice President, (Sir John Barnsley V.D. , J.P) and President/Secretary (D. Gordon Barnsley M.C., B.A.).

The three-storey building, always simply referred to as 'Hatchett St', had a hall, large room and kitchen downstairs with offices on the two floors above including a Chapel on the top floor. An unusual feature was the flat roof, no longer a roof garden which was frequently used for drill instruction.

Boys' Brigade House
Opened by the Brigade Secretary Major-General D. J. Wilson-Haffenden C.B.E accompanied by Batt. President Sir Donald Finnemore and Secretary designate Reg Webb. The day after, The Lord Bruce, DL., J.P. the Brigade President, inspected both a Guard of Honour and the building, (above) and then addressed a crowd of some 200 NCOs of the Battalion.

The Battalion paid £12,500 for it and spent £2,000 on alterations and redecoration although the door-mat with its large 'H H' remained. The Hall was used for badge tests, competitions as varied as Table- tennis, First Aid, Band and virtually all Battalion Meetings. The 'Equipment Department' was able to be re-established in 1966 after a gap stretching back to the bombing of Wrottesley St.. It was always a key meeting place on Saturday mornings for Battalion Officers to gossip over numerous cups of tea being made in the kitchen.

In 1987, the building, now used far less, was sold to the Birmingham Scout Association. Extensive modernisation took place over the next year including a new roof over the hall. Now called 'Centenary House' because 1989, its year of re- opening, was the Centenary of Birmingham's City status. It remains 'HQ' because the Battalion retains two offices for the Battalion Secretary, which were not vacated throughout all the re-building work! Appropriately, 1989 was also the Centenary of The Boys' Brigade in Birmingham.

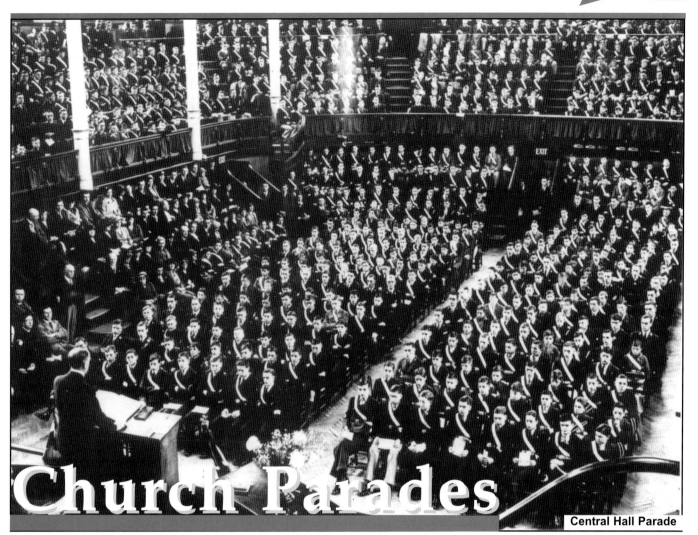

Central Hall Parade

Church Parades

T he Annual Battalion Church Parade is the outward expression of all that the Battalion holds dear. Officers and boys of all ages and denominations worshipping together. Anglicans, Baptists, Congregationalists, Methodists, Quakers gathering to celebrate all that they hold in common as members both of the Brigade and of one of its biggest Battalions - Birmingham.

Just like the proverbial oak tree starting with the acorn the first Battalion Parades were small affairs, but only because the Battalion was small. It has always been the aim that as many members as possible should turn out to bear witness and praise the Lord. For many years Annual Reports proudly announced the exact turnout at Battalion Parades. Over the years the times and format of the Parade have changed. The first report we have is actually from the Second Annual Report (1906-7).

'...most Successful Battalion Church Parade held on Sunday April 14th at Small Heath Congregational Church, resulting in an excellent muster and an impressive and enjoyable service.'

Small Heath Cong. Church was the HQ of the 13th Coy. In 1910-11 we know that the Annual Church Parade took place on Sunday Afternoon March 19th at Summer Hill Wesleyan Church. The Parade State was 430 of all ranks. In 1913 the Annual Parade at Digbeth Institute was being called the 'Spring' parade, but there is no record of another later in the year even though this event on 27th April was completely spoiled by rain with only a few companies turning out. Seven hundred and thirty nine af all ranks turned out for the one Parade of 1914, representing 16 Coys.. The 1915-16 Annual Report mentions that the 'First Founders Day Church Parade' was held on the last Sunday in October at St. Luke's Church, a second parade being held at the Central Hall when Mr Macguire, the Battalion Vice-President, gave the address.

Two parades per year seems to have been regarded as usual by 1917 with the split not only being that of the time of year it was held, but also between Church of England and Non-Conformist. The idea of holding two parades continued until the outbreak of the Second World War. The Cathedral, Carrs Lane, and St. Martin's churches, which would figure stongly in the list of venues for the

Muster for Battalion Parade
St. Mary's Recreation Ground
April 1921

next fifty years, were all used between the wars. In 1919 St. Asaph's Church was used because it was hoped to start a Company there that year. A notable spring parade was held in 1920 at Islington Wesleyan Church where the address was given by Brig. Gen. Sir John Barnsley, Hon. Batt. Vice-President when the singing was led by the Brass Band of the 1st Coy. In the Session 1921 - 1922 the parades were at St. Mary's and the Central Hall. The Rev. Guthrie Gamble, the founder of the 1st Swatow Coy. in China spoke at a special Church Parade in December 1923. In 1924 there was another special parade arranged for the presentation and dedication of the new Battalion Memorial Colours, held at the Town Hall, the first time the Town Hall had been used by the Battalion for a religious service. The Town Hall was the obvious venue for the great Brigade Council Parade of 1927. Mr. Norman Birkett addressed 500 Officers and 1500 boys and the Lord Mayor took the salute at the march-past afterwards.

By the 1930s it became clear that only the largest venues were suitable for the growing Battalion. At a service in the Parish Church conducted by Canon Guy Rogers, (the Rector of Birmingham) it was reported that *'every available seat in the church was occupied.'* By the end of the decade only the Town Hall or Methodist Central Hall would accommodate the whole 2000 plus members of the Battalion who turned out for each parade. In 1935, the day after he had opened the new Battalion HQ in Wrottesley St., Lord Home, Brigade President, addressed the Battalion on the subject of 'leadership' at the Church Parade in the Town Hall.

May 9th 1937 was the date of the special Coronation

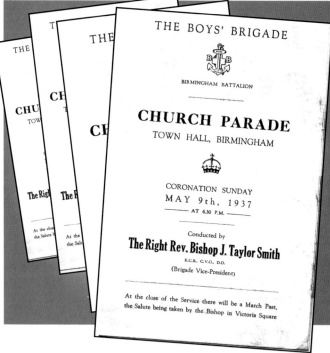

THE BOYS' BRIGADE

BIRMINGHAM BATTALION

CHURCH PARADE

TOWN HALL, BIRMINGHAM

CORONATION SUNDAY
MAY 9th, 1937
—— AT 6.30 P.M. ——

Conducted by

The Right Rev. Bishop J. Taylor Smith
K.C.B., C.V.O., D.D.
(Brigade Vice-President)

At the close of the Service there will be a March Past,
the Salute being taken by the Bishop in Victoria Square

Sunday Church Parade. Bishop J Taylor Smith took an Evening Service at the Town Hall (See Prog. Front). Unfortunately, the weather was bad and a March Past afterwards, impossible. There were 'only' 989 on parade because several companies had special services at their own churches. The weather was better in October that year when the last Battalion Church Parade held to celebrate Founder's day was held at the Central Hall. The address at this service being given by the somewhat aptly named Rev. A Perry Park. MA. In spring 1938, the Divisions held Church Parades instead of the usual sec-

Marching through Victoria Square in the 1930s
Inset: Inside the Town Hall

ond Battalion event. The Founder's day parade on October 30th was also a Divisional event allowing the Annual Church Parade to be moved to Summer of 1939. The war seriously interrupted the pattern of Annual Church Parades, none being held in the 1939 - 1940 session. Under severe pressure and with much reduced numbers the 1941 Service took place at St. Martin's with 1200 of all ranks being present, which was rightly regarded as an outstanding success. The Diamond Jubilee of the Brigade was not forgotten with a special Thanksgiving Service held at the Central Hall on 4th July 1943. The parade orders regarding dress make interesting reading:

'All Officers and boys will parade in correct uniform. Attention must be carefully given to the white piping and white braid on all uniform caps. If wet, coats will be brought, if not worn will be carried folded over the left arm. <u>Gas masks should be carried with slings over left shoulder.</u> All ranks to wear collar and tie.'

Both the Lord Mayor and Archdeacon of Aston took part in the service.
The 1945 Annual Church Parade held at Carrs Lane Church was attended by The Lord Mayor, Alderman W.T.

Wiggins-Davies (Ex 1st Birmingham BB) who read the lesson; there were 1228 all ranks on parade. Divisional Parades were also held again that year.

After the war, parades started to return to normal with the 1946 service being a special re-dedication of the Battalion Colours in memory of those members and ex-members of the Battalion who had lost their lives in the conflict. Fifty four companies, totalling 1411 all ranks, were on parade at St. Martin's Church. After the service a new form of march-past formation was adopted, 'Divisions in sixes' with the salute being taken by Major-Gen. R. Eric Barnsley C.B., M.C., K.H.S. Major-Gen. Barnsley a former officer of the 8th Coy. was the brother of the Battalion Secretary. The new parade formation was *'favourably commented upon'.*

By the late 1940s the number parading was regaining its pre-war level. When, in 1947, the Annual West Midland District Conference was held in Birmingham a record 2220 were on parade. The Brigade President, Sir Joseph P Maclay K.B.E., read one of the lessons and the address was given by Councillor A. G. B. Owen, O.B.E., J.P.. There was also a 'normal' Battalion Church Parade in 1947. The Brigade Council Church Parade of 11th Sept. 1949 had 2180 members of the Battalion plus 572 visiting officers parading to The Town Hall and the Central Hall with the lesson being read by the Brigade President at the Town Hall and by The Brigade Secretary at the Central Hall.

Eyes right! Passing the saluting base, District Church Parade 1967

In 1950, for the first time, two churches were used concurrently for the normal Annual Parade in July; St. Martin's North Divisions, and Carrs Lane South Divisions received 1900 all ranks. During the next year when the Cathedral and Central Hall received 2031 all ranks the NE and SW Divisions shared the Cathedral and NW and SE Divisions the Central Hall. The Battalion in its Jubilee Year 1952, reported record strength of 3312 plus 1754 Life Boys so it is not surprising that St Martin's and Carrs Lane were well filled with 2145 all ranks. The Founders Day Divisional Parades saw 2160 all ranks parading. The Town Hall was filled with 1950 all ranks for the Coronation Year Service. Perhaps the wettest Parade was that of July 3rd 1954 at St Martin's and Carrs Lane. Deluge descended as the Boys assembled in the Car Park. A march to church was impossible, so boys went independently. Many were drenched and having sat in wet clothes for the service it was considered advisable to cancel the march past which was the first time in living memory that such a decision was made. There was another service in October 1954 at the Central Hall in celebration of the Founder's Centenary. Next year the summer was a little drier with the Divisions again being 'rotated' between the churches.

An innovation was made in 1957 at the President's suggestion. The usual split, geographically between the two churches, was done by age. Seniors 15 + went to St Martin's, Brigade Sec. D.J. Wilson-Haffenden C.B.E. gave the address suitable to their age while the Juniors went to Carrs Lane

and the Rev. R.F. Clarke gave a suitable talk. It was repeated in 1958 with Seniors at St Martin's and Juniors at the Central Hall. Mr E. R. Staniford (Editor of 'Stedfast Mag') addressed the Juniors in 1959. The Senior/Junior split was continued until 1963.

Central Birmingham on Sundays in the 1960s and 70s was, to say the least, quiet. This was before 'Sunday Trading' of any kind was commonplace. The city centre on Sunday was normally virtually deserted, that is except on one Sunday, usually in either May or June for the Annual Battalion Church Parade. From 1960 - 1964 a giant parade of some 2000 plus Birmingham BB boys was split between St Martin's-in-the-Bull-Ring and Carrs Lane Church, moving to The Town Hall from 1965 - 1971. In the decade from 1972 to the 1982 the Methodist Central Hall was the favoured venue. Before the parade the four Divisions would fall-in, each in a suitable side-street near the city centre and the Divisional Band would form up at its head. At a pre-determined time, published on Battalion orders from the President, the separate parades would set off each with more than 500 boys usually led by a band of fifty or sixty players. How those drums and bugles would echo from the canyon-like Victorian and Edwardian buildings, which gave way to newer skyscrapers as the parades approached their destination. The whistles would blow and bugle tune instructions would be yelled by each bandmaster over the crashing noise of their young enthusiastic percussionists. The few people who were about, generally friends and family of the BB members found strategic positions to watch the parades, always keeping one eye on the watch so as to take a short - cut to the Church or Town Hall to be sure of securing a reasonable seat.

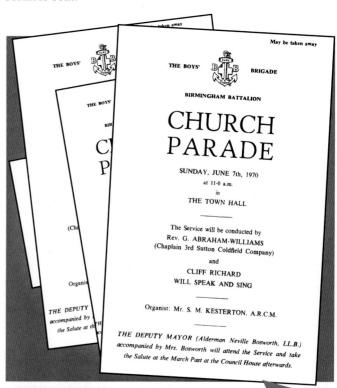

The Battalion would take some time to be seated and settled and it was always every officer's dread that his boys would let down the company so we were always given strict instructions about behaviour, NCO's being reminded of their role and officers seated amongst the boys, not all together. In the Central Hall at least a third of the congregation looked directly out upon another third, if your own officers were not watching you those from another company, seated opposite, were! Proceedings would commence with a great organ - voluntary played by an eminent organist such as Messrs. S. M. Kesterton, A.R.C.M, Stanley Mountford, John Harrison or Richard T. Popple M.B.E. This background music would always tend to drown any banter which eminated from the assembling mass of Brummie boyhood. Generally I remember it was usually all quite reverent and restrained. Only 'Company' section boys were present, The Life Boys, later 'Junior Section', having their own Parade on another occasion. Everyone had a printed service sheet which had 'May be taken away' in the top or bottom corner, and they usually were, but I suspect that they may have still been taken if it had said 'Please do not take away'. Perhaps not as we were all very obedient and honest BB boys.

The congregation would rise and the platform party would make its entrance, usually including the Lord Mayor or The Lord Mayor's Deputy, Battalion officers and those conducting the service. The Battalion Colours, carried and escorted proudly to the front by officers and boys of the champion drill company, would be received and the colour party turned about to the barked whisper of the officer in charge.

The service began. The format was usually three hymns, prayers, a collection in aid of the International Extension Fund, Bible readings and the address. Well - known Birmingham clergy conducted the services, Canon Bryan Green, Rt. Rev. Laurence Brown M.A. Bishop of Birmingham, Rev. Ronald W. Frost, B. D. (notably the father of famous son David), Rev. Alan Broadbent (for many years Battalion Chaplain) and many others. Sometimes the speaker would be a layman, The Hon. Sir Donald Finnemore, Battalion President (1960), E.R. Staniford, Brigade Executive, Editor Stedfast Mag. and Capt. 1st Bletchley Coy. (1962) Cliff Richard, Brigade Hon Vice President, (1970) to name but a few. I can remember the people, but not very much that was said. I guess it did us all a lot of good at the time and no doubt changed a few lives. The sight and sound was certainly an impressive experience. At the end of the service the colours were withdrawn and everyone filed out of the building.

Divisions were re-assembled with their bands and prepared for the grand march-past. Company Captains carefully checked the uniform of the boys. Only boys in correct uniform were allowed to take part in the march-past.

new recruits who had been given the opportunity to parade to the church now had to watch from the pavement. A 'static' band was positioned outside the Council House in Victoria Square, not pedestrianised in those days. Only the static band would play as each Division marched past. The whole parade formed up and marched along Colmore Row, Divisional bands being silenced before approaching the saluting base. The Lord Mayor and other dignitaries watched as the giant column of thousands of boys made its way past. This was both the city honouring the BB and the BB symbolically paying its respects to the city. Usually the BB flag would fly from the mast on the Council House.

After our Division had dismissed, I remember a quite surreal experience. Here was this giant city of Birmingham seemingly inhabited only by BB people. It was a sort of living BB dream. All the bus stops had groups of boys and officers in uniform, buses passed by full of BB boys. Every car was driven by a BB officer. Street corners had small groups of BB folk standing around in deep animated conversation. A company, no doubt based in the central area, marched past, led by its own small band. A stack of drums awaiting transport blocked part of the pavement watched

"Formality"
The Battalion Colours are paraded at the 1997 Villa Park Celebration Service

and a sad reflection upon the warped priorities of a so called 'modern' society. A selfish society which spends billions of pounds annually trying in vain to solve the problems caused by disaffected youth, but not prepared to spend a few hundred pounds and suffer minor inconvenience to encourage those who are not so inclined.

In 1997 the BB & GB got together again for an Annual Church Service at Villa Park with a new name 'Annual Brigades' Celebration Service'. This was an occasion at which many local dignitaries were present as well as the National Brigade Secretaries of the BB and GB. The service was also used as an occasion to present the Queen's Badge (BB) and Queen's Award (GB). In 1998, the Celebration Service was held at Symphony Hall as it was again in 1999. A popular musical feature of the service has been the Birmingham BB/GB Worship band - 'b5'.

"Informality"
Making a Joyful Noise...
At the 1997 Villa Park
Celebration Service

over by a very small NCO. A bench by the Hall of Memory was filled with BB boys resting their legs after marching a few hundred yards. I departed this BB idyll still mesmerised by the quirkiness of what I had seen. Eventually, back out in the suburbs, I found re-assurance by witnessing non-BB people driving and walking around. I felt like 'No 6' from the 'Prisoner' TV series, popular at the time, having just made his escape from the Village.

The Town Hall was the venue for the special Centenary Service of Thanksgiving in October 1983, but the Annual Parade Service remained at the Central Hall a location which was retained until 1987. The 1988 Service was held in the Great Hall of the University of Aston, a complete break with tradition. The 1989 Parade was the first of eight to be held back at the Town Hall.

In 1996, although the venue continued to be the Town Hall, there were fundamental changes made in the Annual Church Service. This was the first Joint Annual Service with the Birmingham District of the Girls' Brigade, the GB equivalent of the Birmingham Battalion. The numbers were such that the Adrian Boult Hall was used for BB Anchor Boys, GB Explorers and Juniors of both organisations. It was the last to be taken by popular Battalion Chaplain Rev. David Woodfield, and the last to involve a Parade and march-past. Such had been the difficulties in organising the parade, it was decided that it would not be a worthwhile exercise in future. Escape routes, traffic diversions, parade marshals, police overtime, walkie - talkies... the centre of Birmingham was now a very different place on Sundays from those 'surreal' days of the 1960s and 1970s. The end of a long tradition

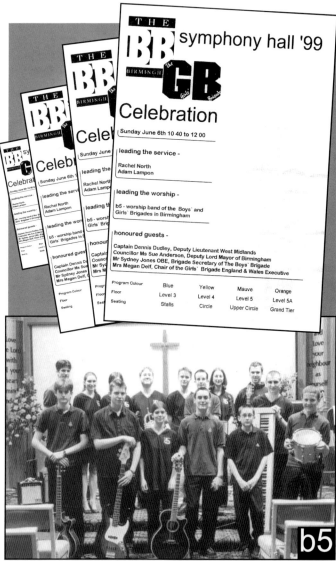

A special combined Youth Organisations Service scheduled for 2000 failed to happen due to venue problems. The 2001 event was held in the Great Hall of Aston University. Symphony Hall will provide the venue for 2002.

Ambulance First -Aid

The Ambulance minute book 1909 - 1913

One of the principal functions of a Battalion is that of administering the award of badges and certificates. The Ambulance Badge was the earliest official national BB proficiency badge, being awarded from 1891. In 1902, the number of badges available to Birmingham BB boys was limited to a three year anchor for service, the Sergeant's Proficiency Star, just introduced that year, and the Ambulance Badge.

Tests for the badge were conducted by examiners, usually doctors, appointed by the Battalion. Ambulance work had to be promoted and encouraged, motivation and incentives provided. The Battalion instituted competitions so that the Ambulance Teams from each company could compete and standards thereby raised. Other than the Drill Shield the two Battalion Trophies, the 'Ambulance Cup' (1908) and the Ambulance Shield (1911) are the earliest.

When the Headquarters at Wrottesley St. was bombed, in 1941, most of the old committee minute books were lost. However one of first minute books of the Ambulance Committee has, miraculously, survived. Entitled 'Ambulance Committee's Reports of Meetings and General Statistics for 1909 - 1910 Session to 1913' it contains details of companies and the workings of the Committee including a record of correspondence. The Companies, 1 - 18 are listed as at November 1909 with seven actually operating Ambulance work. There was no information about the 1st Coy. since the old Coy. had

finished and the new 1st were just about to join. Each company merits its own comment, by the side of the 8th is written *'none whatever'* and by the 10th *'No prospects at all'*. Clearly the whole Battalion was not into Ambulance work! Some companies, notably the 14th (Lodge Rd.), were very keen with six boys having passed the 1st Year exam. and one the 2nd with a further ten under instruction. Not surprisingly the 14th was the company of Ambulance Committee Convener Mr H Caney. It is his hand which records the doings of the Ambulance Committee in its first four years.

There is not enough space to record everything but below are reproduced some wonderful snippets.

'Convened meeting for Jan 4th 1910... P. Card apology from Mr Smith dated 4/1/1910 posted 5th at 9.15 p.m. & received on 6th.'

'Feb. 3rd. Wrote to Blind Institution, Waterloo Passage for 18 Copies of Competition Rules'.

'Recommended that a Doctor be the Competition Examiner & Dr Griffiths (Lieut Colonel South Midland RAMC) highly reccommended'

'P.Card to Mr Barnsley respecting Stretchers & Batt. Marches-out.'

'The Examination for the Cup to take place at Highbury Drill Hall (by kind permission of Capt Drew)...at 8 o'clock...number of questions restricted to 20 with additional 5 Individual Bandages and a Stretcher case. Each company to provide their own Stretchers, Splints, Bandages & a Patient.' The 14th Coy. won but Dr Griffiths in his speech made reference to the closeness of each squad: *'I hope you will never be called upon to attend a case, but if you were called I feel sure the patient would be in good hands.'*

'Caretaker's tip 2d.'

'Letter to Rt Hon J Chamberlain re Shield or Cup'. 'Letter to Barrow Cadbury re Shield or Cup'.

Captain Drew of the 11th Coy had split loyalties, he was a member of the Ambulance Committee and quite willing to offer his church hall for the competition but as often happens things didn't quite work out...as detailed in his resignation letter to Mr Caney:

'I am afraid that your having had the room for the examination has done my company a deal of harm, as the night was arranged for a march out but on account of it being wet of course the boys were brought into the room and were practically driven out into the rain at 7.50 p.m. whereas they should have remained in until it has ceased being kept under command. I shall send in an account to you for the room as soon as I know what we are at loss. we have now missed 2 weeks contributions so we are at a loss of about 7/- we cannot be out of that much. I shall have to return to the boys all the money taken this week as they were crying out about paying a penny for nothing and most of them refuse to Parade on Sunday. Consequently Lieut Baker and I have got to go round and put things right with them on Saturday.'

Even in 1910, the boys obviously knew their 'rights' and a penny was worth a great deal more than it is today. Mr Drew, typical of a dedicated Birmingham BB officer, didn't resign, he was back serving on the Committee by June.

'June 14th 1910. Mr Bradford mentioned two gentlemen who he thought might do some-thing for us in the proposed shield matter.'

'July 18th 10/6 received towards proposed shield from W. Waters Butler.
July 30th Donation of 21/- from Ald. Ansell towards shield.
Selection of design for new shield (messrs Hawkins...)'

'Sept 29th Paid Messrs Hawkins £2.12.6 for shield.
Sept 30th Shield presented to B'ham Battalion at the Pitman Hotel. Messrs Studholme, Beckett & Anderson gave 1/- each towards cost of shield.
Oct. 14th Promise of 2/6 towards Shield from Gordon Barnsley.'

'Oct 22nd. P.C. to Chief Constable re Motor Ambulance inspection.
Oct 24th Telephonic reply from Chief Constable.
Dec. 26th Intimation from Chief Constable that weather is too bad to invite your boys to view Motor Ambulance.'

'Jan 23rd 1911 Letter & enclosure for 3/8 for 5 1st year Certificates 5 Ambulance Badges & Certificates for an Officer who has lost his...'

'April 4th. Mr Hurst made reference to the success of the Ambulance Committees work during the past two years. Arising from this it was resolved that we do our best to waken up the other Committees at our next Battalion Council meeting.'

'May 27th Visit to Duke St. of Ambulance boys from Nos 4, 6, 9, 10 & 14 Companies to Police Ambulance.'

'Jan 9th 1912. Committee suggested that the Convener write to Glasgow & see if a medal-lion or something could be given to induce Ambulance boys to continue their studies a third year.'

*'March 3rd. Meeting of Committee at Pitman Hotel. Present: **Sir Wm. Smith**, A S Hurst, H. Hickman, L..N. Bowen, G. Whitehouse, H. Caney. Sir Wm. Smith advised us to get another team to compete with No 14 for the Shield.'*

'August 16th. Letter to Barnsley re Display. Reply that we cannot get one in with their Company as men will be strapped to horses.' ???

'January 14th 1913 Permission given to buy new minutes book.'

'March 5th Shield Competition Hatchett St Mission.'

'April 27th Doctors Certificate from No 8. Dr Hartley Bunting (1st Years Certificate & Badge) Pvts. A Oakton, G. Oakton, H. Morbey, N. Williams.'

The Annual Reports of the Battalion take us back to 1906-1907 when J. M. Johnson reported that the Committee had been 'reorganised' and Ambulance work was in a 'deplorable state'. One solution was to introduce Competition, (the Challenge Cup Competition with a prize offered by the Battalion President in 1907 was launched in 1908). By 1908 a Battalion Bearer Company had been formed from four stretcher parties, divided into two squads. The boys were picked from the Ambulance Squads of each company. At the Town Hall demonstration in 1908 the ambulance drill exhibited by the boys of companies, No's 3, 6, 7 and 11 was described as 'highly creditable'. In 1909 the Batttalion Bearer Company inspected the Police Motor Ambulance and were instructed how to move injured persons in and out.

By 1914 -1915 some of the skills learnt in the Battalion were being employed on the battlefront in Europe in the R.A.M.C. One member of the 14th Coy's winning Ambulance team, Sergeant Humphries, joined the Navy as Officers' Sick Bay Steward and fell victim to Spotted Fever dying in June 1915. In the 1918 - 1919 Report it was announced that C. R. Bartley who did much for the Ambulance work in the Battalion had died of wounds. Lieut. R. Davey lost his life in the Saltley Gas Explosion.

After the war a number of companies were able to re-start their Ambulance classes but there were only five operating in session 1919 - 1920. In some companies, such as the 1st, it was 1921 before the class could re-start.

Boys of the 3rd B'ham Coy pose for an illustration in the Wesleyan Assurance Society's First Aid Handbook c.1923

In 1924 there were four companies entering the 'Cup' competition for 1st Year boys and three companies entering the 'Shield' competition for second year boys. Judging was by Medical Practitioners with the competition conducted by the St. John Ambulance Association. The 1924-25 Annual Report stated that 'First Aid was again taught in nine of our Companies during the Session and in a few for the first time. The badge was still known as the 'Ambulance Badge' however.

The Ambulance Squad of the 1st Birmingham (Aston) Coy at camp c. 1914.

Union with the BLB, in 1926, gave fresh incentive to Ambulance work since this was one of the pillars of the BLB, its motto being 'To Save Life'. Ambulance drill had from the start in the BLB, replaced drill with rifles as practised in the BB.

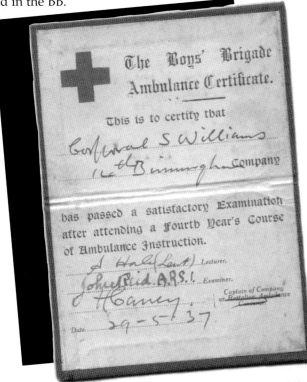

Through the late 1920s and 1930s Ambulance work thrived, but still with certain companies having more than their fair share of the competition trophies, notably the 9th at the Central Hall. Just as many boys had been able to put their Ambulance skills to use in France or Belgium in the Great War of 1914-1918, so too when the dark clouds of war gathered over Birmingham in 1939 many boys, trained in First Aid, found that their services were required, but this time on the home front. Birmingham

endured many nights of 'blitz' conditions when communications were seriously interrupted, hospitals and their patients were particularly vulnerable and communications vital. One BB officer, Mr George Oakton B.E.M., mobilised members of the Battalion to alleviate the problem. George as a boy in the 8th Coy, had gained his Ambulance Badge in 1912, and returned to the Company

Wartime Hospital Messengers from the 1st A Company

as First Aid Instructor after service in the Infantry in WW1. Now, as Captain of the 5th Coy. he was running a messenger service, staffed by BB boys and officers on bicycles carrying information between hospitals, first-aid posts and warden posts through the city's bombed streets. This messenger service involved much danger since the messengers would often be outside during air raids rather than in the safety of a shelter. One night in particular a first-aid post at Kent St. Baths took a direct hit and some of George's boys were killed.

After the upheaval of the war, the Battalion settled down to some degree of normality in the late 1940s and early 1950s. Many senior members were still being called-up into National Service however and rationing was ever-present The reputation for high quality training in the BB was upheld despite difficulties. A tribute to 'BB Training' was printed in the 1949-1950 Annual Report:

Rescue from the Handsworth Park Boating Pool 18th July 1949. '...*two youths, Edward Watson and Maurice Stanley Pallett, by their prompt and efficient rendering of artificial respiration, saved a little boy's life. It is reported that they are both former members of The Boys' Brigade, and their action reflects very creditably on them personally and upon the standard of training given in the Brigade... E. J. Dodd, Chief Constable. Hon Representative of the Royal Humane Society-Birmingham Area.'*

During 1954-1955 there were 50 First-Aid classes operating in the Battalion which before 1960 had risen to 63. It was about this time that the 46th Company from St

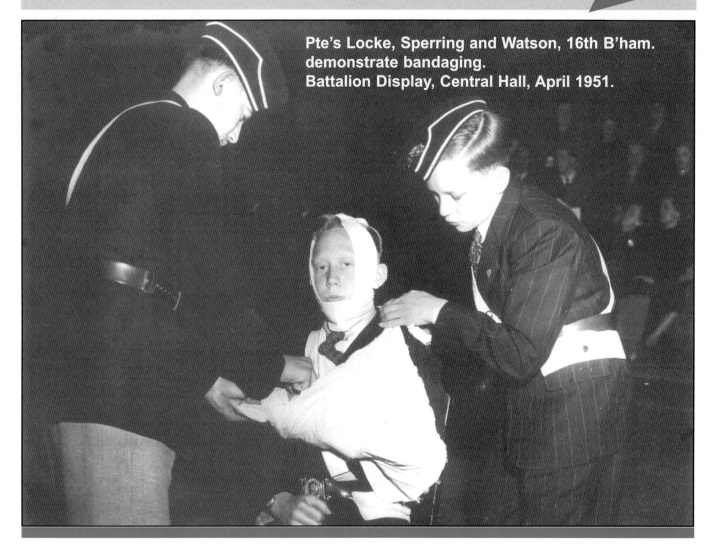

Pte's Locke, Sperring and Watson, 16th B'ham.
demonstrate bandaging.
Battalion Display, Central Hall, April 1951.

Martin's Perry Common began to dominate the First Aid Cup andShield competitions, a situation that prevailed for the next decade. If we can imagine William Smith being present at a First Aid Committee meeting at this time and being asked for advice, just as he was in 1912, we can visualise him saying 'find a team to compete with the 46th!' Eventually, the honours would be spread around other companies, notably the 89th Coy., Kingstanding Congregational. In 1965 the 89th Coy. First Aid Teams were entered by the Battalion in a St. John Ambulance Competition in Kidderminster where they were awarded second place in both Junior and Senior sections, being only two marks behind the winner in each instance. First Aid demonstrations were a feature of the Battalion Displays at the Central Hall with various scenarios being acted out; road accidents, football stand collapses, etc.. The poor 'victims' who were to receive First Aid were always taught to 'yell and scream' just like the real thing but they didn't need a lot of encouragement to do that.

In 1976-1977 the Battalion celebrated its 75th Birthday. There were signs that the 'old order' was in decline insofar as proficiency badgework was concerned. Some even blamed that decline on the tacky new BB 'Barrel' shaped badges which had been introduced in 1969, which in themselves provided no incentive whatsoever. The Morse Cup was not competed for, and the Band Competition was undergoing change. Newer competitions such as Five-A -Side Football, Top of the Form and the Bible Quiz were thriving. The First Aid Cup and Shield, however, were competed for until 1983. It is not clear why such an important activity as First-Aid should become less popular in the Battalion and the Brigade as a whole. Generally it is accepted that First Aid instruction was more readily available in Schools, colleges and workplaces and those young people who were interested in taking it further would join the St. John Ambulance Brigade instead of the BB. First - Aid has continued to run in the Battalion but not as a competitive activity.

Let's Follow the Band...

In the early days of the BB in Birmingham it was company bands which were of great importance. The 1st Aston Manor had a fife and drum Band from November 1897 while drum and bugle bands were also started in other companies. By 1900, bugles had taken over from flutes in the 1st Aston Manor the Bandmaster in 1903 being a Mr Charles H.B. Dunn. The Battalion did not run a band until many years after its foundation. The earliest Band Committee recorded is that for 1906-1907, probably the first, it comprised of Messrs Robert Dry (13th Coy), H. Grimmett (6th Coy) and Mr Butler who was described as 'Bandmaster' and not connected with a particular company. There was a 'Hand-Bell' item by the 2nd Coy. at the Annual Demonstration at the Town Hall in 1908. On a cold December day in 1908 the Battalion went on display at the Aston Villa Football Ground during the interval of a match versus Middlesbrough, the '...*massed bands of the Battalion*' marched around the arena, but the result of the match was not recorded in the Annual Report. However, the introduction of the official BB Buglers' Badge in 1909 gave the Band Committee with Mr Bates, Lt. 2nd Coy., as Convener an increased role. Other members being Messrs Smith and Bowen from the 6th and 10th Coys respectively. The award of Bugle Badges, by decision of the Battalion Council,

required proficiency in eighteen bugle calls examined by the Committee. Sound advice (literally) about Band Playing was given in 1909:

'*The utmost care and discretion should always be observed in order to prevent annoyance to the public through band-playing at inopportune times. Band-playing on Sundays should be reduced to a minimum, and under no circumstances should a Band be allowed to play in the streets later than 10 p.m.*'

The 1910 - 1911 Annual Report lists the Battalion Committees, but there is no Band Committee. Was it missed out or, with apologies for the pun, 'Dis-Banded? The band of the 7th Coy. was chosen to play the General Salute at the Annual Demonstration at the Town Hall in 1911 it needed to be note-prefect in the presence of the Founder Sir William A Smith. The 1913 Demonstration featured renderings by the fife bands of the 9th and 19th Coys.. By 1916 the Band Committee is listed again in the Annual Report with a young Mr L. G. H. Alldridge as its Convener. (Twenty seven years later he was Lord Mayor of Birmingham). In the 1917 - 1918 Annual Report the work of the Band Committee was reported. During the First World War the Battalion had suffered a loss of leadership and a small number of boys, due it was stated, to excessive hours of work in armaments factories. Mr MacGuire, Battalion

Vice President and Capt. of 1st Coy., presented a shield to be competed for, the first winners being the 14th Coy. from Lodge Road Congregational Church. The session 1918 - 1919 was described as one of the best, if not the best, that the Battalion had had in band work. A hall in Bath St. Schools was rented for a combined Battalion Band practice with five companies taking part. The practices were held every month until May. Three company bands entered the Band Competition held in March at which a Mr. Winfield undertook the judging. Out of 80 points the results were: 1st Coy.- 68, 14th Coy.- 58, and 7th Coy.- 58. The practices seemed to have worked since it was reported at the Church Parade held in May that...

'...a marked improvement was shown in general appearance, in smartness, and also in the quality of the music, as compared with the previous parade.'

The 1st Coy., as winners of the Shield, played the competition marches at the Battalion Demonstration. The Buglers' Badge examinations were also going well with sixteen out of seventeen boys passing. The 12th Coy. from St. Cuthbert's Winson Green, had four boys who played every call through without making a single mistake! Mr E. Fox, 1st Coy., was the Band Committee Convener.

Aston Bands Rule !

The Brass Band of 1st B'ham (Aston) Coy. c.1920

A full Brass Band was formed by 1st Birmingham Coy. in September 1919, the only BB band of its type in Birmingham at the time. It played the National Anthem for the Visit of H.R.H. Prince Henry to the City on 14th January 1920. (This had originally been planned as a visit from H.R.H Prince Arthur Duke of Connaught, Hon. Brigade President, who was indisposed at the last minute.) On Sunday April 17th, 1920 the Brass Band played for the singing at the Battalion Spring Church Parade held at Islington Wesleyan Church. The Band Shield that year was won by the 7th Coy. scoring seventy-four and a half marks out of one hundred. (See picture of 7th Coy. about this time, head of page 47).The 7th, based at Alfred Street Council Schools and like the

1st, connected with Aston Parish Church, went on to dominate the competition for the next few years. The 1st's Brass Band ceased to function in 1928.

In 1920, the Convener was Mr A. W. Gabb, Captain of the 9th Coy. who was, no doubt, pleased to read in the Annual Report for 1920 - 1921 that: *'The Battalion Band showed great progress in playing during the session'*. By 1921 the Band Convener was Mr A. Bryant from 2nd Coy. St. Clements Nechells and two Battalion band practices were held. During the session 1921 - 1922 Mr A. B. Carden who was, for several years, Battalion Bandmaster, died. The fact that Battalion Band practices could only be held twice during 1922 - 1923, due to the scarcity of rooms, was now considered to be a problem which would seriously affect the band. Mr. H. Bonaker of the 7th took over as Convener during 1923 - 1924. On 1st October 1926 The Boys' Brigade united with The Boys' Life Brigade and nowhere was that marriage better consummated than in Birmingham.

The BLB, of course, had bands similar to those in the BB. The 6th Birmingham Coy. BLB at Kings Heath had a Brass Band in 1924 which unfortunately ran into trouble with the Church authorities because, in order to pay for their instruments, they needed to take paying engagements- one of which had been on a Sunday afternoon in Kings Heath Park. This was enough for the church to seek disbandment of the Company! The Captain and senior Lt. resigned so the Company was saved, less one band.

The enlarged Battalion, by 1928 some fifty-six companies, had the use of its new Headquarters in Whittall Street. This venture aided all the Committees of the Battalion.

The First Battalion Band, rather than simply a 'combined band', was Formed in 1932-33. Mr Eric Terry was appointed Bandmaster with one of the first performances being at the 1933 Display in the Central Hall. On that occasion the Band played the old time March "Old Woolwich Common" and the modern March "Our Founder". Among its ranks was Alf Smith from the 32nd Coy. who would, some thirty years later, be in charge of a similar band in the same arena. Mr Terry's name lives on in the individual awards for Bugle and Drum called 'Terry Trophies'.

The period which starts in the 1930s is within living memory for a few Birmingham Band veterans. One such is Mr Les Green, now living in Lancashire. We can follow his progress along with that of the Battalion Band. Les first heard a BB band in 1934 at the Sunday Enrolment of his company, the 63rd B'ham at Harborne Baptist Church. This band was the 22nd Company from Bearwood Baptist, who had marched 5 miles complete with Bugle Band. (Batt. Band Champions that year?)

'I can still see in my minds eye the 22nd coming around the bend in Harborne High Street with dress cords on their dide drums swinging to and fro.'

Les transferred to 64th later in 1934 when it was formed at his own church. He attended his first Battalion Parade to the Central Hall with the 64th. The 64th joined with the 63rd and marched from Harborne via Five Ways to join up with S.W. Division, then to the Central Hall, about 5 miles in all (and marched back afterwards!).

'The service amazed me, the size of the congregation and the volume of sound from the singing was awesome. I remember telling my mother when I got home that the Brigade was wonderful enough to have its own hymns, we had sung 'Underneath the Banner' during the service.'

In 1936, Les made his first visit to the new Headquarters in Wrottesley Street...and there saw *'a huge figure of a man in Bandmaster's uniform'* who was to teach us 'Last Post'. That man was 'Jack' Mulingani.

The band final was at Wrottesley St. in 1936 with the 9th and 46th as finalists. The 46th from Perry Common won the shield, its bandmaster being Mr Burrows. Battalion Bandmaster Eric Terry, brought a large measure of uniformity to coy. bands in Birmingham. He wrote down some really good bugle Marches, 'Over There' and 'The Old Woman from Ireland' being good enough to stay in the repertoire of many Companies until the 1970s. He contributed the solo Drum and Bugle trophies to the Battalion. An example of a typical band display was in 1938 at the Annual Battalion Display at Alexander Sports Ground, Perry Barr when the massed Battalion band played the 'Echo' March, 'Sherwood Foresters' (Slow March & Jig) and 'The Old Woman from Ireland' (March).

In 1939, the job of Battalion Bandmaster became vacant and a small team of instructors was assembled, Frank Allbut (7th Coy.), Arthur Hale (14th Coy.) and Alf Smith (32nd Coy.) However, with the outbreak of war and the call-up of young men there was no one available. There were priorities more important than Bands. Mr J. M. Johnson (Coy? 64th or 67th) is listed in the 1938/39 Annual Report. Like many activities, Band was on 'hold' during the hostilities.

In 1945, Les re-joined his old Coy. after seeing and hearing the Central Hall Display. The Band had played 'Robin Hood'. Battalion Bandmaster was now Mr H. J. Lee (6th Coy?), who was by inclination and experience a Choirmaster rather than a Bandmaster, and had been given the job of looking after the band during the war years. The Band was called upon to take part in the Victory Parade on 29th September where a contingent of 250 boys drawn from all companies marched past the Lord Mayor.

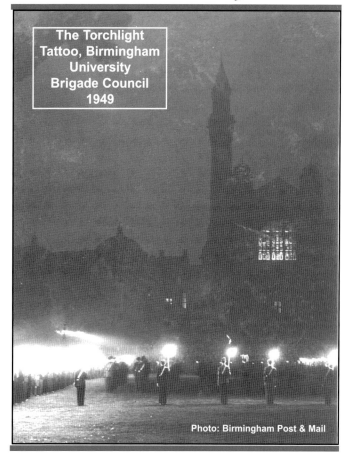

The Torchlight Tattoo, Birmingham University Brigade Council 1949

Photo: Birmingham Post & Mail

Les remembered the Batt. President Mr Anderson from the 4th Coy. described as 'a wonderful bloke' who, he believed, died at a Church meeting three or four years after his meeting him (26th February 1947).

In 1947/8 Les was the Rep. for the S.W. Division on the Band Committee. H. J. Lee was the still in charge at that time, but he gave over to Jack Mulingani in the 1948/49 session.

Torchlight Tattoo

1949 was the year of the Torchlight Tattoo for Brigade Council. Band members practised for some three months twice per week mainly at Nelson St. School Spring Hill. Instructors, included Jack Mulingani (in charge), Alf Smith (drums), Norman Ravenhall (bugles), and Les Green (bugles). The initial letter from Jack Mulingani, in April 1949, detailed the strict requirements. A band in excess of 250 players would be required, but that would be no problem. Returns had been received from 40 companies to date with numbers available as follows: Mace Bearers 11, Bass Drummers 41, Side Drummers 139, Buglers 258, Tenor Drummers 5, Cymbals 14, and there were still 25 companies to reply! Presentation of the display was directed by Mr McTavish, Bandmaster of 39th, who had been the pipe major in the Argyll and Sutherland Highlanders before coming to B'ham. to be a Prison

Officer at Winson Green. A rehearsal was held on the Wednesday night of 7th September, the actual event being on Saturday 10th Sept.

The night of the tattoo came and initially, car-headlights provided some illumination, then flaming torches were lit by paraffin blow-lamps and the 'square' of boys marched out round the outside of the arena. Headlights were turned off and through the darkness at 8.15 p.m., the huge Battalion band entered the arena led by five or six Drum - Majors who each had small electric lights on the ends of their maces. The performance opened with a fanfare and 'Retreat' followed by a Bugle Flourish and the clear crisp sound of the Drummers Call. There then followed a series of Bass Drum Beats, drum rolls and single notes all played at the halt. On the oder 'Quick March' the massed bands lead by the Senior Drum Major set off playing the march "Jubilee". This was followed by a period of slow marching and then the march "The Musketeers" which was repeated. Even being by torchlight with torches carried by 200 boys, it still meant that much of the band was in total darkness for much of the time and Alf Smith remembers running along between the ranks reminding players when to come in with their part! The march "The Musketeers" was written by Norman Ravenhall. The event was a 'one - off' which left its mark upon all who were present. One young man who was particularly excited to be chosen as a drummer was Jack Mulingani's son, Donald. Don, then a boy of 15 yrs, remembers waiting in a side street near the ground. *'In our company we wore a uniform of short trousers, long socks, uniform shirt, cap, belt and haversack, we were proud to wear that full uniform'.* That night they all felt more proud than usual. *'It was my joy to have taken part in this event, under the direction of my Dad.'* Don eventually went on to be Captain of the 72nd Coy. for some eight years. Today Don recalls that he went on to wear the full uniform, with pride, until he was 18 yrs old, not something which could be done easily today for fear of embarrassment and ridicule.

Jack Mulingani (on right) leads the Battalion Static Band during the March-Past of the Brigade Council Parade in 1949 opposite the Municipal Bank in Broad Street. Alf Smith can be seen keeping an eye on the drummers.

The Battalion Band was chosen from all those who had taken part in Tattoo. Don Mulingani was one of the drummers. The standard was high and as a result the band was asked by the Royal Marines Commandant from Sutton Coldfield to Beat Retreat at the Hall of Memory in place of the Marines - it was done in front of a large audience.

"...the Trumpet call obey,"

One time Les visited the *'wonderful Major Gordon Barnsley'* at HQ in Union Street (early 1950s) D.G.B. mentioned that he had a letter from a missionary in Southern India asking for help in finding some manner in which he could call his flock from the village to come to worship. Les had at that time a Selmer trumpet that he had used throughout the war years, so asked if that would help in any way. Needless to say Les' old Selmer went to India and Gordon had many letters from his missionary friend saying how pleased he was with it and how the villagers responded to its call.

'Mad' Mulingani

Jack Mulingani developed a 'reputation' as a great bandmaster, being known affectionately by many boys as 'Mad' Mulingani. Norman Ravenhall, a Brass Band man, didn't miss out on the epithets either, being christened 'Ravin' Ravenhall by the boys. The two must have really made some impression!

Battalion parades were quite a triumph, logistically. Each of the four Divisions made its way to the Central Hall, St. Martin's Church or Carrs Lane Church from a different location, led by its Divisional Band. After the service the Divisions would follow each other with a static band playing opposite the saluting base. To make matters worse the whole Battalion could not fit into one church, being some 3,000 strong. Les remembers a slight problem during one parade:

'I got into hot water one year by letting the buglers play when going through the Minories en route to the Central Hall. The tremendous echo they set up put half of the division , just arriving at church, out of step and that didn't go down very well.'

Les began training a bugle band for the Girls' Life Brigade with Miss Betty Bardell from Quinton. It eventually paraded with the 54th, his own BB Coy. Band. Jack's eldest daughter Barbara was a bugler in that band. It was quite common for BB bandmasters to run GLB bands and in many cases a joint BB/GLB band was run. In the 1950s this was regarded as quite 'daring' - a long time before 'Joint-Activities' were common. For most of the 1950s, the 1st Coy. from Aston were once again the leading band in the Battalion.

The F.D.F. National Band

On the 21st October 1953 the Battalion played host to the 'National Orkester of the Frivilligt Drenge-Forbund', The Danish Boys' Brigade, which performed at the Central Hall. Some 41 guests were accommodated by various Birmingham officers. The concert, one of a series of five in the UK, was a great success. The only sad note sounded at the concert was that Battalion Secretary Gordon Barnsley, who had made all the arrangements for the trip, was too ill to be present.

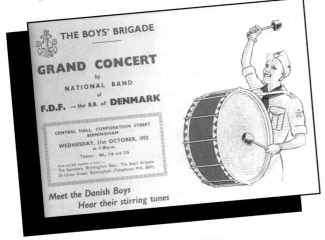

A Proud Record

One of the major influences in BB bandwork in the late 1950s and early 1960s, was an instructional record issued by The Boys' Brigade in order to improve the standard of Bugle Bands. Few people outside of Birmingham (and perhaps many Brummie BB men) will not have known that the record was made in Birmingham. It was made by representatives of the Battalion Band and recorded in Handsworth. We can let Les Green tell the story:

'In 1955 we made a record for the BB at the studios in (Grosvenor Road) Handsworth. All the calls for Buglers' Badge. In those days the first impression for the disc was made on wax and if an error was made the whole thing had to be done again. On the night when we were cutting the master all went well right through to the commentry of 'lights out' when Jack made a mistake; we therefore had to start the whole thing again, against the clock as our time was running out. This resulted in a lip slip in the call 'double' which to my disgust had to remain unaltered and if you have ever heard the record you must have noticed.'

Rudford & Felden

1955 was the year Jack and Les were invited to Abbey House, Westminster (BB HQ) as part of those selected to re-write the Drum and Bugle Band Handbook, the old one having done service from 1922. Les said that he had always thought that the Battalion was honoured to pro-

vide two members from those chosen for the re-write. The two Birmingham men worked with Frank Ketch from the 1st Slough, Chris Williams of 5th London and John Smailes from the 2nd Middlesbrough. Les wrote the popular march 'Rudford', which was included in the Band Handbook. Another march which became popular after inclusion in the new Band Handbook started life on a 'Felden' course. Frank Ketch and Chris Williams attended the Bugle Band Course at Felden Lodge April 16th/17th 1955, then the Brigade's Training Centre for England and Wales, now Boys' Brigade Headquarters. The march was composed for the course and was taught and trialed there. Les Green, Jack Mulingani and Alf Smith were all involved. Alf still has the first pencilled manuscript of the march which was, of course, appropriately named 'Felden'.

L/Cpl. Alton Douglas

There were 56 Bugle Bands in the Battalion in the mid 1950s. One of those bands was part of the 12th Coy., re-started in 1952 by a keen musician, Mr Arthur Garbett, and one of the drummers who came under his influence was a boy named Alton Douglas. Today we know him as the well-loved show-biz personality, musician, humorist and local author. Alton says that he remembers well his time in the Brigade and that it was certainly an influence upon his entry into 'show-business'. *'I wasn't the tallest lad in the band as the photograph seems to suggest, the bugler behind me was much taller'* Alton is keen to point out.

Photograph reproduced courtesy Alton Douglas from his book 'Birmingham at Play'

12th Birmingham Company Band. Blake Lane, Bordesley Green, August 1954. Alton Douglas ...not the tallest boy in the band...

Soggy Jamboree

In August 1957 the great World Scout Jubilee Jamboree was held in Sutton Park. Generally, it had been a wet week, but when the massed Birmingham Battalion Band marched out to perform as part of the BB arena display between 8 - 9.30 p.m. on Saturday 10th, it poured down. Scouts who were present always remember the rain and so do the BB boys! The programme, valiantly completed was a long one. Some who listened and watched said too long:

Fanfare - Retreat. Bugle Flourish - Drummers Call - Rolls and Chords - March - "Jubilee" - Drumming to "Jubilee" - March - "Jubilee" - Drum Solos and repeats. - March - "Kandahar" - Drum solos and repeats. - March - "British Boys"

Strange but true

In hospital, in 1959, following an industrial accident, Les, who had been out of BB work now for a few years, was visited by Stephen Court the young Bandmaster of 12th Coy, at Small Heath wanting help with the band. As he had been told to spend very little time on his feet Les found himself training the band seated in a special armchair! Just one year later the 12th had won the Band Shield. He was presented with an inscribed bugle which served him well training bands in Lancashire since he moved there.

At Christmas time each year the 78th from Smethwick always got asked to join the Father Christmas parade. In 1960 it was suggested that it provide a band drawn from any companies in the area that felt they could help. Les was roped in as Bandmaster. When the day dawned some 40 boys turned up ready to help, thirty-eight of whom turned out to be buglers with only one side drummer and a bass drummer! The sound they made marching along the streets of Bearwood & Smethwick *'I will never forget -it was magic'* said Les.

The 60s & 70s

As the winter of 1959 progressed into 1960 nearly forty Birmingham Bandmasters and prospective Bandmasters attended a course in which, over the weeks, a thorough grounding in the music of bugle bands was top of the agenda. In the 1960s and 1970s the Battalion Band was involved in many fine Displays at the Central Hall under the direction of Bandmaster Alf Smith. Innovative bugle music from Bandmaster Peter Tonks of the 48th (Castle Bromwich) featured in the repertoire. The 1967 Brigade Council in Birmingham and the 1970 Battalion Show at Cadbury's Theatre were great platforms for the Band's expertise. Five drummers from the Battalion participated in the Birmingham Repertory Theatre's production of 'The Recruiting Officer' and took to the stage, with their drums, on different nights dressed in 18th Century costume. Although the Divisional Band system was strong

with Bandmasters such as John Ash (29th & 57th Coys), John Rowlands (2nd Coy.) Ken Gurney (78th Coy.) and many others, it was much more difficult to get together boys from all over the city to participate in a Battalion Band than it had been in the 1950s. There were fewer bands in the Battalion and seemingly far more calls upon the time of both officers and boys.

The period of the late 1960s into the 1980s saw the emergence of one or two large and influential company bugle bands taking a part in Battalion parades and functions. Notably, the 57th Birmingham (Pheasey) and 1st Solihull Companies dominated the Battalion Competition. Due to the influence of the newly formed 'British Youth Band Association' Birmingham BB Bands were now looking further afield for musical inspiration and competition and widening the range of instrumentation to valved trumpets, trombones etc.. The Battalion Band Competition rules were changed in 1978 to incorporate valved instruments as well as bugles with sections for smaller bands and Drum-Majors. The old-style competition where bands would enter an empty hall and play a set routine at the halt with judges sitting behind a curtain was not suitable for modern bands.

Salute to the Queen

It was a Birmingham officer Robin Bolton, Lt. and Bandmaster of the 57th (Pheasey) Coy. who introduced the West Midlands BB Band Contest in 1972. The District Contest, held outdoors, was a great success, and this was followed by his setting - up of the National BB Contest in 1976 at Bingley Hall Stafford, the latter being staffed by many Birmingham Officers. At the time 'The National' was started it was predicted by many, not those in Birmingham of course, that it would be a failure. Twenty five years later it is still a premier event and very popular with Birmingham Bands. Perhaps the major event of the period was the 'Salute to the Queen', the 1977 youth band parade down the Mall in London to celebrate the Queen's Silver Jubilee. On this occasion the rivalry of B'ham's top bands was put aside as a joint band of the 57th and 1st Solihull, which had similar instrumentation, under the direction of Robin Bolton, Ray Elsom and Ken Walker, made up one of the eight BB bands paticipating. H.R.H. The Duke of Gloucester took the salute and the BB Bands were inspected on Horse Guards Parade by Lord Elgin the Brigade President and Alfred Hudson Brigade Secretary. Hon. Batt. Vice- President Mr George Oakton B.E.M., who travelled down with the 57th on that day said that it made him feel proud to be a Brummie!

In 1983, the City of Birmingham Youth Show at the Hippodrome Theatre and the Battalion Centenary Gala Day at the Princess Alice Home, both featured the 57th Coy's Drum and Bugle Corps called 'The Cavaliers' com

The combined bands of 57th B'ham & 1st Solihull - Queen's Silver Jubilee Parade 'Salute to The Queen' 1977

prising nearly one hundred BB & GB members from Pheasey Methodist Church. The year 1983 was also a turning point for Bands in the Battalion. The Centenary Display in the Central Hall that year was a memorable one for Alf Smith because it turned out not only to be his last major event as Bandmaster, but also the last Battalion Band. The boys didn't let him down, producing a spectacular programme.

Into the early 1980s it was the 68th Coy. Band under the direction of Roy Bates which took on the mantle of Battalion Champions. They were followed by the 73rd Coy./2nd Solihull GB for much of the next decade and a half! The 73rd's Bandmaster, John Mendus M.B.E., took over as Battalion Bandmaster in 1983/4 a time when the writing was already on the wall for Battalion Bands. In the last two decades of the 20th century the trend had been towards company bands operated jointly with The Girls' Brigade or even Girl Guides. The wide variety of instrumentaion and music in the modern band lessened the feasibility of running a combined Battalion Band. In 1985, for the BB Brigade Council in Birmingham, bands were heard

and seen in Victoria Square as part of the Civic Reception hosted by the City. On this occasion the Reception was rounded off by Beating Retreat in the square. Bands remain quite popular however, with Birmingham Bands being well represented at the West Midlands and National Band Contests. Flying the flag in recent years, in addition to the 73rd, has been the 51st BB/35th GB and the 3rd Sutton BB/1st Sutton GB 'Chester Road Brigades' bands.

Recently, Victoria Square was again a band venue when in October 2001 another Civic Reception took place, this time for the start of the Battalion's Centenary year. Top Birmingham BB/GB Bands entertained invited guests and members of the public. At the start of the reception the Lord Mayor was greeted with a rousing fanfare specially written for the centenary by Rob Windsor (51st Coy.).

The increasingly popular 'b5', the Battalion's own Music Worship Group, has a number of former and present members who began their interest in music as members of their Company Band.

Beating Retreat, Brigade Council 1985 Victoria Square.

Brum B i t s   'did yer know ...?'

Most Boys' Brigade Badges were and are made in Birmingham. Over the years they have been produced by famous manufacturers such as Thomas Fattorini, Badges Plus, Firmin, H.W. Miller, Smith & Wright, Butler, Dowler, Toye Kenning & Spencer, and many more.

A special Battalion Centenary Badge has been produced and every BB member in Birmingham has one. A badge will also be produced for the Brigade Council to be held in Birmingham this year, 2002.

Judge Finnemore

When the BB and BLB in Birmingham united, in 1926, both Battalion Presidents were Barristers named Donald. Both became Judges and both were knighted.

The Postal Code of the Council House in Birmingham is:

B1 1BB

Private Dennis J. Brown of the 73rd B'ham Coy. (Lyndon Methodist) designed the Brigade Membership Card for the 75th Anniversary Year of the BB in 1958. He was 17 yrs. old and training to be a commercial artist. Allan Jones Capt. 83rd Coy. designed the 1992/93 Card.

A Unique Company

The 83rd Birmingham Coy. (Elmdon) was formed to the minute exactly 100 years after the first Coy in Glasgow, at 8.00 p.m. on 4th October 1983. Probably, the only company in the world to hold this distinction, it originally wanted to be called Coy. No. '100' to celebrate the centenary. This request was rejected by the Battalion Executive so it became the '83rd' to celebrate 18**83** - 1**983**.

In 1948, it was a Birmingham BB Officer, Sweyn E. Barnes, who secured **Felden Lodge** in Hertfordshire for the Brigade. S.E. Barnes was a former Officer and Captain of the 8th Birmingham Coy., and at the time the BB National Secretary for Training. He led the negotiations for the purchase of Felden as a National Training Centre and was widely acclaimed for his persistence and achievement.

Sweyn Barnes joined the 8th in 1910, under the captaincy of D. Gordon Barnsley who couldn't resist producing one of his famous photo-montage's depicting his friend being congratulated at the highest level. Felden Lodge is now the UK & Ireland BB Headquarters.

Battalion Worship Group **b5** got its name from being **BB B**irmingham **B**attalion **B**and. It now includes GB members, but the name persists!

For many years the Birmingham Battalion has enjoyed most friendly relationships with other youth organisations within the city. Naturally, the Girls Brigade, the sister movement of the BB has played a significant role in many activities undertaken by the Battalion in recent years. However, a remarkable friendship between the Birmingham Scout Association and the Battalion goes back virtually to the start of the latter. Over the years there has been much co-operation, help with event organisation and joint charity ventures. Since 1989 the Scouts and BB have shared Headquarters. In 2001, the Birmingham Uniformed Members Party or 'BUMP' for short, attended by many Battalion members, was held at Blackwell Court a facility owned by the Scouts.

Ex - BB Soccer Star

Darius Vassell the Aston Villa and England football striker was a member of the 3rd Sutton Coldfield Junior Section. He left the Company when his family moved house.

By the end of 2002 there will have been **seven** Brigade Councils held in Birmingham: 1912, 1918, 1927, 1949, 1967, 1985, 2002.

The First Council Meeting after the union of the BLB & BB was held in Birmingham - 1927

The 2002 Council Meeting will be the last of its type.

Sports

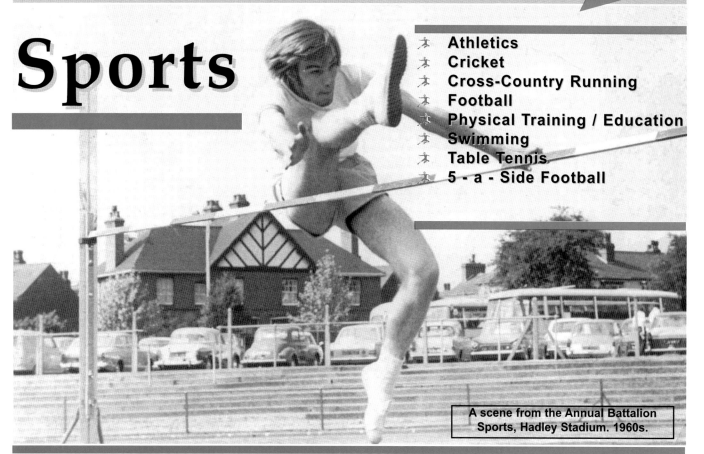

- 🏃 **Athletics**
- 🏃 **Cricket**
- 🏃 **Cross-Country Running**
- 🏃 **Football**
- 🏃 **Physical Training / Education**
- 🏃 **Swimming**
- 🏃 **Table Tennis**
- 🏃 **5 - a - Side Football**

A scene from the Annual Battalion Sports, Hadley Stadium. 1960s.

Before the days of 'Mission Statements' and the like it was the Battalion President, Mr C. J. Cooke, who in 1907 wrote in the Annual Report a few words that certainly echo down the years, a sentiment oft repeated at Battalion events.

'Just a word of advice, while it is essential that the means of obtaining and retaining the interest of the boy, viz; by military drill, ambulance, physical and manual exercises, camps &c., should be utilized to the utmost, that in fact it is necessary to encourage each boy and each company to compete in excellence in all these respects, for his own and his company's honour, yet it is most incumbent upon each company commander, and all officers, to remember that excellence in all these departments of physical culture is not the primary object of the BB., that these means are not to be exalted at the expense or neglect of that primary object viz: the advancement of Christ's Kingdom in the heart and life of the boy.'

Over the years Birmingham BB companies have taken part in a great variety of sporting activities, many nurtured and encouraged at Battalion Level. Badge and certificate tests, Inter - Company and Inter - Battalion events have all served to raise levels of participation and increase standards. Generally, competition is encouraged through team events where the individual boy is given the opportunity to represent his Company or Battalion, thus foster-ing 'esprit de corps' fundamental to the BB method from its foundation in 1883. Individual skills are improved by testing against set attainment standards for certificates and badges.

Athletics

The Battalion 'Sports' Cup first awarded in 1932, which was changed to 'Athletics' Cup in 1974/75, has been dominated by three companies since its instigation; the 1st`A' Coy, 33rd Coy and 6th Coy. to the virtual exclusion of all others. There was, however, 'Sports' activity before 1932.

In 1908 - 1909, a Battalion 'Recreation' Committee was formed with Mr Hill Capt. of the 2nd Coy. as Convener. By 1910 the Convener was Mr S.E. Barnes of the 8th Coy. but it was mainly football and swimming which was formally reported. H. Bonaker was Convener in the 1919-1920 session due to Mr Barnes being involved abroad with the military. A 'Battalion Sports' took place in June 1921. In 1923-1924 Mr W. T. Wiggins-Davies took over as Convener. Mr Wiggins-Davies had been with the 1st Coy. as a boy and would eventually become Lord Mayor (1944-1945). It had probably been the usual thing for the BLB to have an annual sports meeting so when the united

Battalion in 1926 - 1927 held an Athletic Sports in July it was termed 'as usual'. The Sports Ground at Stechford had been inaugurated through the auspices of the BLB and the ground at Perry Barr belonged to the 1stA Coy a former BLB company. The 'Sports' was in fact officially termed 'Review and Sports', a kind of outdoor 'Demonstration'. Entries and numbers were sufficient to warrant two events on following Saturdays. The two north groups at 1stA Coy's ground at Perry Barr, and the south groups on the following Saturday on the Battalions own fields at Stechford. No doubt transport considerations for participants and spectators were also a factor in staging the dual event. This split arrangement certainly continued into the 1927 - 1928 session when, according to the Annual Financial Report it actually made money:

'Athletic Sports Receipts £13. 16s. 0d. Expenses £10. 5s. 11d = Profit £3. 10s. 1d.'

'On your marks...' A scene at the South Group, Battalion Sports held at Stechford, 1928.

It was probably not finances which, by 1931, led to the two Sports events being Combined at Stechford. The facility at Stechford was certainly one of which the Battalion was very proud. However, in 1933, with a record entry of 400 boys and many spectators Stechford's limitations for this kind of event became obvious and the Alexander Sports Ground was chosen for the event.

A proper running track, spectator seating and facilities for 'field' events amounted to a huge bonus. Alexander Sports Ground would be the home of the Battalion Sports right up until the start of the War. Very successful events, despite very poor weather conditions in both 1936 and 1937, fully justified the choice of using a purpose-built stadium. A feature in 1936 was the newly formed Battalion Band leading a parade of competitors. Due to the various problems imposed by the war, particularly a shortage of officers, the Annual Sports in 1940 returned to Stechford. However, Stechford had its own problems, the pavilion was completely burnt-out by enemy action in 1941 and the eleven acres of fields taken- over for food

About to make his mark in the sand. A competitor in the Battalion Sports, Hadley Stadium. 1960s.

production as part of the 'Dig for Britain Campaign'. Sports were still held each year throughout the war and the Sports Cup awarded. Mr Hitler wasn't going to intimidate the Brummagem BB!

After the War, Stechford was still not available for any sporting activities for some years. The pavilion not being re-opened until 1951. Alexander Sports Ground continued to be used for the Annual Sports. In 1949, the year of the great Council meeting at Birmingham University, the University Sports Ground in Edgbaston was used for the second time for the Annual Sports as it was again in 1950.

On May 29th 1950 a Midland Youth Sports Festival was held at the Alexander Sports Stadium, sponsored by The Birmingham Mail. This was the first Sports Meeting ever organised on an inter-organisation basis. Five hundred boys and girls, watched by a large crowd, were competitors. There was representation from most of the City's youth organisations. The results in Boys Section were as follows:

1st Warwickshire ACF
2nd Birmingham ATC
3rd Birmingham BB

The sheer joy of hitting the tape first: Battalion Sports Hadley Stadium - 1960s

Other units were Sea Cadet Corps, Federation of Boys' Clubs, Church army Youth Club, Birmingham County Boy Scouts, Sutton Coldfield Youth Organisation, Birmingham Youth and Sunday School Union, Stonehouse Gang and St. John Ambulance Cadets.

Through the 1950s a number of different venues were used for the Annual Sports. The City Sports Arena Salford, Alexander Ground, New University Track etc. The introduction of an obstacle race and even a Slow Bicycle Race provided 'Humorous Relief'.

In 1962, the Inter-Battalion Athletics and Swimming Championships was started, a new addition to the sporting year, which was eventually to become a regular fixture. The challenge, coming from Nottingham Battalion as part of their 70th Anniversary Celebrations, was taken-up by Birmingham along with Derby, Grimsby and Leicester. As usual, competition bred enthusiasm and the Battalion Sports events had a large entry. During the 1960s the Hadley Stadium at Warley became the choice for the Battalion Sports although Alexander Stadium was still used.

The inter - Battalion event was divided into two age groups, Junior and Senior. Each Battalion took it in turns to host the event, and competing Battalions participated in the organisation. Conveniently, the Battalion Sports was usually timed to occur the week before the Inter-Battalion event. As the inter - Battalion event went into the 1970s, other Battalions such as Sheffield, Liverpool and even some from London took part. By 1974, what had been an occasional event became an annual one involving Birmingham, Grimsby, Liverpool and Nottingham. Birmingham's record in this annual event has been excellent over the years, often winning Junior and Senior titles for both Athletics and Swimming. In 1992, it was agreed to hold events for three age groups,

Junior, Intermediate and Senior. The event today has Birmingham, Grimsby, Halifax, Nottingham and Worcester as regular participants.

The Annual Battalion Athletic Sports, which still takes place on a Saturday in June, has been organised for many years at Hadley Stadium. There is always a wide range of track and field events which are competed for at Junior, Intermediate and Senior levels. The preliminary qualifying events take place in the morning with finals in the afternoon. The printed programme indicates the Battalion record holder and the current holder of the title in each event. Generally the standard is good, but there are just one or two events where the record has stood for twenty years! A tribute to the spectacular athletic prowess of some of the 1980s boys rather than any reflection on current participants.

For most of the 1970s and 1980s the Athletics Trophy competition was dominated by the 6th Coy. with the 66th and 1stA occasional winners. In the 1990s and the new millennium it has been the 4th Sutton Coldfield Coy which has taken the honours and occasionally the 29th Coy..

Cricket

As a Battalion activity, cricket was rather slow to get off the ground, the first competition being organised some twenty years after the Battalion was formed. Quality, has always been a watchword with Birmingham BB as it has been with Birmingham Industry over the years, so it is not surprising to read in the Annual Report of 1912 - 13 that the Battalion had *'Rested on our laurels'* by concentrating

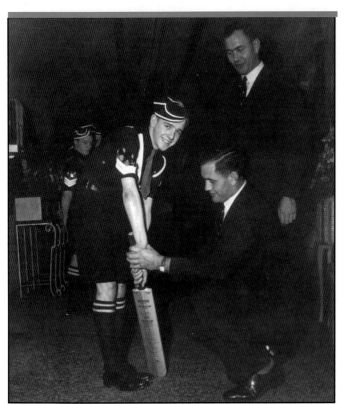

The Bedser Twins offer a few tips to Cpl. Brian Osborne of the 1stA after presenting him with a new Cricket Bat, a prize for winning a 'Stedfast Mag' competition in 1953.

on perfecting the Football League and Swimming Sports. Not that much could be done to remedy this situation between 1914 - 1918. In fact, it was the season 1921 - 1922 that the first Cricket Competition was arranged with nine companies entering and matches played each week throughout the summer. Such a move to diversify sporting activities led the Annual Report to state *'It is the most successful season the Birmingham Recreation Committee have ever had.'*

The subsequent few seasons were not quite as good as had been the launch of Battalion Cricket in 1921 - 1922, with only five teams entered in 1923 - 1924. The union with the BLB in 1926 meant that there was more teams and a Battalion Ground at Stechford upon which to play the games. In the season 1927 - 1928 there was three divisions. Cricket even made a small (very small) profit as laid out in the Annual Accounts:
Cricket receipts £2. 6s Expenses £2. 5s 10d. = profit of 2d.

The 25th Coy. had a good team through much of the 1930s but the league was suspended during Wold War Two. In the season 1944 - 1945 there were 26 companies running cricket teams a number which had risen to 31 by the following season. Running a 'team' and entering it for a Battalion competition are entirely different pursuits. More than half the teams in the Battalion were not able to take

part in the league, which in 1945 - 46 consisted of two divisions with seven and eight companies respectively. Fortunately, most parks and works grounds in the 1940s and 50s maintained a cricket square.

In the 1947 - 1948 season the divisions were increased to three, then four in 1948 - 1949 and five in 1949 - 1950. Fifty companies had cricket clubs and thirty of them were entering the competition. This was the peak of cricket participation in the Battalion in what must have been one of the largest youth leagues in the country. In the season 1951 - 1952 a Weeknight league was started in addition to the Saturday League.

The 1960s brought with it a reduction in teams taking part in the Battalion Leagues which by the end of the decade were less than half the number at the start. A cricket coaching course was attended by 40 boys at the County Ground in Edgbaston in 1963. However, cricket was on the decline, not helped by a series of wet summers in the early 1960s and the increasing lack of suitable pitches. Weeknight cricket was often the victim of the weather with the honours being shared on many occasions. Finishing the weeknight season with an outright winner only became the normal outcome when the league was much smaller .

The Weeknight League attracted many companies over the years with the 6th, 10th, 19th, 39th, 57th, 66th, and 70th Companies being regularly in one of the top three places. This League finished in 1995.

The Saturday League was dominated by fewer companies than the weeknight game with only the 6th, 10th, 62nd & 70th Companies taking the honours after 1960. The League finished in 1981.

 # Cross- Country Running

The first Battalion Annual Cross-Country Run, in 1946, seems to be a good example of an activity initiated at Battalion level. There are no reports of companies entering any similar competitions prior to that date. It was reported as being a great success with some 200 boys taking part in a Senior event of 3 miles and a Junior event of 2 miles. Unfortunately, no venue details are given in the Annual Report. We know that the second event, in 1947, was run in Sutton Park with twelve senior teams and eleven junior teams. As would become the tradition the venue for the third event was a new location, Robin Hood Golf Club Links with a record entry of 34 teams.

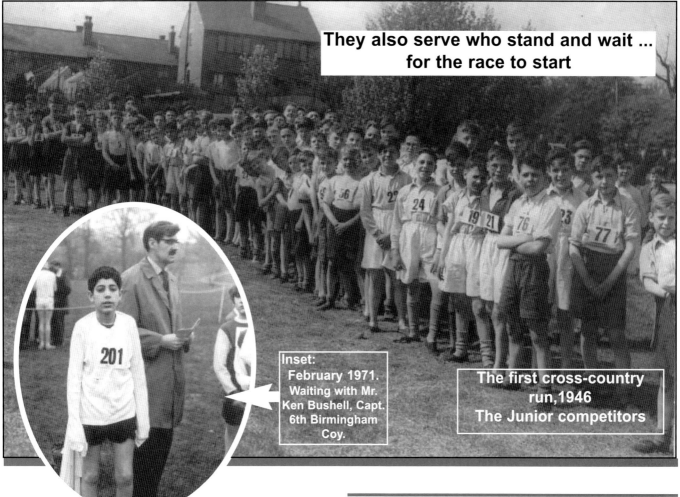

**They also serve who stand and wait ...
for the race to start**

Inset:
February 1971.
Waiting with Mr.
Ken Bushell, Capt.
6th Birmingham
Coy.

The first cross-country
run,1946
The Junior competitors

Harborne Golf Club, Castle Bromwich Area, and Warley Park all provided venues for the runs in the 1950s and 60s Fifty-eight teams entered the 1965 runs along with nineteen individuals. At Warley Park in 1967 the Warley Harriers organised the course and supervised the judging one of many times the Harriers assisted. Foot and Mouth regulations restricted the Sutton Coldfield races in 1968 to school playing fields.

In 1971, an Inter-Battalion event , along similar lines to that already established for Athletics and Swimming, was established in Nottingham. The venue was Woollaton Park, where the championships was destined to remain for the next thirty years. The Nottingham Competition had three age groups, Senior, Intermediate and Junior, so from 1971, the Birmingham Battalion event used these categories. Although Nottingham, Grimsby and Birmingham Battalions have been ever-present in these events, sometimes there has been representative teams from twelve Battalions from as far afield as Scotland and Northern Ireland. In 1974, for instance, the Battalion won the Junior run, Inters run and was second to Belfast in the Senior run. In 2001 this event was cancelled for the first time due to the Foot and Mouth Disease outbreak.

Football

We have no records of Battalion football before 1912, but it would not be difficult to imagine that many companies would have had a team well before that date. Church leagues were some of the earliest to be established in Britain giving birth to many of the great football teams of today. Aston Villa was a fusion of church teams from the Aston and Villa Rd. areas of the city. Many BB companies played in junior church leagues. It was probably the 1st Aston Manor Coy. joining the Battalion in 1909, which led to football being given a higher profile, particularly through its famous old - boy Emmanuel. M. (or 'Man') Roberts as he was known, who had played for Crystal Palace. Naturally, it was the 1st Coy. which was the first winner of the newly presented Football League Shield in 1912. The Annual Report of 1912 - 1913 thanks the 'Sporting Mail' for publishing reports of games. A *source of amusement* was the Officers v Boys Match a tradition carried on for many years, not politically acceptable today. The first Inter - Battalion Match v Wolverhampton was also reported in 1912 and the result was 2 - 2. The

The Battalion Football Team in 1912. Many of the boys were from the 1st B'ham. (Aston) Coy.

same year saw the team lose by six clear goals to the N. Staffs Battalion, probably indicating that, outside of Aston, there were not many companies playing football in Birmingham.

Before the Great War the 1st would win the shield twice more. The war, of course brought with it a few problems and it was reported in the Annual Report of 1918 - 1919 that:

'Owing to the suspension of so many Companies and the extreme staff shortage in the others, not much could be arranged in the sports line. A 'knock out' competition for the Football shield was arranged, however, and six companies entered viz: 1, 2, 7, 18 and 25th. The final was played between the 7th and 25th Companies, the latter winning. The 7th, however, lodged an appeal which was sustained by the Committee, and the match was replayed. This time the 7th were successful, and so were awarded the trophy.'

E. M. 'Man' Roberts pictured at the time he played for Crystal Palace. Emmanuel Roberts was an old boy of the 1st Aston Manor Coy. As a young Lt. he trained the 1st (Aston) Coy football team and eventually became Capt. of the 25th Coy. He took over the 1st Coy in 1936 and was Captain and a Hon. Batt. Vice President until his death in February 1957.

E. M. Roberts (L) and the 1st B'ham. (Aston) Coy c.1917.

**The 10th Birmingham Company, Moseley Rd.
Winners Football Shield Season 1927 - 28**
Five members of the team are wearing their Battalion Team 'Caps'
The Football Shield was presented to the Battalion in 1912 by the 10th's
Captain T. O. Bowen. The Officer on the right is Mr Harold Burnett
who was to become Captain of the 10th, Battalion President
and Hon. Brigade Vice - President.

In the season 1919 - 20 the League was re-started comprising seven companies and was eventually won by the 7th also from Aston. In fact, it was 1923 before another company could get their hands on the shield. In 1920 - 21 another Inter Batt. Football match versus Wolverhampton was held at home, this time the Birmingham Boys won 5 - 1. An away match also resulted in a victory. Perhaps, with ten companies competing for the championship, the selectors had a wider choice of players. The following season brought an increase in competing teams with two divisions being formed. A knock-out competition was started in 1921 - 22 for a cup presented by W. Cook Esq., J.P. Thirteen companies were taking part in the two football leagues by 1924 and Inter-Battalion matches being played against N. Staffs and Bristol. An incentive was introduced for the winners of the two leagues in 1924 - 25 season in the form of bronze medals for each member and a football for each team.

The union with the BLB for the season 1926 - 27 meant a total of between 300 - 400 boys playing football. For the first time the matches could be played on the new Battalion Ground at Stechford. A former BLB Coy., the 4thA, won the Cup. In the following season the divisions were increased to three due to another record entry. For the first time in seven years the Battalion team were defeated by Manchester. According to the accounts football was a profitable activity with receipts totalling £25.5s 6d and expenses being £24. 8s 7d, resulting in a profit of 16s. 11d. In the Annual Report of 1933 - 1934 the Battalion Cup Final is reported to have been played at Villa Park, although it could have been staged there before this time. In the early 1930s the top team in the Battalion was

undoubtedly the 25th from Aston Parish Church, St Peter's Mission, Witton one of the famous footballing Aston companies. Perhaps a decade of Company Captaincy by a certain E. M. Roberts during the 1920s had established the required tradition.

Over the second half of the 1930s the Battalion team was able to redeem itself with regard to the much regretted Manchester defeat. Two matches were played resulting in an 8 - 2 win and an 8 - 3 win. Not all Inter-Battalion matches resulted in a Birmingham win. For instance, in the match versus Northampton on February 19th 1938 the Battalion team were given a 3 - 6 drubbing The match was, naturally, conducted in the very best of spirits.

**The Birmingham & Northampton Battalion Teams.
February 19th 1938.**
The photograph is taken outside the (old) Pavilion at
Stechford.

During the first part of the war the Football League was suspended, but 'friendly' matches were played. Stechford Playing Fields was unable to be used after 1941 due to damage inflicted upon the Pavilion and much of the ground being given over to food production. In the 1944 - 45 season, according to the Annual Report, there were thirty-six football teams. A year later the number had risen to forty - six. Forty - two teams took part in the league of 1945 - 46 which was divided into four divisions.

The increase in the strength of the Battalion in the two decades after WWII was more than reflected in the number of football teams and the popularity of the activity. Before the end of the 1940s there were six divisions and fifty - three teams. The de-requisition of the Playing fields for the 1950 - 51 season added to the impetus as did a series of Lectures which was set up on the work of the Referees Association. Thirty matches each Saturday certainly kept the 'Ref's' busy. A new Challenge Shield was presented in 1951 by the Birmingham Rotary Club. The club also sponsored medals and trophy replicas. The strongest team between 1953 and 1961 was the 1st Walsall Wood company which dominated both the Cup and the League competitions at a time when the number of teams was at its peak.

The 1967 - 68 season signalled change in Battalion football. There were now fewer teams but divisions were retained with smaller numbers in each. Divisional teams were chosen to represent the four parts of the Battalion in the new West Midland District Shield. The N.W. Divisional team being beaten by N. Staffs in the final. A new under 14's League started in 1969 - 70. The Battalion 'team' was now also run in 'Senior' and 'Junior' sections. In 1969, the Cup Final was played as usual at Villa Park but the second half was under floodlights for the first time. In 1974, the 19th Company won the last Battalion Cup Final to be played at Villa Park.

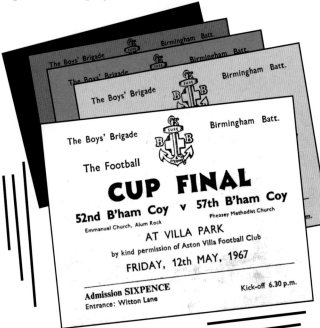

After Stechford Playing Fields was sold football continued on Park Pitches and on many grounds belonging to local industry, viz: Wilmot Breedon, Raleigh Industries, Guest Keen and Nettlefolds, etc.. Pembroke fields at Perry Barr, was also put to much greater use. The Rotary club continued to present medals year by year. Home and away matches were played against Northampton, Bristol, Liverpool, London and Belfast. The Football League winners in the 1980s and 1990s were from a wide number of companies, 6th, 11th, 29th, 34th, 39th, 43rd, 52nd, 57th, 66th and 4th Sutton Coldfield, a very healthy competition. The Cup winners were a rather more select group in both Senior and under 14 competitions. The exception perhaps being in the late 1990s in the under 14 event when the 29th Coy took the honours more often than not winning the under 14 and senior 'double' in 1998 & 1999. A number of events have been run by the Battalion in conjunction with

Aston Villa FC, a good example being a 'Football Soccer School' in August 1997 for eighty boys.

 # 'PT' & 'PE'

The programme for the 5th Annual Demonstration at the Town Hall in 1911, like the previous year, included a number of items which could be classed as 'Physical' although the word 'Training' was not yet part of the vocabulary. It had been common practice for BB companies, like their military counterparts, to indulge themselves in exhibitions of 'Drills' and 'Exercises' which were a part of the weekly programme to promote physical fitness and corporate action. Such 'drills' in the BB, as at school, were often performed to the accompaniment of piano music.

Synchronised activity which would later come under the general term 'Physical Training' was performed with a variety of 'props'. The 8th Coy. performed 'Bayonet Exercises' although the model rifles used would not have had bayonets fixed. The 7th Coy. displayed 'Singlesticks'

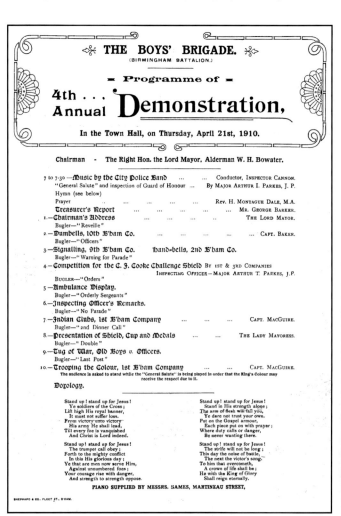

Association. The next decade was one of overall progress in Swimming with Woodcock Street Baths at the centre of events each year for the Gala. In order to maintain high standards, officials of the Midland Counties A.S.A. were brought in to officiate at the Gala. Naturally, the start of the war in 1939 made regular swimming instruction difficult.

The 1944 - 45 Annual Report stated that there were 25 Swimming Classes in operation throughout the Battalion. During the late 1940s and through the 50s the numbers increased to a peak of 57 classes in 1957. This increase reflected both the strength of the Battalion and the emphasis being placed upon young people being able to swim by all the Government Sports bodies. It was not common in the 1950s, or the 1960s for even quite large schools to have their own swimming pool. The work of the Battalion in this area should not be underestimated. In the early 1960s Life - Saving in the water became an important activity, again an activity allied to outdoor pursuits and the D of E Award. The Birmingham City Police gave a display at the Annual Swimming Gala in 1959.

The Inter-Battalion Athletics and Swimming Competition started in 1962; the start of many successes for Birmingham swimming teams. Generally the athletics would take place during the day with the swimming competition in the evening. Birmingham has hosted the event at Solihull on a number of occasions, for instance in 1974 versus Derby, Grimsby, Liverpool, London, and Nottingham the Juniors won and the Seniors finished second. The inter-Battalion event continues and remains popular. The Battalion Swimming Championships is also still keenly competitive. The 6th company, champions from 1975 to 1983, were beaten by the 59th in 1984 and have taken the trophy eight times since. The 4th Sutton Coldfield took the honours five times in the 1990s with the 8th and 7th companies having success. In the case of the 7th, winners in 2001 after a wait of some 80 yrs!

 # Table-Tennis

Table Tennis developed as a popular Company activity after the Second World War. The game had been played in the 1930s in many Church Halls gradually becoming more popular. The English Table-Tennis Association was not formed until 1927 the year after the first World Championships had been held. The game was usually regarded, as it often is today, as a recreation activity for a company 'Clubnight'. As clubnights grew in popularity after the war so did Table - Tennis. Thus, in the BB, Table

- Tennis represented the informality of the 'Youth Club', perhaps the greatest icon of the new Youth Service.

Winners of the under 14 Table-Tennis 2000 & 2001

An ideal activity for a company of any size, but only requiring a small team in order to compete, usually three boys, it is not surprising that a Table-Tennis League was started in Birmingham. The first League ran experimentally in 1947 - 1948 with twenty companies taking part and was won by the 4th Coy.. The next year the competition had grown to thirty-five companies competing. Between 1949 - 1962 both Senior and Junior Cup competitions were run, this being replaced with a system of Divisions between 1963 - 1968. In 1969, another system was introduced dividing the Battalion into North and South sections with no play-offs between the section winners. Generally matches were held at Company headquarters although tables were available at BB House Hatchett St. The most successful company for many years was the 10th Coy which took the honours three times in a row in each of the 50s, 60s and 70s.

Individual Junior and Senior Competitions have been run in addition to the Cup since 1965 and from 1967 an Officers competition. The finals of these individual competitions, for many years, were held at Hatchett St. In 1972, the North & South sections were combined into one competition the 'Table-Tennis Cup'. Table-Tennis remained very popular during the 1970s, moving away from its 'club' image and into the realms of serious sport. The 34th World Table-Tennis Championships were held in Birmingham in 1977 providing an extra stimulus for some of the keener BB players.

5-a-side Football

5 -a- side football, like table - tennis, became popular with many companies because, of course, only five boys and perhaps a couple of reserves were required to make up a team. Additionally, this sport was indoor and made use of many new Sports facilities being constructed around Birmingham, was not subject to the vagaries of the weather and had a comparatively short playing time enabling quite large fixtures to be completed in one day.

In the 1969 - 70 season the National BB Five- a- Side Competition was held at Erdington and this triggered interest in the establishment of a Battalion Senior and Junior Competition first run in 1971. In 1972 there was a West Midland District Competition, won by Birmingham. A major problem for relatively new sports, such as 5-a-side football, is to fit their fixtures into a full sporting schedule, even finding one single free Saturday could prove difficult as demonstrated in the 1975 - 1976 season when Birmingham again hosted the finals for the National 5-a-side Competition at the University of Aston, but on the same day as the Battalion Athletics Championships.

Other 'Sports'

The Tug-of-War Cup was popular between 1950 - 1977 dominated by the 1stA and 6th Coy's., the 1stA winning the Cup 14 times and the 6th 8 times. Tug of war competitions were, for many years, a regular feature of Battalion and Group Camps.

Tug of War, a popular camp activity

A seniors Ten-Pin Bowling competition was started in the Battalion in 1978 with the 70th Coy. as winners in the first year. There have been other similar competitions but nothing organised on a regular basis.

Your move Boris...

They say that Chess is 'exercise for the mind' so perhaps it is not out of place to include it here. It has operated as a competitive activity within the Battalion since 1977 and the trophies in three age groups are always keenly contested. Three or four companies have achieved much success over the years at all levels notably the 55th/16th in the 1970s, 2nd Sutton Coldfield and 73rd in the 1980s, 49th and 59th in the 1990s.

Members of the 29th Coy. Dovedale Expedition 1983

Outdoor pursuits such as hiking, camping, orienteering etc. have always been encouraged by the Battalion. These activities often take place at Annual Camps in the summer or special lightweight expeditions throughout the year. For many years the BB sponsored 'Cleveland Hike', a national competitive outdoor team event has attracted many Birmingham companies to enter, often with some success.

On Target!

Archery Class at the 57th Coy (Pheasey) c.1964

Robin Bolton front right.

Sports Fields: Stechford & Pembroke

The Battalion Playing Fields Stechford.

Summary of an article by D.L. Finnemore from the 'Anchor' broadsheet 1949.

'The Battalion's Greatest Possession'

Out of use since 1941 when a bomb destroyed the pavilion, the 12 acres of land had been cultivated for growing food. Now it is back with us and has been seeded for grass and will probably be in use by autumn 1950.

Bought nearly a quarter of a century ago. (1926) It arose from the 1st World War and the desire of a father to remember his son who, while serving in the R.A.M.C. was killed in action. Mr. H. S. Thompson a well-known accountant gave to the BLB in Birmingham a sum of £250 in memory of his son Maurice Thompson. The Hon. Adjutant and Sec. of the BLB Battalion were anxious that the money should be used for some special purpose and the Battalion agreed to put the money in the Bank towards the purchase of a playing field when that should be possible. Mr Gilbert Southall, who was BLB Battalion Treasurer was equally keen. Several years were spent raising money and looking for a suitable field. Two flag days were held by permission of the Lord Mayor, for one of which an officer broadcast on the old Midland Station. Several hundred pounds were given by B'ham citizens in this way.

The field was found, off Manor Rd. Stechford and some generous gifts, especially from the Society of Friends, enabled the land to be bought and a fine pavilion to be erected. Gas & water were laid on, and there was a large canteen and twelve dressing rooms. Some seven or eight football pitches were laid out and used through the year for football, cricket and sports. Later, six more dressing rooms were added. In 1926 the BLB & BB united and the BB Battalion succeeded to the use of the fields. Unfortunately an Incendiary Bomb reduced the pavillion to

ashes one night in 1941.

'The fields are looked after voluntarily by Mr Babington (of the old 4th & 11th) and his friend Mr Hall of the old 13th. They run the canteen, allocate the pitches, clear the pavillion, cut the grass and maintain order.'

In the 1950 Annual Report it stated that:

Mr C. J. P. Mann, Capt 26th Coy, had been appointed as Warden, and a house adjoining the ground had been purchased as his residence.

The new Pavilion at Stechford, opened in 1951

The new Pavilion was formally opened by Major-General T.N.F. Wilson CB, DSO, M.C. of K. George's Jubilee Trust, on Sat 2nd June 1951. The General was received by the Battalion President Mr R. K. Brown & Sir Donald Finnemore. General Salute was (most appropriately) played. 900 Officers & Boys were on Parade. A Bugle fanfare and the breaking of the BB flag on the flagstaff indicated the formal opening. Throughout most of the next twenty years Stechford Fields were much used. The Pavilion was improved in 1960-61 by the provision of hot water for the showers and space heating for the canteen. By the late 1960s, however, the fields were becoming less well used and the costs of maintenance increasing. Many park pitches which hadn't existed when the field was opened, were now also readily available. An offer of some £200,000 for the land by a house builder, was too good to refuse so the field was sold. Some of the money went toward the purchase and refurbishment of 'Perrycroft' near Malvern.

The Pavilion. Pembroke Fields, Aldridge Road, Perry Barr

Pembroke Fields was presented, in 1923, to the 1stA Company by its Captain, D. L. Finnemore Esq. M.A., being named after his former Oxford College. The Pavilion was presented in 1934 by Old Boys' and friends to celebrate the 21st Anniversary of the Company. Although strictly speaking Pembroke is a '1stA Company' facility it is widely used by Companies in North Birmingham. It was for a few years the home of the North Group of the Battalion Sports. Like Stechford, Pembroke had a resident keeper who lived on site. Mr J. G. Wray who lived in 'Pembroke Lodge' was, for years, Convener of the Battalion Sports Committee. In the mid 1960s the M6 motorway was built over part of the field.

Civic Service

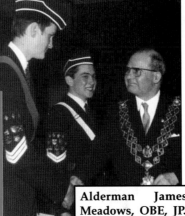

The Battalion has always been very proud of its links with the City. Over the years, Lord Mayors, the personification of the city, have had a close connection with the Boys' Brigade.

From drummer boy to Lord Mayor
—AND TODAY THE BAND WILL BEAT OUT MEMORIES

Birmingham's Lord Mayor, Alderman James Meadows.

WHEN a Boys' Brigade band marches off to ...n parade today, ...m's first citizen ...ring a reflective ...

Lord Mayor of ..., Alderman James ...e sound of the big ...

...fore than 40 years ...y of 13, he was also ...f the Boys' Brigade ...aduated from the ...the bass drum in ...band.

...end, 900 members of ... from all parts of ...n the city for the ...ing of their council. ...be a church parade ...in's-in-the-Bull Ring ...Alderman Meadows ...refers to be known ...ill be shaking hands ...members of the ...om he has not seen

... 65-year-old Mr. ...ll, of Gillott Road, Edgbaston, and 56-year-old Mr. Jim Evans, of Grayswood Park Road, Quinton. Both served in the 4th Birmingham Company with the Lord Mayor — Mr. Wastell as a lieutenant and Mr. Evans as captain from until 1960, when the com was disbanded.

Mr. Evans grew up wit Lord Mayor in Osler & Ladywood, where they next door to one anoth back-to-back houses. Mr. W is now a member of the Midland district executive.

Both the Lord Mayor an Evans attended the com summer camp at Llandu Wales in the summer of 1924.

The Lord Mayor of Birmingham, Alderman James Meadows, was 13 when he attended this 1924 Boys' Brigade summer camp in Wales with fellow-members of the 4th Birmingham Company. He is seated second from the left, and in the centre is Captain Harry Anderson and, to his left, Mr. James Evans, one of the Lord Mayor's schoolmates who will meet him again this week-end for the first time in 40 years.

Alderman James S. Meadows, OBE, JP. Lord Mayor 1967 - 1968. A former member of the 4th Birmingham Coy in the 1920s. (See Press Cutting) He became Battalion Hon. Vice- President in 1968. Alderman Meadows was always a keen supporter of the Battalion.

Alderman Sir Joseph Balmer JP
Alderman Donald Johnstone JP,
Alderman Eric Mole, OBE, JP
Cllr. Edward F. Hanson LL.D (Hon), J.P. FSVA
All the above have been keen supporters of the BB and served as Hon.Vice- Presidents of the Battalion.

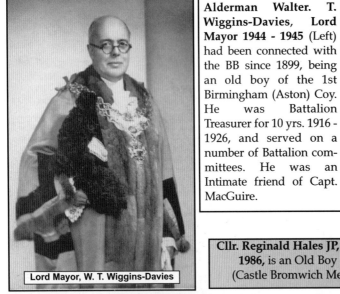

Lord Mayor, W. T. Wiggins-Davies

Alderman Walter. T. Wiggins-Davies, Lord Mayor 1944 - 1945 (Left) had been connected with the BB since 1899, being an old boy of the 1st Birmingham (Aston) Coy. He was Battalion Treasurer for 10 yrs. 1916 - 1926, and served on a number of Battalion committees. He was an Intimate friend of Capt. MacGuire.

The Battalion has many other links with the City, for instance as orderlies for the City of B'ham Show. Many thousands of pounds have been raised by the Battalion over the years in support of Lord Mayors' Charities

The Council House and Art Gallery were built by the firm of John Barnsley & Sons. The Barnsley family had a very close association with the Battalion. Sir John was an Hon. Vice President and both his sons were BB Officers, one of whom was Battalion President and Secretary during nearly 50 yrs of service.

Cllr. Reginald Hales JP, Lord Mayor 1985 - 1986, is an Old Boy of the 48th Coy (Castle Bromwich Methodist Church).

Alderman Charles V. G. Simpson. Lord Mayor 1968 - 1969. An Old Boy of the 10th Coy. He was a Battalion Hon. Vice President who always took an active interest in BB work.

Lord Mayor Alldridge Inspects

Alderman Lionel. G. H. Alldridge.
Was for 30 yrs a BB Officer, and Captain of the 36th Coy. **Lord Mayor 1943 -1944** .
He was awarded the OBE 1944-1945.
A report of his funeral service from July 1966 stated that representativess of local & national bodies were present including Mr Reginald Eyre MP (Ex. Boys' Brigade member), *'Conspicuous in their smart navy blue uniforms were members of the Birmingham Battalion of the Boys' Brigade, of which Ald. Alldridge was Vice President.'*
Lionel Alldridge had two Special Interests, The Boys' Brigade & the City's Hospitals. He was described as 'The Lord Mayor of Youth' a title he treasured. Regularly taking his Sunday morning BB Bible Class, he had a deep religious faith. No-one could speak ill of him as he made an outstanding contribution to life of city.
He was a member of the congregation of St. Germain Edgbaston.

The Joys of Camp

From the 1890s the Aston Manor Companies, held a regular joint summer Camp. There is no record of other Birmingham companies camping until the first Battalion Camp held in 1902. As this report from the BB Gazette of October that year revealed, enthusiasm for camping was somewhat dampened:

'The first camp of the Birmingham Battalion took place at the park of Sutton Coldfield near Birmingham. The use of the park kindly allowed for the purpose by the Sutton Town Council. Unfortunately the weather was most unpropitious, nearly the whole week. Necessitating constant rearrangement of sleeping quarters.'

Further Battalion Camps were not contemplated and it was 1908 before a group of companies got together for another summer camp. The 6th Coy. along with 8th and 13th camped together under the command of Capt. C. J. Cooke, Capt of the 6th and Battalion President. It was the first time the 6th ever encamped. The Camp was at Kenilworth on a field loaned by a Mr E. Gee. It is interesting for us today to realise just how much of an 'adventure' this was for all concerned, Kenilworth must have seemed like another world. Local residents offered fruit, flowers and entertainment. Lord Ernest Seymour and Lady Seymour entertained the Companies to tea on the lawn at their residence, and Lord Seymour reviewed the Companies, afterwards inspecting the camp. The 7th and 11th companies also camped, the 7th on Cannock Chase and the 11th at Dodderhill common (near Hanbury). By 1913, 16 Companies in the Battalion were camping, most at Company Camps.

Scouting

From about 1909 many Birmingham Companies were keen to involve their boys in the new 'Scouting' activity. Scouting was very much desired by the boys who saw the outdoor life, survival and tracking as being the very latest up to the minute craze. Naturally, Camp was a great time to do Scouting, but some companies, such as the 8th from Islington Wesleyan Mission under Capt. D. G. Barnsley organised special Scout Camps. BB Boys who were scouts would wear their special BB Scout uniforms for scouting activities. George Oakton was one of the Scouts in the 8th in 1912 who looked forward to the special Scouting activities held on Saturdays. *'We never wore our Scout Uniforms for BB Parades'* said George. Scouting was an activity for which there was a 'costume' just as there was for football or swimming. Boys' Life Brigade Companies were also very much caught up in the Scouting phenomenon, particularly as 'Scouting' was being marketed as a pacifist pursuit. The 1st Birmingham Coy. BLB, a Quaker Company, left the Brigade to become 'Peace Scouts' in 1913, eventually re-joining the BLB in 1922 as the 19th Birmingham Coy.. The 19th, from the Friends Institute Moseley Road, became the 19th Birmingham BB upon union in 1926.

Scouts of the 8th Birmingham Company in 1909.
Company Capt. D. G. Barnsley, standing back right, was in charge but he didn't wear a Scoutmaster's uniform.

Scout sections were not encouraged in the BB after 1926. The Introduction of the Wayfarers' Badge in 1927 along with other 'outdoor' activities rendered scouting as a separate activity obsolete within the BB.

Camp 1914

The BB Gazette of 1st May 1914 made the announcement that... *'After a Lapse of about ten years, a (Birmingham) Battalion Camp, which promises to be largely attended, is being arranged'.*

The 1914 Battalion Camp was held at Teddesley Park, Penkridge, Staffs. Commanding Officer was Capt D. G. Barnsley of the 8th Coy.

Before the start of the camp the boys paraded in full uniform at Thorp St Drill Hall with Haversack rations being carried. Boys had been strongly recommended to have their hair cut short and to have had a bath before proceeding to camp. The Camp Orders stated that In the interests of general health any boy who was not perfectly clean would be dismissed from camp. Strict silence had to be maintained whilst entraining. On arrival, boys detrained when the 'advance' was sounded. The boys then fell in on the platform previous to marching on markers in the station yard. Packed kit bags had been taken in advance (the night before) to the HQ of 3rd Coy in Dalton St.. Once the boys had arrived at their destination it was important that they knew when and how to come and go, the orders were clear:

'No boys must quit the camp except at times named in daily orders without a pass signed by his Camp Captain and countersigned by the C.O. or Adjutant. All passes will be given up to the sentry on returning to camp.'

For daily tent inspection at 7.30 a.m. kits were laid out outside each tent and dressed by the right. Full uniform was worn. Any 'defaulters', for instance, arriving back at camp late, were sent to the Guard Tent. Officers of the Night Guard came off duty at 6.30 a.m., but only after seeing that the flag was hoisted for Reveille and that the Bugle Band Paraded. Guard 'beats' lasted two hours, with the Guard parading in uniform with 'Arms'. Again there were detailed instructions:

'Sentries walking backwards and forwards on their beat must do so in a brisk, soldier-like manner, and must on no account quit their arms, lounge, or converse with anyone…'

Officers Mess Orderlies paraded in the Officers Mess at 7.00 a.m., and remained on duty until 7.00 p.m.. They laid and cleared the tables, washed up, kept clean the tent and waited at table wearing full uniform.

Bathing was done by half companies, swimmers right half and non-swimmers left. Boys entered the water when 'advance' was sounded. Swimmers bathed within a space marked by red flags, non-swimmers within a space marked by blue flags. Each boy had a bathing 'pal' and the two stayed together whilst bathing. At the sound of 'Fall In' all bathing ceased. The Camp Orders stated that Bathing pants must be worn.

The Canteen was closed half an hour before meals and was not open on Sunday. There were two 'Visitors Days' when relatives of the boys were invited to inspect the camp; Teas being provided for them at 6d each.

Playing cards were strictly forbidden. The whole experience sounds somewhat 'regimented' by today's standards, but camp routine was modelled on that of the military camp and that is what the boys expected and just what they wanted. Unfortunately, a few of them would be getting the 'real thing' sooner than expected during the next few years.

Wartime Camping

Due to the war, camps were not held by the Battalion, although some companies did arrange their own. It was difficult to get equipment for a large camp. The annual Camp Appeal launched by the Battalion prior to the 1914 camp was discontinued with any donations received being given proportionally to poorer companies which were holding camps of their own. In 1918, 150 boys from four companies spent a week in camp during the August Bank Holiday in spite of increased wartime difficulties; they were getting the 'camping bug'!

One company, the 9th from Belmont Row Mission, really got into the swing of things whilst camping at Coleshill in 1917. Like many companies before and since, the boys wrote their own song. The tune was 'So early in the morning' the words paint fascinating portraits of the boys who attended the camp, their nature, exploits and employment in local business.

> 1. Capt. Davey is his name,
> In the 3rd & 9th he won a fame.
>
> Chorus: Hurrah for Camp at Coleshill,
> Hurrah for Camp at Coleshill
> Hurrah for Camp at Coleshill
> And the good old 9th BB.
>
> 2. S. Sgt. Williams is a sport.
> We called him Toffee-De-Lux for short.
>
> 3. Harry Bissell is an officer great,
> His pineapple chunks for tea we ate.
>
> 4. The N'C.O's are a fine good lot,
> They turned up well to clean pan & pot.
>
> 5. Sgt. Porter is his name,
> By flirting he has many a game.
>
> 6. Sgt. Smith is quite a tike,
> Always on Stan Tromans Byke.

7. Cpl. Adams is in the Cadets,
An all night guard is what he suggests.

8. Cpl. Troman is a 'Kenrick Boy'
But his holiday at Camp he means to enjoy.

9. Cpl. Bradbury from Stewarts and Lloyds,
Is the typing king for parody guides.

10. Cpl. Warder the prospective Jew,
Will endeavour to amuse both me & you.

11. L.Cpl Mackley is as dry as chips
His Submarine Lancers gives us the splits.

12. L. Cpl. Bannister is a runner sublime,
His name for the staircase race is fine.

13. L/Cpl Prosser the bread yeast man,
Is no relation to the flying man.

14. L.Cpl. Adams the minor brave,
The life of a rat he could not save.

15. Pte. Loach when he paid his fare,
They called him the Woodcock St. Lord Mayor.

16. Pte. Burns & Masons Stores,
Were always getting into the wars.

17. Pte. Bonnalls trousers let in air,
Where his seat ought to be, he discovered a tear.

18. Pte. Boswells dad came to see him one day,
So Boswell decided to run away.

19. Pte. Bott & Hemming went to the C.W.S.
And came back dripping in a terrible mess.

20. Pte Vernon had a cold in his head,
Took 'Tincture of Benjamen' when going to bed.

21. Pte. Hitchman's Ma' brought sweets one day
Which he changed for cash his fare to pay.

22. Pte. Paget led a hermits life,
With his kitten in the small barn far from strife.

The Boys' Brigade,
Birmingham Battalion

Camp Orders
AND
Regulations,
1922.

BINTON, Near Stratford-on-Avon.

FRIDAY, AUGUST 4th to
SATURDAY, AUGUST 12th.

Fields kindly lent by
Mr. T. HODGES, Binton Hill Farm.

An informal group at the Battalion Camp 1920, Teddesley Park. These boys are wearing armbands with numbers, suggesting some kind of duty, possibly 'orderlies'.

Like most camp songs the 9th's epic went on a bit and meant something to the boys who sang it. The same boys, of course, usually find that they cannot sing when it's time for hymns at a camp service. The officers always got a mention, as here, sometimes favourable! Camp food, rarely escaped mention in such songs. There is a choice collection of Birmingham employers mentioned, Masons Stores, C.W.S., Stewarts & Lloyds, and Kenrick's.

Arrival at camp 1926

After the war there was no holding back the enthusiasm for camping with six companies forming a 'Battalion Camp' in 1920, and returning to Teddesley Park. There were 175 boys at the camp. Six other company camps took place that year with 509 boys in the Battalion attending a

Camp 1921 Teddesley Park . The Advance Party.
It was the job of the Advance Party to go ahead of the Camp and erect the tents, equip the marquee, dig pits, put up signs, and generally prepare for the arrival of the main party.

camp. The success of the 1920 venture was followed in 1921 by 260 of all ranks attending Battalion Camp, which was again held at Teddesley Park. A further eight companies camped in such out of the way places as Hopwas, Canwell and Hill Hook, making a total of 618 of all ranks in the Battalion attending Camp that year.

Between August 4th and 12th 1922, the Battalion Camp was held at Binton near Stratford Upon Avon. There were 350 boys including detachments from Kidderminster, Coventry and Leeds. That year other companies camped in six separate locations with a total of 526 B'ham boys spending a week at camp. A seaside site was chosen for 1923, to be held at Clarach Bay, Near Aberystwyth. This camp, from August 4th to the 11th, combined seven Birmingham and four Kidderminster companies. That year 465 Birmingham boys attended camps. The 1924 Camp, was held at Hunstanton Hall, Norfolk between August 2nd - 9th and termed a 'Birmingham Group' camp. Some 447 boys attended camps that year.

The following year a further 'Group' Camp was held at Hunstanton Hall , Norfolk from Aug. 1st - 8th. In 1927, the first 'United Battalion Camp', was held at Penmaenmawr, with some 350 Officers and Boys. In total 700-800 boys in all the Battalion camped that year. Wales was chosen again in 1928 with another united Battalion Camp held at Harlech from August 4th - 13th having a record-breaking 410 Boys on camp. Altogether 800 B'ham BB Boys spent a week at Camp in 1928. The C.O. for the Battalion camp was D. L. Finnemore, M A. Capt. of 1stA Coy. with S. E. Barnes Capt. 8th Coy. as Adjutant. The camp was formed into 4 Coys A, B, C, & D. The

Bandmaster was D. Shock (Lt). It is interesting to note the costs, for boys 12, 13 & 14. 23/-. (£1.15p). Even then, it was an affordable holiday. The 1929 and 1930 Camps were held at Criccieth with over 300 boys at each. The 1932 Annual Camp was a return to Penmaenmawr in August. A total of 823 B'ham boys were at camps that year.

Camp often provided an opportunity to do things you couldn't do back home in the city

With the Battalion growing in size and upwards of 1000 boys attending company camps, no Battalion camp was held after 1932. The logistical problems of catering for the needs of such large numbers put such massive camps out of the question, except for great International events.

Departing for Camp in the 1930s
Boys (in full uniform), officers, baggage, tents, groundsheets, buckets, pots, pans, sports equipment, food...sometimes even the piano from the Church Hall, all loaded on to an open truck courtesy of a local business.

Birmingham Group Camp, 1977 Isle of Wight

More Group Camps

Strong companies often preferred to camp alone or in 'Groups'. Group Camps, started early in the Battalion's history, remained very popular after the Second World War with the same five or six companies camping together each year, often choosing a different site each time. These Group Camps cannot be classed as 'Battalion' Camps, but often they were of similar size to that which many smaller Battalions could muster. Perhaps the most enduring group started camping together in 1950 on the Isle of Wight. Started by Mr Bill Ball Captain of the 67th Coy. followed eventually by the indomitable Mr Stan Stebbings when he took over as Captain of the 67th Coy.. The 67th were joined by three or four other companies, which having learnt how to camp from the 'experts' sometimes went on to run their own successful company

OI! SIR, WHO IS MR STEBBINS!

Cartoon from the 1983 Group Camp Booklet

camps. This was certainly the case with the writer's former company because after a shared experience on the

Isle of Wight in 1960 the 57th Coy went on to run successful company camps for more than twenty years. Stan Stebbings (see photo page 103) sadly, died in 1997, but many will remember his 'presence' characterised by an enormous genuine ex-RAF handle-bar moustache which grew larger as the years went on. Previously C.O. and

Picture: Birmingham Post & Mail

The 1st (Aston) Coy. board a plane at Elmdon Airport to go to Camp in Jersey, July 1959.
The first Birmingham Coy. to travel to camp by air.

more recently, Chaplain, Ken Powell or Bishop Ken Powell, as he should be addressed, has attended most of the Camps. Other companies not mentioned above, which have been part of this group included the 18th, 27th, 44th, 52nd, 58th, 61st, 70th, 75th, 3rd Sutton Coldfield, 1st Polesworth, 1st Tamworth, 1st Oxford, 1st Witney, 136th London and a Jersey Coy.. The 1st Sutton Girls' Brigade have also attended in more recent years. A special Get-Together and Parade Service, with the Lord Mayor in attendance, was held in 1990 to celebrate 40yrs of the Group Camp. Needless to say many memories were re-kindled at that event; the boy who broke his leg on the first day in 1966, or the camp at which two officers ended up in hospital. Fresh in their minds was the previous year at Woolacombe when all were shown just how much camp means to some boys... a young man, although dying, was determined to attend. His doctors said that he could not take the rigors of the long journey. The group pestered and cajoled 'til they arranged a helicopter to take him to camp for the day. Great excitement and a tear jerk-ing experience for all. Camp means so much for old and young BB members and the older you get the more likely you are to recall those camp tales. Perhaps it is best to let Mr Stebbings sum it up as he did in the 40th Anniversary programme:

'...a celebration of the joy of 40 years, an opportunity to remi-nisce to retell those anecdotes that have bored our families all those years. Yes, it's sheer self-indulgence but with a pur-pose...to thank OUR LORD for His blessing, and to provide the present generation the depth of the appreciation that we all have of our time at Boys' Brigade Camp'

International & National Camps

Birmingham boys were not slow in coming forward when large 'Special' camps were being organised on a National or International basis. Sharing a camping experience with boys from all over the UK, at a camp with special National significance, was simply too good an opportunity to be missed. One of the first such events to be arranged was to coincide with the great Jubilee Celebrations in Glasgow in 1933, the Jubilee Camp at Dechmont. Alf Smith, an NCO in the 32nd Coy was lucky enough to go, representing his Company and of course, Birmingham Battalion. Upon his return to Birmingham young Alf put pen to paper:

'After a long and rather tiring journey we arrived with boys from several other companies in Glasgow about seven o'clock on Friday morning. In the station there was a little, neat stall, draped with scotch plaid. Here were the transport officers and they directed us to the train to Dechmont. We were on the train bar-ley fifteen minutes when we found ourselves walking up the drive only to find a stream of motor buses to meet us. This was the final stage of the journey and when we came in sight of the vast number of tents I wondered however I was to find my own. This had all been arranged and when I <u>did</u> get to my tent we all exchanged conversations with one another.

In our tent were boys from Birmingham, Glasgow, Sunderland, Newcastle and London. After breakfast we were all dished out with a ground sheet and blankets which occupied biggest part of the morning. In the afternoon there was a trip round Glasgow by bus. There was a concert in the evening and the casket was sealed containing the signatures of the boys representing the different nations, and the officers were solemnly charged not to break the seal till 1983. "Lights out" that night went at about 11 o'clock and I think everyone was glad to get a good night's rest after all the excitement of the day.

Revellie 7 o'clock, and after washing, dressing and folding our blankets ready for tent inspection we had breakfast at 8 o'clock. after tent inspection there was a rehearsal for the review. Then came the review itself. We all marched to our positions at Queens Park Recreation ground. Prince George drove to his posi-tion by car and as he did so a great roar went up from the crowd. It must have been a glorious sight, just try and picture it for yourself 30,000 boys all in uni-form manoevering forward. There were 60,000 spectators and I am sure every-one including the prince himself was greatly impressed by it, and when tried to picture the total strength of the B.B. and all had risen from those thirty boys.

On Saturday evening there was another concert, given by the New Vagabonds, and there was also a great deal of excitement caused by a push ball lent by the "Daily Mail". At the back of the camping ground there was a large hill and after a lot of persevering they managed to get the ball to the top of this, and let it come tearing down again. One day they got it in between two lines of tents and being unable to steady it, it came in contact with a bucket of water used in case of fire and somebody's kit-bag got a trifle wet. On Sunday morning there was a drumhead service conducted by the camp chaplain the Rev. Joseph Gray and was attended by the Right honorabl;e the Lord Provost of Glasgow. On Sunday afternoon there was a Conventicle at Hampden Park, the Worlds largest football ground, and the address was given by the Right Rev. Lauchlan Maclean Watt. There was 100,000 people present, another 100,000 people turned away, and that many fainting cases that the ambulance men could not cope with them and the Staff-Sergeants had to help.

On Sunday evening there was, what seemed to me the most fascinating thing of all- the Fire of Friendship. At Dusk we were all mustered on to the side of the hill singing the "Anchor Song" and all the senior boys were each given a torch to light the way. It was a glorious sight and must have been seen for miles around. First of all we sang the hymn "Underneath the Banner" and then a short talk by the Chaplain. During the first singing of the chorus representatives from the Original Glasgow Company, India, Africa, Canada and the Channel Islands came round the fire. During the second singing of the chorus representatives from The Irish Free State, Northern Ireland, Wales, England and Scotland came round the fire. Then we sang the Jubilee Song and at the end the reprrsentative boys thrust there torches into the fire and it soon bacame one big blazing mass. While it was still burning we sang "Onward Christian Soldiers" and then there was a single note on the bugle and it could be plainly heard echoing over the hills. This was a signal for a silent prayer at the close of which was the Lords prayer. After this everyone had to stare into the fire for two minutes and think their own thoughts. It seemed marvellous the silence that reigned over such a vast crowd, not a whisper, not a murmour or sound of any kind except the rumble of the trains in the distance. We closed by singing "Abide with me", which was followed by the retreat played from the very top of the hill. The fire would die out in the early hours of the morning, but it would still burn in our hearts for ever. At night in Scotland it is very cold and I think most of us felt it that night more than ever.

On Monday morning we were aroused from sleep somewhat earlier than usual by an officer and we were told to get dressed immediately if we wished to go on the excursion through the Kyles of Bute. when we got outside, however, everywhere seemed deserted and the washing place too, that was generally crowded was empty, but we wasted no time and we were ready a long time before the others. Those who were leaving that night had to pack their kit bags after breakfast in case we were late coming home from the trip. As soon as we had finished this we had to fall in and we were each given a box containing 4 ham sandwiches, 2 cheese sandwiches, a cake, an apple, a biscuit, a cardboard cup and a ticket bearing a stamped number.

We marched to the station and took a train from there to Wembys Bay which took about an hour and a half. We boarded the boat and soon we were steadily steaming down the Clyde. The secenery was undescribeable. All hills and valleys for miles and miles, and in some parts purple heather could still be seen in bloom. And so farther and farther down the Clyde until we came to Ockenlocken where a maroon was fired from the pier as we went past. Time went very quickly and we were soon having our dinner and the ticket that I mentioned previously was given in exchange for milk served in the cardboard cup. It did not seem long but we found ourselves going back again, past the hills, past Ockenlochen and back to the landing stage. We had to rush and crush to get to the train, for in our carriage we had to have sixteen. One on each of the racks and seven on each side, a bit crushed yet funny enough everyone of us went to sleep which made time pass very quickly. When we arrived it was getting rather late and we only had time to have a last look round camp, a meal, and so home again better fitted to carry on with our work.'

In 1954 the Centenary of the birth of the Founder, Sir William A Smith, was naturally celebrated in many ways throughout the world. The major event of the year was undoubtedly the great International Camp held on the

Eton Camp From the air

Playing Fields of Eton College from 12 - 21st August, when some 2,500 boys from all over the world came together to honour the memory of the Founder. Birmingham boys were present, of course, but perhaps most significantly the whole Camp was under the command of Birmingham Officers. Sir Donald Finnemore, then Battalion Hon. Vice-President was Commandant, Mr R. K. Brown, Battalion President, was Camp Adjutant; Mr R. H. Webb, Battalion Adjutant in Charge of Entertainments and Mr S. H. Gilbert responsible for hospitality, particularly for those boys remaining in the UK beyond the camp dates.

Sir Donald Finnemore (in white shirt)
with the Founder's Sons
Mr G. Stanley Smith, OBE, MC (Left) and Mr D. Pearson
Smith (Right) at the Eton Camp 1954

The Lord Mayor, Alderman J. J. Grogan, MBE., JP hands over his message to be presented to the Mayor of Kingston and St. Andrew, Jamaica. The four boys who will represent Birmingham are wearing their special CariBBean Camp Uniform. Sir Donald Finnemore, Battalion President, and Mr W. Gordon Innes, Battalion Secretary, look on.

Brian Stansbie and David Hewston were two boys from the 43rd Coy. selected to attend. Brian remembers being assembled in eight camp companies and watching the flag run up to the strains of the pipe band.

'Our tent was situated in Company 8, Tent 1, Line D and consisted of 3 from Canada, 2 from Glasgow, 1 from Worthing and 2 from Birmingham. We experienced many activities, Morning Service in the Eton College Chapel, Visits to London Airport, Windsor Castle, Westminster Abbey, Buckingham Palace, St Paul's Cathedral etc.' Quite an experience for Brummie boys in 1954! *'There was a Grand Finale, a torchlight procession through Windsor on the last night, to a great Camp fire...'*

In 1958 the BB was 75 yrs old and to celebrate there were two camps! One was the CariBBean Camp in Jamaica and the other a special training camp for 750 senior boys, held at Lilleshall Hall called, surprisingly, the '750 Camp'. Four Birmingham boys and the Battalion Secretary attended the Caribbean Camp in April and 35 Birmingham boys went to the training camp in August. The leader of the Lilleshall Camp was Sir John Hunt, who had been in charge of the British Expedition to Mount Everest 1952 - 1953 and was then Secretary of the Duke of Edinburgh's Award. The 750 Camp was so successful that a similar venture was organised in 1961, simply called the 'Senior Boy Training Camp' There were more than thirty Birmingham Boys at the 1961 Camp. The Training Camps

Birmingham Boys at the Senior Boy Training Camp August 1961

were designed to raise the skill level of senior boys who would then take that expertise back to their companies. Football, Archery, Weight-Lifting, Badminton, Judo, Golf, Lawn Tennis, Rugby Union, Gymnastics, Basketball and Fencing were all on the menu. The venture for Seniors was continued in 1963 with Birmingham boys again taking part in an International Camp at Glenalmond, Perthshire in August.

Twenty years passed before Birmingham Boys were again involved in a great BB International Camp. The Brigade Centenary celebrations, marked all over the world in 1983

featured many outstanding events, the International Camp held at Scone Palace, Perth for ten days in August, was amongst the finest. In a departure from all previous Camps, BB uniform was not worn, there being a special informal Camp dress. The camp was divided into 'Clans' each with its own Chief. In charge was the Chieftain - Col. Charles H. K. Corsar, OBE, TD, MA, JP, DL. Paul Stansbie from the 4th Sutton Coldfield Coy was one of the 26 Birmingham boys selected to attend, following in the footsteps of his father who had attended the Eton Camp. Paul says that alongside his pride in achieving both the President's and Queen's Badges his time at the Scone Camp comes top of his BB experiences. *'My first impression of the camp was that of apprehension...I remember sitting on my case and being struck by the sheer size of the project. The friendliness and efficiency with which I was assigned camp uniform (a commemorative sweatshirt), a tent and an adoptive clan soon settled me down. The Camp was attended by approximately 1800 officers and members from 36 different countries... although most of the interest was focussed on a group of Swedish girls! I was able to make new friends and learn new skills by getting involved in numerous activities, in particular a camp award for participation in sports, arts & crafts etc. Almost twenty years on its only now I can really appreciate what a great opportunity this was and how fortunate I was to be part of it.'*

There have been other great Camps since 1983, but nothing on the scale of the Centenary event. The 1986 Centenary of camping at Rozelle, Ayr and the 1991 International Camp at Aberdeen.

The Future of Camping

The introduction of the Duke of Edinburgh's Award in the late 1950s provided an opportunity for 'lightweight' camping. Expeditions for a few days in North Wales or the Peak District have often supplemented but not replaced the static summer camps. These small camps are organised almost entirely on a Company basis but training and testing are done at Battalion and national level. When organising trips to mountainous terrain it is vitally important that the correct safety codes are observed. For some, the Boys' Brigade will provide the only opportunity to participate in such activities.

For most Birmingham boys there is still much to be gained by a simple change of environment and responsibilities. Living as part of a large family, sharing the duties, respecting the countryside, walking, seeing the stars at night, and a thousand other advantages that any BB officer who has been to camp will tell you. In 2002, Birmingham companies still go to Annual Summer Camp the experience is very much valued and likely to continue.

Camp 1933 aboard the 'IMPLACABLE'

HISTORY OF THE IMPLACABLE

The Battleship Implacable, which became one of Englands 'Wooden Walls' was launched in 1800 under French colours as the 'Duguay-Trouin'. With Capt. Claude Touffet in command and 650 men on board, it engaged HMS Victory at Trafalgar surviving the battle only to be captured two weeks later. The re-named 72-gun Prize Ship fought as part of the British fleet until 1842 when it became a Training Ship for boys. It was ordered to the scrap heap in 1908, but the order was countermanded by King Edward VII. In 1912, Mr G. Wheatley Cobb and Mr W. L. Wylie saved the vessel.

The Admiralty gave her away in 1925 after which she was operated by the 'Implacable Committee' as a place where city boys could take a holiday and 'taste the sea'. The ship lay in H.M. Dockyard Portsmouth alongside the old 46 - gun Frigate 'Foudroyant'. It was commanded by Lt. Col. Harold Wylie an archaeologist and 'the greatest living authority on old-time sailing ships' who was slowly restoring her just as he had HMS Victory little over a mile away.

In the early 1930s, BB boys were given the chance to have their Annual Camp on the ship after making application via Capt Ridge of the 1st Enfield Coy..

In 1933, the 32nd Birmingham Coy. were part of the 'crew' of 120 BB boys who had paid their £1 for the week. Activities available included Diving, Swimming, Water-polo, Rowing, Sailing, Seamanship, Signalling, Marine Motor Engines. Visits to 'Victory', Submarine Base, Battleships etc.. Games and Sport. The Birmingham Boys joined in enthusiastically with everything. They slept in hammocks, washed and scrubbed the decks, saluted in memory of Nelson and pretended not to be 'landlubbers'. At the end of the week they were sorry to depart from what had been an 'unusual' camp.

Scrubbing the decks in the morning

Whatever happened to the Implacable?

The fate of the ship was rather sad but full of naval tradition. She was taken back by the Admiralty in 1941 as a Training Ship. But on December 2nd 1949, after a number of attemps to save her, the world's oldest floating warship was towed into the channel proudly flying the French Tricolour alongside the White Ensign and blown up in 36 fathoms of water. On her last voyage she passed the new 'HMS Implacable' - an Aircraft Carrier, as a band played the National Anthem and the Marseillaise.

Alf Smith, one of the Birmingham Boys on the ship in 1933 kept the press cuttings about the end of the ship in the back of his photo album. The Implacable may have gone forever, but the memories of that camp live on.

'Flies in the milk' Attempting to row a 12-oared Cutter

The 32nd with Lt. Col. Wylie

Battalion Camp Criccieth 1929

A Distinguished Visitor ... Lloyd-George

Delivering some of the famous oratory

The 'Welsh Wizard' arrives

David Lloyd-George (Prime Minister 1916 - 1922) lived in Criccieth N. Wales so he was very much on home ground when he visited the Birmingham Battalion Camp in 1929. He was, of course a great national personality and received a big brummie welcome upon his arrival, a distinct contrast to the way he had been received when speaking at Birmingham Town Hall some three decades earlier when he had made his escape, dressed as a policeman, from an angry crowd of some 30,000 Brummies!

From The Boys Brigade Gazette 1st Oct 1929:

'The Birmingham Battalion Camp at Criccieth was honoured by a visit from Mr Lloyd George, who inspected the camp and addressed Officers and boys, giving them a hearty welcome to this beautiful spot, and recalling happy days of boyhood when he roamed free over beach and countryside. He congratulated them upon the condition of the camp and upon the ideals of the BB, which would develop the best in a Boy's character, and said that true happiness could only be attained by service for others-

their Companies, their homes, cities, country, and the great brotherhood of mankind. Three rousing cheers brought the characteristic "L.G." smile.'

The uniforms worn at the camp reflect the variety used in the Battalion at the time just three years after union with the BLB. In 1929, uniform was worn for most camp activities other than swimming or some of the dirtier parts of fatigue duty. Trips were organised to the Ffestiniog railway and local beauty spots.

The Camp C.O. was Donald Hurst with S.E. Barnes as Adjutant. George Oakton, Captain of the 5th Birmingham Coy. and an officer at the Camp, recalls that food was as usual at the forefront of discussion amongst the boys but for two very different reasons. A somewhat negative reaction followed from when Cyril Mann, during his first stint as duty officer had managed to pollute the porridge with paraffin. Much more positive comments came from the group of boys detailed to act as Stewards for Lloyd-George at his 'open-house' that week, in fact they had never stopped talking about the 'colossal' tea which was so generously provided for them.

Cadbury Garden Party 1932 Bournville

Three Cheers for Mr & Mrs Cadbury!

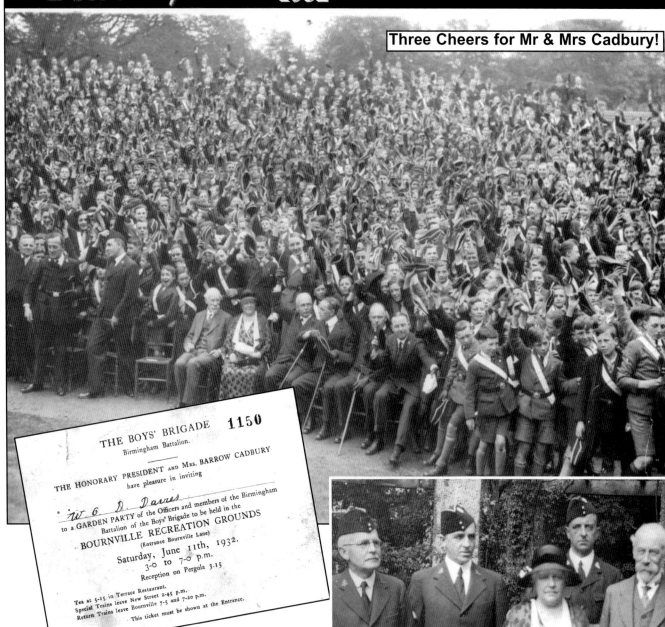

THE BOYS' BRIGADE 1150
Birmingham Battalion.

THE HONORARY PRESIDENT AND MRS. BARROW CADBURY
have pleasure in inviting

Mr G. D. Davies
to a GARDEN PARTY of the Officers and members of the Birmingham
Battalion of the Boys' Brigade to be held in the
BOURNVILLE RECREATION GROUNDS
(Entrance Bournville Lane)
Saturday, June 11th, 1932.
3-0 to 7-0 p.m.
Reception on Pergola 3.15

Tea at 5-15 in Terrace Restaurant.
Special Trains leave New Street 2-45 p.m.
Return Trains leave Bournville 7-5 and 7-20 p.m.
This ticket must be shown at the Entrance.

Pictured at the Garden Party. Left to right:
Mr Gilbert Southall (Battalion Treasurer), Mr Donald Hurst (Hon. Batt Vice-President), Mrs Geraldine Cadbury, Mr Donald Finnemore (Battalion President), Mr Barrow Cadbury (Hon. Batt President).

The largest BB Garden Party ever held.

Saturday June 11th 1932,
Bournville Recreation Grounds.

Special trains were laid-on to get the Battalion to Bournville. All the boys enjoyed a tour of the factory and received a box of chocolates.
More than 2000 Officers and boys sat down to tea in one great hall. A truly memorable occasion.
There was even sports equipment laid on for the use of the boys.

The *Cadbury* Connection

Friends Hall & Institute, Moseley Road.

When the first Company of the Boys' Life Brigade in Birmingham was founded on 21st March 1901 at the Friends' Institute Moseley Road, Mr Barrow Cadbury, a member of the famous Chocolate making family, was pleased to be appointed President. As a Quaker, he was a committed pacifist and keen to support a Brigade which sought to:

'...lead our boys to Christ...by means of drill - not associated with arms, but with instruction and exercises in the saving of life from fires, drowning, and accident.'

At the age of eleven years, young Barrow Cadbury was sent to a *Realschule,* a state elementary school in Germany. Drills and military exercises were part of his training. According to Percy W. Bartlett, his biographer, whilst attempting to explain Barrow's involvement with the BLB and BB in later life; *'pacifist as he was he could not forget his German quasi-military drill!'*

Between 1909 - 1910 the 1st Birmingham Coy. BLB, like much of the Brigade movement, was keen to adopt the latest craze of Scouting. The BLB companies in Birmingham were encouraged to affiliate their scouting to the National Peace Scouts (formed in 1910). In 1912, 'British Boy Scout troops' (Peace Scouts) could register as BLB companies and unofficial 'Boys Life Brigade Scouts' were starting up. The company, which met in the Drill room of the Mission Hall in Upper Highgate St., wanted to become just 'Peace Scouts', so it relinquished the title '1st Birmingham BLB' altogether. Mr George Cadbury, Barrow's uncle, and Chairman of the family business before Barrow, was a great supporter of the British Boy Scouts. Thus, there was, no doubt, little objection to this development from within the Cadbury family. The title

'1st Coy. Birmingham BLB ' was given, in 1913, to the new Baptist Coy. in Hockley, formed by Mr. Donald Finnemore. In 1919, the BLB Company at the Friends' Hall was re-formed as the 19th Birmingham with Barrow Cadbury remaining as President.

A great supporter and benefactor of the Boys' Life Brigade nationally from 1922, in Birmingham Barrow Cadbury became Hon. Battalion President of the new united BB Battalion after 1926. He was always supported in his generosity by his wife Geraldine. Geraldine's brother, Mr Gilbert Southall, was an officer in the 19th Birmingham BB at the Friends' Institute and Treasurer of the Birmingham Battalion. Gilbert Southall was responsible for overseeing the successful purchase and development of the Stechford Playing Fields.

In 1932, Barrow Cadbury decided that he would like to celebrate the approaching Jubilee of the Boys' Brigade in 1933. Before retiring from his position as Chairman of Cadbury's Chocolate at Bournville in July 1932, a post he had held for ten years, he arranged a massive Garden Party in June of that year. The whole of Birmingham Battalion, more than 2000 Officers and boys were invited to the party. Everyone sat down together for tea in one hall, and according to Sir Donald Finnemore writing Barrow Cadbury's obituary many years later *'...all will remember the kindness and graciousness with which everyone was received by Mr & Mrs Cadbury.'*

When, in 1935, the Battalion was looking for new Headquarters Mr Cadbury was to provide a considerable slice of the money required to buy the Wrottesley St. premises. He then went on to make a personal appeal on the radio for more. Mr Gilbert Southall was again involved with the finances for this project, making a sizeable contribution himself. Barrow Cadbury continued to support the Brigade financially and influentially as a Freeman of the City.

Dame Geraldine Cadbury, the first Lady Magistrate in the City of Birmingham, died in 1941. Barrow Cadbury continued with his generous support, being made Honorary Brigade Vice President a position he retained until his death aged 95 in 1958. One of his final acts of benevolence was to enable four boys to represent Birmingham at the CariBBean Camp. (See picture on page 78)

The 19th Company, in 1983, when the Moseley Rd. premises closed, removed to the Friends Meeting House at Colmore Road Kings Heath and is now the only remaining Quaker Company in Birmingham.

The Boys' Brigade King George V Silver Jubilee Run
April 1935

The BB nationally organised a series of 'runs' whereby five copies of a loyal message were conveyed by hand to The Duke of York, Chairman of the Boys' Brigade Jubilee Display at the Royal Albert Hall, via routes starting all over the British Isles. The Duke would personally give the message to the King who had been Patron of the BB for all of his 25 yrs as Monarch. Specially chosen boys, holders of the King's Badge, would have the honour of bearing the message in a silver baton flanked by two other runners as escorts. The North-Western message which started from Londonderry on April 24th arrived in Birmingham on April 30th via Glasgow, Liverpool and Stoke. It was carried accross the city by twelve Company Teams each bearing the baton for about four miles. A special ceremonial exchange was organised at each transfer, at the one outside the Council House the message was read aloud by The Lord Mayor. A Roll of bearers was signed by each Kingsman as he took custody of the message. 2106 boys took took part nationally covering a total of 2, 309 miles.

Signing the Roll

The Lord Mayor Reads the Message

10th & 33rd Coys Changeover at Meriden Cross

Border Changeover West Bromwich Boys hand to B'ham.

Leslie Harrison, George Tucker & Jim Tucker 32nd Coy.

Young Brother

From Boy Reserves to Junior Section

A simple list of 'Sections' and the emblem of the 'Boy Reserves' (as above) is all that appeared re. the BR in the Battalion Report of 1918-19. This general understated approach to what was considered to be a 'fringe' activity epitomised Battalion Annual Reports for many years to follow. The picture was not much different nationally. An organisation had been started for 'little boys' who wanted to be in the Boys' Brigade, but were not old enough. There was no way that the Boys' Brigade would let them be part of the organisation so they remained on the outside.

There was nothing new in this disinterested attitude. The Aston Lads' Brigade, some thirty years before, as the available photographic evidence seems to suggest, had a large number of younger boys. This younger age - group both delayed ALB membership of the BB and reduced numbers joining. Perhaps it is not surprising that of the seven B.R. Sections listed in 1918 - 19, three were from Aston.

The first Sections were 'connected' with a BB company, having the same number designation, they were the 1st, 7th, 9th, 11th, 12th, 18th and 19th. Known as 'The Training Reserve of The Boys' Brigade' they catered for the boy aged 9 - 12 yrs (Sometimes 13 yrs). Founded by Mr F. C. Carey Longmore in Warley, Essex in 1917, the method was to provide '... a religious atmosphere of happy hours of recreative training...'. The analogy used at the time was that of 'lambs' requiring food. It is perhaps difficult to imagine the average 13 year old Birmingham boy today being regarded in quite the same way!

By 1919 - 20 there were still only seven Sections, two closed, the 11th and 12, and two new ones the 2nd and 19th started. Three sections had entered for a 'Challenge Shield', which was awarded to the 1st. (See Photo). This 'Efficiency Shield' donated by Capt. Anderson of the 4th Coy., and only ever won by the 1st Section would cause a

'Leading Reserves' of the 1st Birmingham Section with their Hon. Instructor and the Anderson Efficiency Shield. May 18th 1920.

degree of controversy in subsequent years. The picture of the 1st Section in May 1920 shows clearly the uniform with naval pattern caps. The jerseys were blue with a woven or metal badge (These are woven). The 'Leading Reserves' have the addition of a shoulder cord to indicate their status. The cords were replaced in 1922 by white lanyards. Albert Morris, the Leading Reserve sitting front left, wrote on the back of this picture postcard: 'notice my Drum Strap'. It was possible for Reserves to have their own band, as did the 1st, but on no account were they allowed to participate in any BB Company activity, including Church Parade. Everything was organised entirely separate from the BB.

Interestingly, the 'Boy Reserves Birmingham Battalion Minute Book 1921 - ' still survives, giving us a closer look at the doings of the 'B.R. Battalion' in its formative years. The initial meetings were held at Alfred Street School (Aston), and were chaired by Mr Bonaker. The first meeting agreed to form a League for football, arrange a Church Parade to Dyson Hall on Founders Day Oct. 30th and request a grant of £2.00 from the BB. At the next meeting, November 1921, the rules for the Efficiency Shield were reviewed, as they would be subsequently on a regular basis. Letters were to be sent to the BB with a view to providing a football shield and to Carey Longmore regarding a visit to Birmingham as an Inspecting Officer. The grant from the BB was obviously forthcoming since it was put into the hands of Mr W. T. Wiggins- Davies. Following the lead given by the BB, the BR formed an Executive Committee and a Recreation Committee in addition to the Battalion Council. The third meeting of the Council, in January 1922, suggested that a proposal be put to Mr Longmore that a pennant be used to distinguish each section. (The idea was soon taken - up, an example of Birmingham forward - thinking!).

Mr Longmore, who agreed to come to Birmingham was requested to wear his new 'Grey' uniform for the occasion. We don't know whether or not he was in 'grey' but we do know that he addressed a special devotional meeting laying great stress upon the fact that the younger boys wanted variety and not too much of the same old routine. He also added that he was very pleased with all he had seen.

Although Mr Hankinson was 'Chairman' in 1922, it was during that year the posts of Sec. and Chairman were amalgamated and Mr A. R. Dudley became 'BR Convenor'. The 1922 Church Parade was held at the Ellen Knox Hall and lead by the band of the 1st Section. Football friendlies were started before Christmas with a league starting in the new year. A draughts and skittle league was also proposed. The Executive committee reviewed the shields for Efficiency, Cricket and Football and decided to withdraw them. The BB officers were getting worried that there were too many awards which would lessen the impact required when boys transferred to BB. The BR Council didn't approve and asked for a review. The Efficiency Shield was to be retained with modified rules. By August 1925 however, Mr C.L. Beckett, Battalion BB Sec. who was chair of the BR meeting, reported upon opinions expressed at the recent national BR meeting at Windermere that there was a tendency for Reserves to do too much on the lines of the BB. It was proposed that the Efficiency Shield be withdrawn.

In 1925 the eight BR sections now operating in Birmingham wanted to hold a joint Display. Digbeth Institute was favourite, but not available, Kyrle Hall in Sheep St. was not suitable, the Friends Institute was regarded as being too far out and only the last choice, the Gymnasium at the YMCA was available. All the problems with the venue meant that enthusiasm had lapsed and the event scheduled for January 30th 1926 was postponed. The Leaders 'social' also in January did go ahead with the newly appointed national 'Lady Demonstrator' (Miss

Webb) as the speaker. 1926, was destined to be the last year of the Boy Reserves.

The Boys' Life Brigade held its 21st Anniversary 'Coming of Age' meetings in Birmingham between 10th - 12th September 1920. The Council House was the venue for the BLB Annual meeting itself, but many other meetings took place. At 4.30 p.m. at the YMCA on the 12th by invitation of the Birmingham Adjutant, one Captain D. L. Finnemore, tea was taken followed by an Informal Conference on the 'Junior Section'. Well, the discussion was held and the outcome was the formation, in 1921, of 'The Lifeboys'. So there we have it - The Lifeboys, conceived in Birmingham. As for 'Junior Section' a longer wait of 46 yrs, but at least we can say 'You heard it here first'!

The Lifeboys

The Lifeboys, the Junior League of the Boys' Life Brigade, was set - up to do for the BLB what the 'Reserves' was doing for the Boys' Brigade; providing a fun activity for little boys not old enough to join the Brigade. The Lifeboys was divided into 'Teams' each team being connected with a BLB Company. The programme mirrored the four-sided programme of the BLB: Social, Spiritual, Physical and Educational, hence the 'Square' divided into four which made up the centre of the emblem. Like the Boy Reserves' naval hats and anchor, the Lifeboys drew

Left: Wilfred Booth Taylor's Lifeboy Registration Certificate as Leader of the Sparkbrook Team (2nd B'ham.BLB) 1923.

Right: A picture postcard sent, in 1924, to Donald Finnemore's sister by her Lifeboy Leader friend in Southend - on - Sea. The uniform worn by the boys and leaders can be clearly seen. The boys' jumpers are saxe blue with a woven badge. Caps are worn with an enamelled metal badge on the front.

upon nautical analogies using a 'Lifebuoy' as the outer part of its emblem. We know very little about the progress of the Lifeboys in Birmingham. With the enthusiasm of Donald Finnemore, driving the Battalion, it is likely that there were at least as many Lifeboy Teams in Birmingham as there were Boy Reserve Sections, by 1926, possibly many more.

The Life Boys

In October 1926, The Boys' Brigade and The Boys' Life Brigade united to form one organisation; The Boys' Brigade. The two Junior organisations also merged with 'The Life Boys' (now three words not two) as the new title. The BR pattern sailor hat was retained in the new uniform and the dark blue jumper, although the old LB cap was phased out gradually. Metal or woven badges with the new combined motifs of anchor and lifebuoy were worn on the jersey. Blue pennants indicated the Team number. Much of the new Life Boys programme and ethos was inherited from the old BLB Lifeboys, eg. the motto 'To

Play The Game'. There were, however, clear differences in the methods adopted. The new Life Boys, for instance, would not be allowed to hold a Camp, a luxury previously enjoyed by the Lifeboys.

The new Birmingham Life Boy set-up called 'The Birmingham Life Boy Area', the equivalent of the BB Battalion was able to report 'real progress' at the end of its first full year. The person in charge, now known as 'Supervisor' was Miss Burrows. The Hon. Sec. of the Life Boy Area Council was C. H. Hankinson. Council Meetings were held every two months. During Brigade Council Meetings in Birmingham a Demonstration, Tea and Conference were arranged for Life Boy Leaders of Birmingham and Miss Webb, now 'Lady Demonstrator' to the Life Boys, took charge of a Team made up of Leaders and boys from various Teams in the area, and a practical programme was given. The first Session closed with a 'Sportagama'. The minutes tell us that the Kyrle Hall was available at £2 per hour, Woodcock St. Assembly Room £1 Per hour or the Central Hall for £8.00 per night.

The Life Boys
Left: The Official Picture 'The smart young fellow'
Centre: The Life Boys Emblem
Right: 'The Little Devil' As drawn c.1937 by a BB Officer - Mr. D. Gordon Barnsley, Birmingham Battalion Sec.. Mr. Barnsley was, in fact a great supporter of the Life Boys, as the Captain of a BB Company (54th B'ham) with a Life Boy Team which was run by his wife.

The relationship between the Life Boy Area and the Battalion over the years was to become generally quite cordial. However there were many BB Officers who looked upon the Life Boys as 'little boys who get in the way of real Brigade work'. There were occasions when the Life Boys seemed to be encroaching upon the domain of the BB. The big concern was always to limit the activities done by The Life Boys so that they would look forward to joining the BB Company. The other essential was to keep them well away from the older boys who wouldn't stay in an organisation full of little kids. Some conflict was thus almost inevitable.

The 33rd B'ham Life Boy Team
enjoy a day out in 1929. Note the caps still in use as an alternative to the naval pattern hat.

Needless to say it was at Woodcock St. Assembly Room that Teams gave varied items dealing with all sides of LB work. Mr Carey Longmore was the visiting Officer and Mr S.E. Barnes chairman. 'Sportagama' initially seems to have been used to describe any Life Boy event, whereas later it became descriptive of an outside event involving, as the word suggests, just sports and games. The numbers certainly seemed to indicate that the new Life Boys organisation was becoming popular. In 1927, compared with the previous year, there were 31 Teams, an increase of 9, 44 Leaders an increase of 17, and 550 boys an increase of 120.

Over the years, the Life Boys and later the Junior Section, would increase both in size and in the variety of activities undertaken. The major events, sometimes annual and later with some on a three year 'cycle' reflecting the Four-Sided programme. The Spiritual event was the Annual Parade Service, for many years held at the Digbeth Institute. Physical events included Sports and Sportagama's. All events could be said to include the Social side of the work, but the great outings and trips would be perhaps the clearest manifestation of this element. The Educational side was again inherent in the way most of the other activities were performed, but specific Festivals and Competitions would encourage this aspect of the programme.

By the 1927 - 1928 session the pattern of Birmingham Life Boy work was settling down. Miss Webb was back in town holding a Leaders Training week which finished up with a paper entitled 'The problem of the awkward Boy'. A Sports Day was organised at the BB Batt. Sports Ground with 16 Teams taking part, this was to be the first of many such events. A 'United Display & Inspection' was held at the Central Hall. There were now 875 boys in 36 Teams. The new BB Battalion HQ in Whittall Street meant that all LB equipment was now conveniently available in the BB shop. There was now a place in which to hold all Executive and Council meetings. In 1930 Miss Winnie Devey took over as Area Supervisor but the annual activities of Display and Sports continued. The Battalion Annual Report carried the following message:

'A delightful atmosphere pervades a 'Life Boy' Team, a happy and radiant spirit characterising its meetings. At the age of 12 a 'Life Boy' is transferred to a 'BB Company' and many of the finest fellows in the senior movement have been drafted from the 'Life Boys'.

The 6th Annual Display, 1932, was reported in the BB Gazette, still confusing displays with 'Sportagama's'!

'The Sportagama held in the Central Hall on the 10th February was witnessed by a large and much interested audience. Mr D.L. Finnemore, Battalion President, was in the chair, and the Visiting Officer was J. H. Early, Chairman of the Life Boy Committee. Many interesting items were given by various Teams, and these included sea shanties, Indian camp, bull fight, musical ball, relay games and exercises, sack football, figure marching, etc., which were all thoroughly enjoyed by the spectators. Mr Early said that he had had a very delightful evening, and that the atmosphere was just right-jolly, light-hearted, and young-boy-like.'

In 1933 the first 'Outing' took place on 27th July. The boys went to Manor Farm. (Dame Elizabeth Cadbury's Home) The outing was to become one of the most important events in the programme. There were 40 Teams, 100 Leaders and 1097 boys by 1935.

The Display at the Central Hall had become something of an Institution in the LB Area. Mr W. H. McVicker, Mr

Life Boys Rehearsing for a Display Item c.1936.
The good ship 'BOLOBO' was named after the first BB National Training Centre, in Edgware Middx.

Barrow Cadbury and Mr Dennis Webb had all either chaired the proceedings or acted as 'Visiting Officer'. The Annual Church Parade too was becoming one of the established annual events. In 1935, the Annual Church Parade was held at Digbeth Institute.

A new BB Battalion H.Q. opened in 1935, in Wrottesley St. provided even better facilities than at Whittall Street. The new Battalion Secretary, Gordon Barnsley realised that the building was surrounded by an area which needed a Boys' Brigade Company. He formed the 54th which was officially based at St. Martin's, but met at the HQ during the week. Mrs Barnsley took charge of the Life Boys. On the meeting night she would have their uniforms laid out and the kids were made to change there and then. When

their meeting was over they changed back into their own clothes and the uniforms were stored away for use the next week. This was the kind of area it was around Wrottesley St. in the 1930s.

At the end of the 1930s there were 50 teams and 1318 Life Boys in the Birmingham area with Miss Devey, now a member of the National Life Boy Committee, still in charge. Mr Rupert Wastell, Leader in Charge of the 4th Birmingham Team was appointed one of the District organisers for England and Wales. Mr H. Anderson, BB Batt. President was elected to the office of Chairman of the Life Boy Committee of the Brigade Executive. Now Birmingham was really in the driver's seat. In 1939, the 'Display' at the Central Hall, took the form of a Pageant.

Many Life Boy activities were curtailed during the war years. With Churches being bombed, evacuation, blackout, and some Leaders away in the army, the number of teams reduced, but the work carried on. A survey was made to find out which teams were able to continue. The results confirming that the teams in the Central Area were being particularly badly affected. In 1943, Mrs H. Blackham, from the 18th Team, came on the scene as Secretary just as long - serving Supervisor as Miss Devey retired. Mrs Barbara Nash, who would more than twenty years later take up a similar position, remembers well as a very young leader, her first encounter with Mrs Blackham 'A large lady in a bus conductors uniform'. The war had brought all sorts of shortages and official uniforms for Life Boy Leaders were not available. Barbara satisfied herself with a bus conductors tunic and a girl guide hat turned up on three sides just like the official 'Tricorn' model. It was the late 1940s before the correct hats were available.

Mr Wastell, termed 'District Organiser' rather than 'Supervisor' had taken over from Miss Devey with Mrs Blackham as Secretary. It was Mrs Blackham who first suggested a Training Course be run and in 1945 the first Leaders Training Course was held at the HQ of the 55th Team. All the more remarkable because it was held before any similar course had been run by the Boys' Brigade Battalion! It was this kind of progressive thinking that caused the Birmingham Life Boy Area to grow throughout the 1940s. By 1950 there were 55 Teams, 112 Leaders and 1269 Boys. The Central Hall had to be used for the Annual Service as well as for the display. In 1949 Mrs Blackham had to stand-down as Secretary and was replaced by Mrs Irene Bartlett. When Mrs Bartlett took over as Sec. there were four major events taking place each year, Service, Sports, Outing and Display- not to mention events just for Leaders. With increasing numbers during the 1950s the three-year cycle for some events was introduced. After all, it was argued, that boys are Life

Life Boy Leaders line up outside the Municipal Bank in Broad Street. 1949 Brigade Council Parade

Boys for three years before being transferred to the BB, so they will all have the opportunity of taking part in a variety of major events.

Outings

The 1950 'Annual' Outing to Liverpool was the first of the great post-war logistical extravaganzas. 579 Boys and 129 adults went on a specially chartered train. The advance instructions stated that there should be one Leader for every six boys. The decision was made that on this occasion uniform would not be worn but that LB badges would. This lack of clear identification proved to be a real problem, making 'rounding up' of strays very difficult - future trips would be in uniform. The railway engine given the task of transporting this mass of Bubbling Brummie Boyhood was resplendent with a large Life Boy emblem affixed to the front. This was, of course, the age of the newly created British Railways and of noisy, dirty, smelly, but to boys (and adults) 'exciting' steam trains.The trips were filmed by BB Battalion Secretary Mr W. Gordon Innes, one of the many guests who accompanied the mass exodus. Even the choice of destination was to some extent in the hands of BR, the availability of trains and carriages to carry such large numbers being paramount. The LB emblem would be 'worn' on the front of the 'Outing' train for many years, until the advent of diesels and a change of name made it impossible. Coaches or buses would be hired at the railway terminus for local excursions. In 1957, trips from Weston to Cheddar were cancelled because of petrol rationing!

Rosalie Roughton reported the trip to London Airport and Battersea Pleasure Gardens in 1960 in the BB Gazette. Detailing all the arrangements that had been made and how successful the event had been, she included a picture of the train which had been eagerly awaited, she wrote: *'What a cheer went up as the Station Announcer declared that*

the *"Life Boy Special" to London was arriving!'*. In the 1960s the trips to Liverpool included a ferry trip over the Mersey and a trip through the tunnel, with lots of transport and was somewhat 'risky' logistically. There were however no losses of boys. The 1962-63 Annual Report says:

'With the supreme courage which seems to be characteristic of Life Boy Leaders, over 400 Life Boys were taken by special train on a day's outing which included visits to Liverpool and New Brighton. Weather was wonderful. Not one boy got lost...'

Destinations such as Weston Super Mare, London Airport, and Battersea Pleasure Gardens, Liverpool, New Brighton and Southport featured in the three year cycle which, until 1981, were all served by train. Train journeys did come with a few problems: in 1969, for instance, the Trip to Weston - super- Mare lost one boy and his mum. After a period of 'free time' near the end of the day they returned to the wrong station and waited, wondering how it was that everyone else was lost! In 1966, the outing to Colwyn Bay took organisers by surprise when 700 booked to go. However, train journeys by diesel in the 1970s had lost much of the attraction of steam and booking a complete train for 500 boys was becoming difficult. The Triennial Outings continued in the 1980s by bus rather than train, with the Theme Parks, Camelot and the American Adventure being favourite. The last outing was in 1990.

Displays, Pageants & Festivals

In 1952, as the first of the new three-year cycle of events, a second Pageant, was held at the Central Hall. It was called 'Far Round the World' and featured items in National Costume from those countries where Life Boys existed. There was also a uniformed item performed with each national presentation. In 1955, it was back to a more conventional Display at the Central Hall which was continued in 1958. The '58 event being paised for the wonderful finale 'Building a Church'. The 1965 Display 'A Life Boy Pie' at the Central Hall was to be the last. Appropriately, the Central Hall was filled to capacity with the chief guest being Mr David White the National Life Boy Secretary.

The Junior Section

From 1967, the Life Boys were 'Junior Section BB' and as such were invited to take part in the annual BB Display, also at the Central Hall. The young brother emerged in force at the 'Best Sellers '67' BB Display, wearing the old LB uniform minus the brass badge and his sailor cap- tally bearing the words 'The Boys' Brigade'. Sixteen sections took part in that event. The Juniors had their own items each year which were usually amongst the most popular on the programme. The Junior Section provided items for

The 'Life Boy Special'

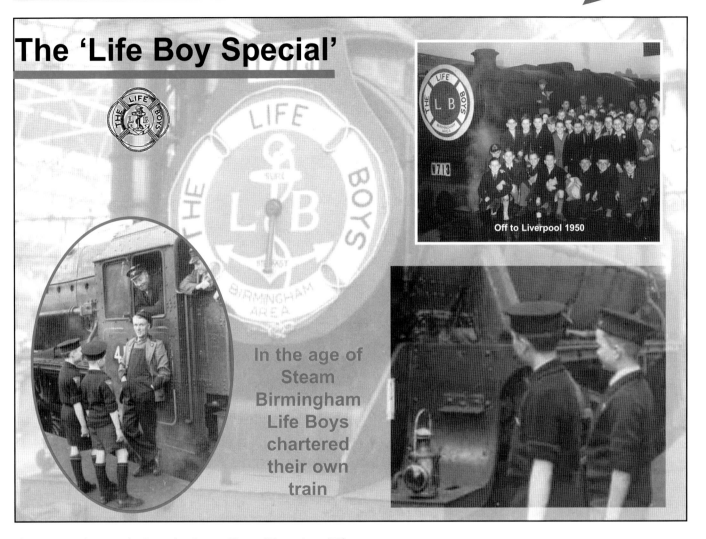

Off to Liverpool 1950

In the age of Steam Birmingham Life Boys chartered their own train

the BB Displays including the Stage Show 'Showtime 70' (1970) at Bournville Theatre. The last of the traditional Displays took place at the Central Hall in 1983. The Central Hall was the venue for the special 'Brum Beat' show in 1985 on the occasion of the visit of Brigade Council which included a strong Junior Section component.

The 'Educational' side of the new Junior Section programme, rather than being restricted was expanded. In addition to tha Annual BB Display, in 1968 the first Triennial Festival of Music Arts, Crafts and Cake Making took place with 300 Boys and Parents attending. The event, held at Rea St. School in March and replacing the former Life Boy Display, was a great success. The second event, in 1971, attracted over 700 entries and was held at the Friends' Institute Moseley Road. The 1974 event attracted 23 Sections and 800 entries taking part in singing, marching, crafts, etc.. Outgrowing the Institute the event moved to the Central Hall, but attracted fewer entries in subsequent years. The last Festival took place in 1983. Through the eighties, nineties and into the new millennium the system of major events every three years was breaking down. The reason for this change being the

THE LIFE BOYS
The Junior Reserve of The Boys' Brigade

OBJECT : The advancement of Christ's Kingdom among young Boys and the training of a body of suitable Recruits for The Boys' Brigade.

Birmingham Area Council

DISPLAY

CENTRAL HALL, BIRMIN
Wednesday, February 16th, 1955, at

Chief Guest : *Mrs. A. G. B.*

PROGRAMME THREEPENCE

THE BOYS' BRIGADE
THE LIFE BOYS
The Junior Reserve of The Boys' Brigade

Birmingham Area Pageant
"FAR ROUND THE WORLD"
CENTRAL HALL, BIRMINGHAM
WEDNESDAY, MARCH 12, 1952
at 7.30 p.m.

PROGRAMME · THREEPENCE

NO EXIT

'Far Round the World'
The Finale

Life Boy Pageant 1952   Central Hall

move towards a programme similar to that used successfully for the older sections of the BB. The whole idea, of giving the boys a wide variety of activities and competitions which had been thrown out in indignation in the 1920s, was now taken up with enthusiasm. The purpose was now to retain boys in what had become the largest section in the Brigade. There was no point in 'saving' activities for the Company section if boys left the BB after only a year or so into their Company Section membership. The Juniors of the 1990s were much more sophisticated than the 'little boys' of the 1920s and 30s and required far more than Games, and stories to keep them interested.

Preparing for
'Kitchen Cantata'
Display 1969

Sportagama's

Although 'Sportagama' was the Life Boys own word for a Sports and Games event, usually indoors, it was initially not used in Birmingham to label any Life Boy event. It was used, however, by those reporting nationally on the Annual Battalion Display which included many team games. From 1928 until the War, there was an 'Annual Sports' which was re-vitalised in 1953 to become the first proper 'Sportagama' as part of the Triennial event system. The first Birmingham Sportagamas were outdoor events which made use of the Battalion Field at Stechford, back in use after its wartime role as a giant vegetable patch.

Potted sports and games rather than traditional athletic events were on the menu of the Sportagama. In 1959, despite being a hot dry summer, the Sportagama was held on one of the few wet Saturdays, the rain being ignored by the boys. Often with more than 200 boys taking part the event was always a great success. The rain was so heavy on the day of the 1970 Sportagama that it was cancelled and typically, the sun came out in the afternoon. The 1973 event, with over 300 boys from 24 Sections, was famous for the 85th Section's canteen running out of pop before the first race was run! This event was the first to be held at the new venue of Digbeth in the Field, Yardley.

Sportagama 1964

By 1979 the name 'Sportagama' had been replaced by 'Sports Afternoon' with a change in format but still at Yardley. In 1987 it was re-christened 'Fun Day' another was held at Lyndon School in 1989 and although entries were rather disappointing a good time was had. In 1991 another 're-launch' as a 'Sports Fun Day' at Pembroke Field included, Dribbling, Egg and Spoon, Welly Throwing, Potato Race, Unihoc stick dribble, etc.. There

The Scene at a Junior Section Sports Event

were three age groups for the sports. Essential items such as the Tuck shop and Refreshment Marquee were not forgotten. The Sports Fun Day was repeated in 1992 with the 7th Section winners of a 'very successful day'. In 2001 the morning of the BB Athletic Sports was reserved for Junior Section Fun Races and Sports.

Annual Services

The Annual Service was not part of the Triennial system because it was an annual event usually held in April. For instance, in 1950 it was held at the Central Hall and at St.

Martin's in 1951. A Carol Service was held in 1960 at St Martin's starting a tradition continued throughout the 1960s with the service remaining in November. The collections at these services were donated to the care of a number of boys and girls suffering from leprosy who received successful treatment as a result of the donations. Later, the collections went to local Birmingham charities. The Cathedral was used in 1967 when 450 Boys and officers made up the congregation. By 1969, the numbers had risen to over 800. In the 1970-71 Session there were two services because the time of year they were held was changed from November to May. In 1972 the Service at St. Martin's was described as being in the 'Modern Idiom'. Participation was at the core of the services, for instance in 1974 everyone brought home made percussion instruments, sticks and shakers full of dried peas...quite a noise!

In 1975, the Annual Service moved to the Central Hall where it continued through the 1970s and 1980s. From 1979, the Anchor Boys now had their own service at St. Martin's. The last Central Hall Junior Section Service with 788 people present was held in 1987. In 1988 a special service to celebrate ten years of the 'Anchor Boys' was held at the Great Hall of Aston University when Anchors and Juniors combined. In 1989, a Joint Service of all Sections was held in the Town Hall conducted by Rev. Ken Powell, the hall was nearly full and the service rated as 'excellent'. The Junior Section Activity Committee recommended to the Executive that in 1990 and thereafter a joint service be held. The request was granted. In 1996 because of the link-up with the Girls Brigade the Adrian Boult Hall was used in addition to the Town Hall for the Juniors of both organisations.

Just Like Big Brother

Outside of the 'Triennial System' and the Annual Church Parades the Life Boys during the 1950s and 1960s in Birmingham was an eager young movement which naturally evolved into a fully fledged section of the BB. Under the direction of Mrs Bartlett and for a few years Miss Roughton; numbers and activities continued to expand. To get a degree of uniformity a resolution was passed at a meeting of 29th November 1954, that ' *All Life Boys in Birmingham will wear Shoulder Pennants'*. In 1959 there were 74 Teams, 168 Leaders, and 1714 Boys.

When Eric Thomas took over from Mrs Bartlett as Supervisor in 1963 the excitement of change was in the air. The BB Haynes Committee were producing a Report that would bring in the end of The Life Boys. A Special Life Boy Council Meeting was called to discuss the implications of the proposals in the Report. By 1965, the implications were clear as Eric Thomas reported: *'Even if we lose our identity, our work will continue as effectively as ever.'* Eric's valediction to his last 'Life Boy' Report, in 1966, says it all:

'This Session is a notable one inasmuch as at its close a lot of things near and dear to so many of us cease to exist. Not the least of which is our Name and our Motto, "Play the Game". We feel the poorer for it but realise that these changes are for the good of the Boy. Meanwhile, we continue as always in our endeavour to attract and hold Boys in the hope that they may be drawn into Christ's Kingdom.'

Edwin Hale took over as the first Junior Section Chairman. Initially, the boys' uniform remained virtually the same as the Life Boys but with a new Cap Ribbon 'The Boys Brigade' and a woven BB Badge on left breast. In 1968 a new 'Dynamic Duo' took over the Juniors, Mrs Barbara Nash as Chairman with Mrs Brenda Davies as Secretary. The Junior Section boys were now to wear Shoulder Titles instead of Pennants. (Some Battalions had used titles since 1958 and LB days but B'ham had consistently used Pennants). Worn on the left Shoulder, the correct wording was eg. '1st Birmingham' which did not include the word 'Company' In 1970 a single new pattern hat was introduced for all sections with Juniors wearing a yellow backing behind the badge. A new uniform Jersey was available from 1972 along with a new Lady Officers' uniform, the outcome of a committee which had included Mrs Irene Bartlett.

was organised by Clive Andrews. A 'Top of the Form' competition was started in 1970 by Olive Woolass, which attracted 17 entries in its first year. In 1980-81 Mr R. S. (Bob) Herbert became Chairman, a position he occupied for four years, until Roger Green took over between 1984 - 1989.

Kate Smith was the last Chairman of the Junior Section Committee when the Battalion administration was re-structured in 1993. In 1999 a new uniform was introduced (Left), very similar to the previous one except for the lighter blue jersey and the hat now being optional.

85th Coy. Winners J/S Five a Side 2001

Mr Clive Andrews presents the 1994 Junior Section Football Cup to the 67th Coy.

The Junior Section in the 1970s started to develop a wide range of activities which mirrored those of their older brothers in the Company Section. The First Junior Section Swimming Gala was held in 1978 at Saltley Baths. This event would remain amongst the most popular, and noisiest, for the next 25 yrs. From 1980 it has been held at the Aston Newtown Baths. In 1970, Two Football Leagues were established (North & South) and the first Indoor Five - a side knockout competition, another favourite,

The Anchor Boys

Before the 1950s, the idea of a Pre-Junior section for boys aged 6 - 8 yrs would have horrified even the most ardent supporter of the Life Boys. The arguments put forward against the Boy Reserves in 1917 were that bringing in these 'Little boys' would ruin the movement for the older members and the young boys should wait and look forward to the time they could join the BB. Exactly the same points were made by those in the BB and Life Boys/Junior Section when 'Pre-Junior' groups started to appear.

Birmingham was not at the forefront in the establishment of pre-Junior groups. For a start, it was considered to be 'against regulations' and a big Battalion with full time staff was relatively easy to 'police'. The Life Boys, (and later the Junior Section,) numbers were strong and there was no 'competition' at the pre-Junior age range from other similar organisations. There was, it seemed, no need for such a group. However, in other areas of the UK, by the 1960s, pre-Junior groups were becoming popular. Perhaps the most famous being the 'Cabin Boys' in the London area and 'Robins' in Northern Ireland. Lots of other names were used, 'Anchor Boys', 'Imps', 'Pilot Jacks', 'Pirates', 'Bandits', etc..

The Rev. Stephen Winwood had seen the Cabin Boys and Robins operating in London and suggested to Pat Thomas of the 4th Sutton Coldfield Coy that such a group be started. So, in 1970, Birmingham's first pre-Junior section christened 'The Imps' was started. The uniform consisted of the old Life Boy hats (which had ceased to be used that year) with a white band and the words ' The Imps', white shirts, blue shorts and a blue tie hand embroidered in white by Pat with 'The Imps'.

In the early 1970s other companies in the Battalion began to take-up the idea of a Pre-Junior group. The 29th and 57th Coys being pioneers. In 1976-1977 the Boys' Brigade officially recognised `Pre-Junior Groups' aged 6 - 8 yrs, as being 'Part of the BB Family'. The first five Groups 29th, 56th, 57th, 75th & 4th S/C were registered. Outcasts no longer, there would now also need to be a 'Pre-Junior Committee' to co-ordinate activities. Pat Thomas, Gill White & Dorothy Clive made up that first 1978 commit-

tee, meeting in Pat's front room. Mrs Pat A. Thomas formally became the 'Battalion Co-ordinator for Anchor Boys' in 1979, later called 'Anchor Boy Chairman'. The name 'Anchor Boys' was officially adopted for the Battalion. The uniform of a red jumper with BB cloth badge was instituted. The number of Anchor Boy sections continued to grow, there being twenty by 1979, the 'International Year of the Child'.

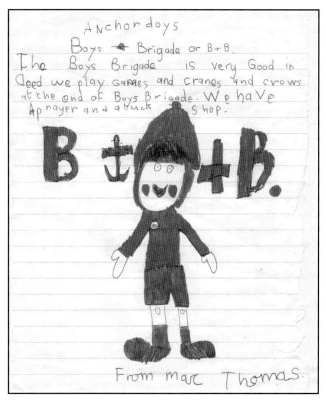

Activities such as an annual 'Fun Day', the first being at Digbeth in the Fields in 1979, Colouring Competition, Outing to Wicksteed Park, Christmas Party at Hatchett St, and the first Annual Anchor Boy Service at Sutton Baptist Church were organised, these events setting the pattern for years to come.

An Anchor Boy Carnival Float 1982

An Anchor Boy Five-a-Side Team 1992

Lord Thurso at the special 1988 Anchor Boy Service

In 1982 Pat Thomas was invited to serve on the (National) Pre - Junior Section Programme Committee. That year the name 'Anchor Boys' was adopted by the whole of the Brigade as the title for the 6 - 8 yr old pre- Junior Section. In 1984, Jackie Morris (56th Coy) took over as Chairman. However, by March 1985 Mrs Dorothy Clive (57th Coy) was elected to that post. Anchor Boys performed two numbers from 'Oliver' at the 'Brum Beat' show for Brigade Council. In 1985, dirty faces were OK!

Concerned about the loss of potential Anchor Boys to the 'Beavers' and following a request from Birmingham to reduce the joining age to 5 yrs the BB Executive, in May 1989, authorised the Battalion to enrol 5-yr-olds. Shirley Taylor and Martin Hayden followed Dorothy Clive into the Chair of the Anchor Boy Committee before it was absorbed into the Battalion Activity Committee in 1993. Anchor Boy activities have been popular with the Divisions and many competitions have been organised over the years.

Anchor Boy 'Urchins' ready to sing for their supper in 'Brum Beat' 1985

Food Glorious Food ... This time for real.

In 1988, the Anchor Boys section was 10 yrs old. Lord Thurso, the Brigade President, attended as Guest of Honour, a special Junior Section and Anchor Boy Service on Sunday 15th May at Aston University.

Brummie BB Heroes

Private Dennis C. A. Haile 16th B'ham. Cov.

On 28th November 1951, Pte. Dennis Haile aged 13, a member of the 16th Birmingham Company, was on his way to school when he met a man shouting that some children were trapped in a fire. Dennis saw smoke pouring from an upstairs bedroom window of a nearby house. Two children were at the window screaming. The man went to call the Fire Brigade. Dennis immediately climbed the iron work on the front porch of the house, straddled across a wide gap, and put one foot on a three-inch (750 mm) ledge at the top of the window.

Clinging to the narrow bedroom window-sill with his fingers, Dennis edged his way along so that he was under the open window. He took the small boy of six on his back and carried him to the porch, handing him to someone below. He then went back for the girl of four, and brought her safely down.

It was not until nearly six months after the incident that the news of the brave deed leaked out. Dennis told no one, not even his friends.

Dennis Haile was awarded the Boys' Brigade's highest honour, the Cross for Heroism, sometimes called the 'BB VC' (pictured above).

On Sept. 23rd 1952 he was presented with the medal by the Lord Mayor of Birmingham Ald. W. T. Bowen. This was the fifth such award made to a Birmingham boy, the first for 40 yrs. He was also presented with a wrist-watch by the Society for the Protection of Life from Fire, and a Bible from his Church, South Yardley Methodist.

Dennis shows his medal to the two children he rescued

Brummie BB Heroes

The Boys' Brigade

This is to CERTIFY that

BEN WILSON (16)   73rd Birmingham Company

was awarded
The Boys' Brigade Cross for Heroism

on the ...1st........... day of ....December 1997.....

for   the courage and presence of mind he showed in going to the assistance of another member of a small party climbing Mount Snowdon who had fallen for some 300 feet and sustained serious injury.

In poor weather conditions and over very difficult terrain Ben made his way down to the injured person and gave first aid assistance until the Mountain Rescue Team arrived.

Ben placed himself at significant risk but his actions were a crucial contribution to the eventual recovery of the injured person.

_____   *Brigade President*

_____   *Brigade Secretary*

The Boys' Brigade Cross for Heroism is awarded for a signal act of self-sacrifice for others, heroism in saving or attempting to save life, or marked courage in the face of danger.

L/Cpl. Ben Wilson 73rd B'ham. Coy. (Right)

James suffered a broken knee, abrasions to his head, bruises all over his body and shock. His Company Captain said: *'Ben knew what he was doing, comforted him and kept him awake and alive ... any one of our company would have undertaken the same procedure, we prepare for the D of E Award from age 11, so in a way Ben is receiving it on behalf of us all.'*

Ben officially received his Boys' Brigade Cross for Heroism from the Mayor of Solihull on Monday 19th January 1998. This was the 198th award to be presented since its institution in September 1902, only the sixth to a Birmingham Battalion member. The year 2002 as well as Birmingham Battalion centenary is also the centenary year of the Cross for Heroism. It is appropriate then that Ben is the latest boy to join that select band of recipients.

Sunday 13th July 1997 was both unlucky and lucky for 17 Yr old James Whitehouse (pictured left above) undertaking his Duke of Edinburgh's Award Gold level Expedition on Mt. Snowdon. A freak gust of wind blew him off the notorious Crib Goch ridge and down a 300 ft. sheer rock cliff face where he disappeared into the mist. The lucky part was that he didn't crash to his death and that his friend and fellow 73rd Company member 16 yr old Ben Wilson, saw him fall and in spite of the obvious danger, immediately went to James' assistance.

With the party leader, BB Officer Mike Shaw, Ben scrambled down the mountainside towards his friend lying seriously injured below. Ben first heard and then spotted James through the mist and immediately started to make him comfortable, stemming the bleeding and applying dressings and pressure, using first-aid techniques learnt in the BB. For more than two and a half hours, although frightened and cold Ben stayed with James, keeping him talking and covering him with a foil blanket. Eventually assistance arrived despite the bad weather conditions. James was carried further down the mountain, winched aboard an RAF Sea King rescue helicopter and flown to Gwynedd Hospital in Bangor.

Brummie BB Heroes

Cross for Heroism:

1907 - Sgt. William David Burgess
Age 17, 5th Birmingham Coy.

Sergeant Burgess was returning from work on the evening of July 11th when he was told of the peril of a boy, aged 6 years, who had fallen into the canal. Running to the spot, he plunged in and succeeded in bringing the boy ashore in an unconscious condition. Other helpers were at hand, and they were successful in their efforts to restore animation. Sgt. Burgess was awarded the Royal Humane Society's Testimonial on vellum, previous to the presentation of the cross which he received from the hands of the Battalion President, at the annual Battalion Parade at Curzon Hall.

1910 - Pte. Harry Bosworth
Age 13, 14th Birmingham Coy.

For saving a boy from drowning in the canal, Western Rd Birmingham, 2nd Dec 1909. Pte Bosworth was also awarded a certificate of the Royal Humane Society for this act.

1912 - Pte. William Bednall
Age 16, 5th Birmingham Coy

For attempting to rescue a girl from drowning in the canal at Birmingham.

1912 - Pte. Arthur Jones
Age 12, 10th Birmingham Coy.

For attempting to rescue a child from drowning in the River Cole.

Cross for Heroism
This cross is awarded from Headquarters 'to any boy who, being a member of the Boys' Brigade, has performed a signal act of self-sacrifice for others, shown heroism in saving life or attempting to save life. Or displayed marked courage in the face of danger.'

There have been Six Crosses for Heroism awarded to B'ham Boys. The other awards detailed here should be regarded as representative.

Brave J/S Boy Simon Wright ▶

Diploma for Gallant Conduct.

1946 - Corporal Raymond Leslie Hadley, aged 15, of the 39th Birmingham Company, for saving a dog from drowning at Witton Lakes, Birmingham on January 19th, 1946

1949 - Lance Corporal Raymond Cyril Fox aged 17 & Private Frank Jeanes aged 16, both of 33rd Birmingham Coy., for rescuing a boy from drowning in the sea at Lidstep Haven, Pembrokeshire, on 30th July. 1948

1951 - Cpl Donald Bevan. 20th Birmingham Coy. Rescued a five yr old boy from under an oncoming bus in Corporation St. on the way to his Company meeting. Although he was knocked over by the wing of the bus, Sgt. Bevan attended the drill parade without telling anyone of the incident. Nothing was known until the grandfather of the boy, who had noticed his cap badge, wrote to Battalion Headquarters.

1951 - Pte. David Parker of 35th Birmingham Coy. Saving a small boy from drowning in an aqueduct at Shirley 3rd July 1951.

1955 - Pte. Keith Davies 55th Birmingham Coy. For rescuing his friend from drowning in the river avon when their canoe capsized.

The Brigade President's Commendation - For Gallant Conduct

1984 - J/S Simon Wright (aged 8) 67th Birmingham Coy.
For saving his cousin Andrew (aged 5) from serious injury. Andrew was savagely attacked by a neighbour's large Alsatian Dog which gashed his back and leg. Simon went to Andrew's assistance and pulled the dog off his victim. Simon's prompt and courageous action undoubtedly saved Andrew from even more serious, and possibly fatal, injury.

The Battalion Drill Competition Colours

The 8th Company, Islington Wesleyan Church.
The first winner of the newly presented Battalion 'Colour' 1911
The Colour, given to the Battalion by Major D. G. Barnsley, was presented to the
8th Company at its Annual Inspection on Wednesday May 17th by the Battalion President Mr A.H. Angus.
The eight foot high pole can be clearly seen.

Here the boys of the 8th proudly display the new colour. Informally (above left) and in a more formal pose, by providing an escort, complete with model rifles! (above right)

Annual Battalion Inspection, Saturday June 28th 1913 in Summerfield Park.
The Colours are Trooped in slow time, all ranks standing at the salute:
Slow march played by the Massed Fife Bands of the 9th and the 19th Companies under Lieut. A. W. Gabb 9th Birmingham Company. One of the two colours is probably a company colour.

The Present-day Battalion Colours

First presented on 27th April, 1924 at the Town Hall and dedicated to the Immortal Memory of Officers and Old Boys of the Battalion who fell in the Great War of 1914-18.

The Colours were dedicated by Rev. Owen Spencer Watkins, C.M.G., C.B.E. assisted by Rev. H. S. Astbury, M.C. and the Rev. Ivory Cripps, B.A.. The Colours being handed over to the care of the Battalion by Lady Bowater.

The colours are made from silk poplin. The first, or King's/Queen's Colour is a modification of the Union flag. In the centre of the Union is a circle bearing the title of the Brigade and the date, 1883, enclosing the Brigade crest; below is a scroll, bearing the designation of the Battalion. The second, or Battalion Colour, is the crimson cross of St. George of England, on a white field. At the centre is the Brigade crest, contained within a circle, which bears the designation of the Battalion. Encircling this is a wreath of laurel, surmounted by the crest of the City of Birmingham, over a scroll bearing the city motto, "Forward". Below are the dates "1914 - 18" & "1939 - 45" and underneath these a scroll bearing the words - "In Memoriam". The pikes are of polished mahogany, and bear on their tops the lion, the National Emblem, in moulded brass gilt.

Initially, the King's Colour & Battalion Colour were awarded separately. From 1927 they were awarded to the winners of the Battalion Drill Competition.

Today, the Colours are awarded to the 'Most Efficient Company' in the Battalion.

The dedication ceremony in the Town Hall

Restoration of the Colours.

After suffering damage in World War II the King's Colour was 'mended' having also a red cross added to the emblem. In 1975, due to excessive wear, the Battalion Colour was completely re-made as an exact replica of the original.

By decision of the Battalion Council, the scope and intention of this cherished Memorial was extended to cover also the World War of 1939-45. The re-dedication of the Colours was carried out by the Rector of Birmingham, Canon T. Guy Rogers, M.C., B.D., Brigade Vice-President, at the Annual Church Parade of the Battalion, held at the Parish Church of St. Martin, on Sunday afternoon, 14th July 1946.

Major A. H. S. Waters, V.C., D.S.O., M.C. taking the salute at the march past which followed the dedication, 27th April 1924.

'Perrycroft' Malvern

The Battalion's Country House 1971 - 1998

The story of 'Perrycroft'

Designed, by leading Arts and Crafts Architect Charles F. A. Voysey, and built in 1895 by Broad of Malvern on the Western slope of the Malvern Hills near Upper Colwall in Worcestershire. The house was built for Mr John Wilson of Albright and Wilson Chemicals at a cost of around £5000. John Wilson was involved with the Great Western Railway and much other Midlands industry. He was a J.P. and M.P. for North Worcestershire. Although John died in 1932 Perrycroft remained in the family until 1950. The estate then included seven cottages, two coppices and extensive pasture land.

During the Second World War Perrycroft was used to house children evacuated from Birmingham. The evacuees attended the local Downs School in Colwall and amongst them were boys from Hockley, members of the 1stA Birmingham Coy. BB. After the war, Donald Finnemore, Capt. of the 1stA, maintained the link with the Downs school by bringing his boys to the school to use as a base for their summer camp.

In 1950, the house was sold, much of the surrounding Malvern Hills having been given to the Conservators. The Perrycroft estate was split into ten lots with the lodge, stables and coachhouse together, with Garden Cottage and Perrycroft coppice remaining as part of the estate. The new owners, Mr and Mrs Clark sold further portions of the estate and, in 1954, had a new drive made to by-pass the Lodge. Colonel and Mrs Phillips bought the house along with ten acres of land in 1955. Col. Phillips was a former High Sheriff of Radnorshire. The Phillips' stayed until 1961 when they sold Perrycroft to William and Susan Gibbs. William was from a tile-making family from Bromyard and Susan had a fortune inherited from her Grandfather, a member of the McAlpine construction family. The tennis court was built and the gardens were well maintained. William and Susan's marriage broke up in the early 1960s and the house became empty.

In the mid 1960s, Birmingham Battalion were looking for a property which could be used by boys of the Battalion. A location near the Malverns was favoured because of its accessibility after

the opening of the M5. The Malverns was an area of outstanding natural beauty, popular with people from Birmingham, which would be an ideal location for a house where members could enjoy a time of fellowhip in a homely atmosphere. It was hoped that such a house would be an ideal base for the increasingly popular Duke of Edinburgh's Award Scheme. The money to buy the house would come from a Battalion Trust which had recently sold the Battalion Playing Fields at Stechford.

Sir Donald Finnemore, still Captain of the 1stA Coy who had originally negotiated the purchase of Stechford Playing Fields in 1926, was amongst those given the task of searching for a house. When Perrycroft came on the market, seeing its potential, he proposed that enquiries should be made. The house was sound, but in a run-down dilapidated condition, having been empty for about five years. Perrycroft was purchased and a small committee formed to assist the architect with restoration, adaptation and furnishing. It was adapted and modernised to accommodate 36 boys and Staff along with a resident Warden.

On the Battalion's Birthday, 1st May 1971, Perrycroft was opened by Sir Donald, in his capacity as Battalion Hon. President, a dream come true. For more than a quarter of a century the house provided an opportunity for boys to escape from the city into the wonderful Hereford/Worcestershire countryside. Facilities were excellent with well equipped rooms including a basement 'Club' area. The House, being set in more than 10 acres of ground directly adjoining the hills, was an excellent base for some outdoor pursuits, for a while having its own 'Assault Course'. It was more like a 'hotel' than a hostel and many visitors simply could not believe that it was regularly used by boys!

However, needs do change. A smaller Battalion, more widespread travel, and rival facilities meant a change in the way Perrycroft was run. The house was opened up to other Christian groups, schools, and colleges. Day conferences, receptions, visits from architectural study groups etc., all were catered for. BB use was mainly at weekends and in holiday periods. As a 'listed' building modifications and adaptations to the structure, required for its new users, could not be easily undertaken and the building was losing money. Sadly, the house was sold in 1998. The happy memories of times spent at Perrycroft will last for many years.

Perrycroft Scrapbook

The 2,500th member of the Battalion to stay at Perrycroft was Pte. Ivan Higgins of the 38th Coy. in August 1973, only two years after it had opened!

Mr. Hywel Hughes outside Perrycroft — the new Birmingham Boys' Brigade "adventure hotel" — today.

Adventure hotel for Boys' Brigade

DREAM COMES TRUE FOR SIR DONALD

Evening Mail Reporter

A RETIRED High Court Judge will see a life-long ambition realised on Saturday when he opens Birmingham Boys' Brigade "adventure hotel" on the Malvern Hills.

Sir Donald Finnemore, at 83, thought to be the oldest Boys' Brigade company captain in the country, advocated a permanent base in the countryside for the Birmingham Battalion.

The chance came when a builder offered £200,000 for the Boys' Brigade 10-acre playing field off Manor Road, Stechford, which Sir Donald had purchased 25 years ago.

£1 EACH

The money has now been used to buy, equip and finance a country mansion, Perrycroft, set in 10 acres of woodland on the slopes of the Malvern Hills near Upper Colwall.

For £1 each for £4 for a week be used for Birmingham members panies.

About buying nisation to ac

The by Ch leading is listed

THE BOYS' BRIGADE
Birmingham Battalion

Perrycroft

CONFERENCE, TRAINING and RECREATIONAL CENTRE

Mrs. Hughes preparing o opening

Photo: Berrow's Newspapers

Mr George Oakton B.E.M. Batt. Hon. Vice- President plants a tree at Perrycroft in 1978 assisted by members Darren Nichols & Nigel Hudson of the 67th Coy with their Captain Mr Stan Stebbings, Batt. Vice-President. This was one of six trees donated by Mrs I Wilson whose late husband had built Perrycroft.

Birmingham Celebrates the BB Centenary 1883 - 1983

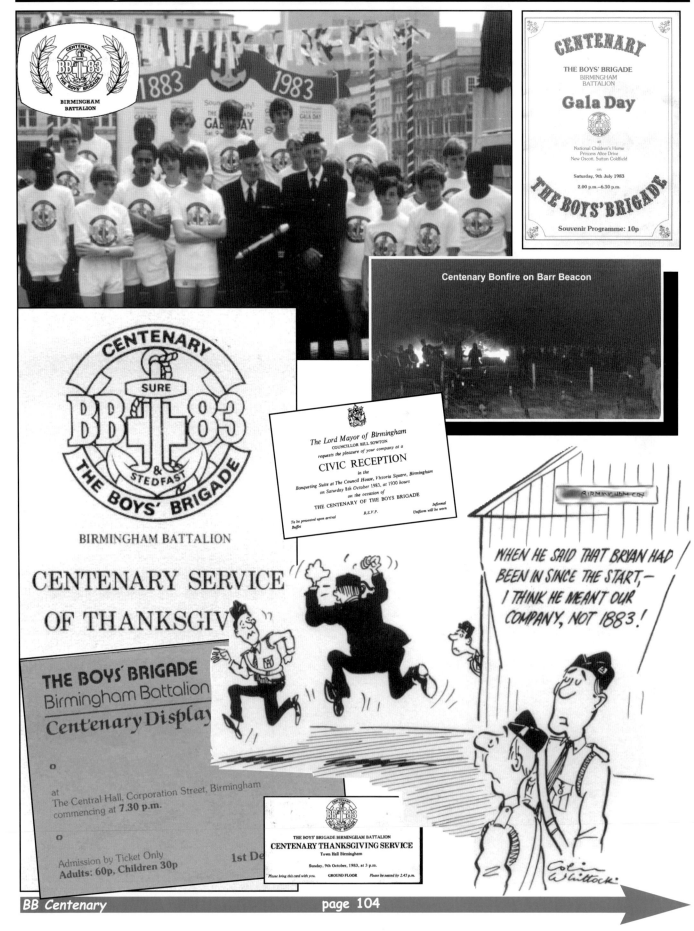

BIRMINGHAM BATTALION

CENTENARY
THE BOYS' BRIGADE
BIRMINGHAM BATTALION

Gala Day

at
National Children's Home
Princess Alice Drive
New Oscott, Sutton Coldfield
on
Saturday, 9th July 1983
2.00 p.m.–6.30 p.m.

THE BOYS' BRIGADE

Souvenir Programme: 10p

Centenary Bonfire on Barr Beacon

CENTENARY
SURE
BB✝83
& STEDFAST
THE BOYS' BRIGADE

BIRMINGHAM BATTALION

CENTENARY SERVICE
OF THANKSGIV

The Lord Mayor of Birmingham
COUNCILLOR BILL SOWTON
requests the pleasure of your company at a
CIVIC RECEPTION
in the
Banqueting Suite at The Council House, Victoria Square, Birmingham
on Saturday 8th October 1983, at 1930 hours
on the occasion of
THE CENTENARY OF THE BOYS' BRIGADE
To be presented upon arrival   R.S.V.P.   Uniform will be worn
Buffet   Informal

WHEN HE SAID THAT BRYAN HAD
BEEN IN SINCE THE START, —
I THINK HE MEANT OUR
COMPANY, NOT 1883 !

THE BOYS' BRIGADE
Birmingham Battalion
Centenary Display

o

at
The Central Hall, Corporation Street, Birmingham
commencing at **7.30 p.m.**

o

Admission by Ticket Only
Adults: 60p, Children 30p   1st De

THE BOYS' BRIGADE BIRMINGHAM BATTALION
CENTENARY THANKSGIVING SERVICE
Town Hall Birmingham
Sunday, 9th October, 1983, at 3 p.m.
Please bring this card with you.   GROUND FLOOR   Please be seated by 2.45 p.m.

Colin Whittock

AMICUS
PART OF THE **BB** FAMILY

The Amicus Group at the 6th.

The Amicus Group at the 80th.

The First Amicus Group in the World!

I n the Spring of 1994, the 6th Birmingham Coy at Kings Heath and Moseley Baptist Church, 'ever ready to explore new avenues of work with young people', decided to take up a scheme, details of which were first published by the BB in Summer 1993. That scheme was called 'Amicus' (Friends).

In their words, 'We decided to move forward...' and the group at the 6th became the world's first Amicus group, the leaders being Mike Evans and Paula Booth.

So what is Amicus?

Amicus is an alternative programme to meet the needs of older teenagers. It is available to male and female on an equal basis aged between school year 9/10 and 22 yrs. The idea is to utilise the expertise of single-sex organisations such as the BB or GB in a mixed gender setting over an extended age range at a time when many young people leave the church.

Groups determine their own programme which is structured, progressive and demanding. Uniform is optional.

The Duke of Edinburgh's Award has been a major part of the 6th's Amicus programme from the start. Amicus groups have operated at a number of companies within the Battalion. In 2002, they are part of the 6th, 80th & 3rd Sutton Coldfield companies.

CHARITY

The Battalion has raised many thousands of pounds for many worthy causes over the years. Collections from Church services, Special fund raising events such as Sponsored walks, Camp collections, Band appearances, in fact, far too many to list here.

Among the most long supported charities are the Denominational Missionary Societies; Baptist, Methodist, Anglican etc. For example the Leprosy Hospital in Dichpalli, India, has been supported by Methodist BB companies through the BB Branch of the MMS. In the late 1940s and after, run from the West Midland District BB Office shared with the Battalion at 24 Union St. The hospital had two BB companies, a GB company and a large Brigade Hall.

Members of the Battalion have performed duty as Stewards at the annual 'Friends of Vellore Concert' at the Town Hall, for more than 20 years and assisted at the National Fund raising Day for St. John Ambulance at the NEC, organised by Lady Penelope Cobham.

For the **Children in Need Appeal 2001**, at the start of the Centenary Session, a target of £2002 was set, and was exceeded!
Here (right) some of the boys of the Battalion, who took their cheque to the BBC at Pebble - Mill, are seen waving to the cameras along with BBC celebrities including Pudsey Bear.

The Visit of Her Most Gracious Majesty Queen Victoria.
13th January 1989

IN CELEBRATION OF THE
VISIT OF
Her Most Gracious Majesty
Queen Victoria

on Friday,
13th January 1989

On the evening of 13th January 1989 Three-hundred Birmingham BB Boys formed a Guard of Honour for 'Her Majesty Queen Victoria' on the occasion of her visit to the City as part of its Centenary Festival. The BB formed up complete with Brass Band on the forecourt of Snow Hill Station and along Colmore Row. Earlier, they had paraded from the Gas Hall watched by thousands of sightseers. Everyone was wearing the dress of 1889 for the re-enactment.

Actually...we are quite amused !

B.U.M.P. = Birmingham Uniformed Members Party

Saturday 30th June 2001
Blackwell Court, Blackwell, Bromsgrove.

Little People:
Anchor Boys, Explorers, Rainbows & Beavers

Middle People:
Juniors, Brownies, Cubs.

Big People:
Company/Seniors, Seniors/Brigaders,
Guides/Rangers, Scouts/Ventures.

Colour-coded T Shirts with the BUMP logo were
worn by each of the three age groups.

The afternoon party (Little & Middle People)
had 1500 members taking part, with the evening
party (Big People) having 400 members.

This was the first combined event for the four
organisations in Birmingham.

**There was a massive menu of fun
activities. The sun shone and a great time
was had by everyone.**

Battalion Competitions and Trophies
Excluding 'Divisional' Competitions and Trophies

Ambulance Cup
Presented by Capt. C. J. Cooke.

1908	7th Coy	1947	6th Coy
1909	3rd Coy	1948	10th Coy
1910	14th Coy	1949	10th Coy
1911	9th Coy	1950	69th Coy
1912	3rd Coy	1951	39th Coy
1913	14th Coy	1952	28th Coy
1914	14th Coy	1953	6th Coy
1915	14th Coy	1954	46th Coy
1916	14th Coy	1955	46th Coy
1917	5th Coy	Now known as 'First	
1918	9th Coy	Aid Cup'	
1919	7th Coy	1956	46th Coy
1920	7th Coy	1957	1stA Coy
1921	10th Coy	1958	46th Coy
1922	10th Coy	1959	29th Coy
1923	1st Coy	1960	46th Coy
1924	1st Coy	1961	46th Coy
1925	1st Coy	1962	46th Coy
1926-		1963	34th Coy
1927	10th Coy	1964	46th Coy
1928 -		1965	89th Coy
1929 -		1966	89th Coy
1930 -		1967	89th Coy
1931 -		1968	94th Coy
1932 -		1969	4th S/C Coy
1933 -		1970	35th Coy
1934	15th Coy	1971	58th Coy
1935	10th Coy	1972	59th Coy
1936	10th Coy	1973	89th Coy
1937	9th Coy	1974	89th Coy
1938	1st Coy	1975	58th Coy
1939	65th Coy	1976 -	
1940	9th Coy	1977 -	
1941	N/A	1978 -	
1942	N/A	1979	33rd Coy
1943	10th Coy	1980	33rd Coy
1944	55th Coy	1981	89th Coy
1945	23rd Coy	1982	78th Coy
1946	10th Coy	1983	78th Coy
		Not awarded after 1983	

Ambulance Shield
Presented by the Ambulance Committee

1911	14th Coy	1948	69th Coy
1912	14th Coy	1949	69th Coy
1913	14th Coy	1950	69th Coy
1914	14th Coy	1951	69th Coy
1915	14th Coy	1952	39th Coy
1916	9th Coy	1953	19th Coy
1917	9th Coy	1954	6th Coy
1918	14th Coy	1955	28th Coy
1919	14th Coy	Now known as 'First	
1920	9th Coy	Aid Shield'	
1921	7th Coy	1956	46th Coy
1922	10th Coy	1957	28th Coy
1923	7th Coy	1958	39th Coy
1924	10th Coy	1959	46th Coy
1925	8th Coy	1960	46th Coy
1926		1961	46th Coy
1927		1962	46th Coy
1928		1963	46th Coy
1929		1964	46th Coy
1930		1965	46th Coy
1931		1966	89th Coy
1932		1967	89th Coy
1933		1968	89th Coy
1934	9th Coy	1969	89th Coy
1935	15th Coy	1970	35th Coy
1936	9th Coy	1971	35th Coy
1937	10th Coy	1972	35th Coy
1938	9th Coy	1973	58th Coy
1939	9th Coy	1974	58th Coy
1940	9th Coy	1975	58th Coy
1941	N/A	1976	58th Coy
1942	N/A	1977 -	
1943	10th Coy	1978 -	
1944	55th Coy	1979	33rd Coy
1945	10th Coy	1980	78th Coy
1946	10th Coy	1981	78th Coy
1947	69th Coy	1982	78th Coy
		Not awarded after 1982	

Drill Colours & Shield
Colours only until 1947.
Harry Anderson Memorial Drill Shield presented 1947 and awarded from 1948

1923	10th Coy	1948	10th Coy	1974	33rd Coy
1924	10th Coy	1949	10th Coy	1975	33rd Coy
1925	4th Coy	1950	33rd Coy	1976	33rd Coy
1926 -		1951	10th Coy	1977	33rd Coy
1927-		1952	10th Coy	1978	33rd Coy
1928-		1953	10th Coy	1979	57th Coy
1929-		1954	9th Coy	1980	73rd Coy
1930-		1955	1st A Coy	1981	73rd Coy
1931-		1956	10th Coy	1982	-
1932-		1957	10th Coy	1983	73rd Coy
1933-		1958	59th Coy	1984	29th Coy
1934	33rd Coy	1959	59th Coy	1985	73rd Coy
1935	33rd Coy	1960	59th Coy	1986	73rd Coy
1936	33rd Coy	1961	1stA Coy	1987	73rd Coy
1937	10th Coy	1962	10th Coy	1988	29th Coy
1938	46th Coy	1963	10th Coy	1989	73rd Coy
1939	46th Coy	1964	10th Coy	1990	29th Coy
1940	33rd Coy	1965	10th Coy	1991	29th Coy
(Platoon Drill)		1966	10th Coy	1992	73rd Coy
1941	N/A	1967	94th Coy	1993	73rd Coy
1942	N/A	1968	94th Coy	N/A 1994.	
1943	33rd Coy	1969	94th Coy	See Battalion Efficiency	
1944	46th Coy	1970	94th Coy	Trophy.	
1945	4th Coy	1971	94th Coy		
1946	1st A Coy	1972	94th Coy		
1947	10th Coy	1973	94th Coy		

Efficiency Shield
Presented by W. T. Wiggins-Davies Esq.

1920	1st Coy
1921	1st Coy
1922	4th Coy
1923	10th Coy
1924	10th Coy
1925	10th Coy

Cooke Drill Shield
Presented by Capt. C. J. Cooke.

1907	3rd Coy
1908	3rd Coy
1909	2nd Coy
1910	1st Coy

(and Battalion 'Colours' from this year 1911.)

1911	8th Coy
1912	10th Coy
1913	8th Coy
1914	10th Coy
1915	10th Coy
1916	10th Coy
1917	1st Coy
1918	25th Coy
1919	1st Coy

Battalion Colours only (Drill without Arms).

1920	1st Coy
1921	4th Coy
1922	10th Coy

New Memorial Battalion Colours
(see separate list)

Cooke Shield Drill with Arms

1920	1st Coy
1921	10th Coy
1922	10th Coy
1923	10th Coy
1924	10th Coy
1925	4th Coy

Shield Finished when Rifles given-up.

Efficiency Trophy
Presented by R. George
Winners parade the Battalion colours.

1993	4th S/C Coy	1998	4th S/C Coy
1994	4th S/C Coy	1999	4th S/C Coy
1995	6th Coy	2000	4th S/C Coy
1996	4th S/C Coy	2001	4th S/C Coy
1997	4th S/C Coy		

An exhibition of trophies in 1952

Richard Greening

29th Coy.

Winner of the Terry Trophy

1985, 1988, 1989 & 1990.

Drum Challenge Cup (Individual)
Terry Trophy

Year	Coy	Year	Coy
1943	43rd Coy	1974	45th Coy
1944	6th Coy	1975	39th Coy
1945	43rd Coy	1976	48th Coy
1946	43rd Coy	1977	48th Coy
1947	55th Coy	1978	73rd Coy
1948	32nd Coy	1979	68th Coy
1949	1st Coy	1980	68th Coy
1950	39th Coy	1981	38th Coy
1951	1st Coy	1982	68th Coy
1952	39th Coy	1983	?
1953	1st Coy	1984	29th Coy
1954	9th Coy	1985	29th Coy
1955	54th Coy	1986	8th Coy
1956	54th Coy	1987	73rd Coy
1957	39th Coy	1988	29th Coy
1958	8th Coy	1989	29th Coy
1959	39th Coy	1990	29th Coy
1960	10th Coy	1991	51st Coy
1961	10th Coy	1992	40th Coy
1962	66th Coy	1993	3rd S/C Coy
1963	1stA Coy	1994	73rd Coy
1964	1stA Coy	1995	2nd S/C Coy
1965	94th Coy	1996	80th Coy
1966	10th Coy	1997	80th Coy
1967	10th Coy	1998	80th Coy
1968	48th Coy	1999	73rd Coy
1969	48th Coy	2000	73rd Coy
1970	48th Coy	2001	80th Coy
1971	78th Coy	2002	51st Coy
1972	78th Coy		
1973	78th Coy		

Bugle Challenge Cup (Individual)
Terry Trophy

Year	Coy	Year	Coy
1952	46th Coy	1977	58th Coy
1953	14th Coy	1978	73rd Coy
1954	2nd Coy	1979	38th Coy
1955	1st W/WCoy	1980	38th Coy
1956	1st Coy	1981	38th Coy
1957	8th Coy	1982	73rd Coy
1958	1st W/W Coy	1983	73rd Coy
1959	1st W/W Coy	1984	73rd Coy
1960	1st W/W Coy	1985	43rd Coy
1961	1st W/W Coy	1986	29th Coy
1962	1st W/W Coy	1987	4th S/C Coy
1963	48th Coy	1988	4th S/C Coy
1964	78th Coy	1989	73rd Coy
1965	78th Coy	1990	51st Coy
1966	78th Coy	1991	51st Coy
1967	78th Coy	1992	3rd S/C Coy
1968	66th Coy	1993	33rd Coy
1969	57th Coy	1994	61st Coy
1970	66th Coy	1995	80th Coy
1971	10th Coy	1996	73rd Coy
1972	2nd S/C Coy	1997	22nd Coy
1973	57th Coy	1998	73rd Coy
1974	1st S/C Coy	1999	73rd Coy
1975	1st SolCoy	2000	73rd Coy
1976	48th Coy	2001	3rd S/C Coy
		2002	3rd S/C Coy

Band Shield
Presented by Capt. C. A. MacGuire

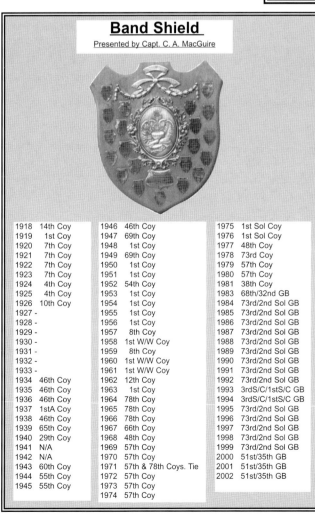

Year	Coy	Year	Coy	Year	Coy
1918	14th Coy	1946	46th Coy	1975	1st Sol Coy
1919	1st Coy	1947	69th Coy	1976	1st Sol Coy
1920	7th Coy	1948	1st Coy	1977	48th Coy
1921	7th Coy	1949	69th Coy	1978	73rd Coy
1922	7th Coy	1950	1st Coy	1979	57th Coy
1923	7th Coy	1951	1st Coy	1980	57th Coy
1924	4th Coy	1952	54th Coy	1981	38th Coy
1925	4th Coy	1953	1st Coy	1983	68th/32nd GB
1926	10th Coy	1954	1st Coy	1984	73rd/2nd Sol GB
1927	-	1955	1st Coy	1985	73rd/2nd Sol GB
1928	-	1956	1st Coy	1986	73rd/2nd Sol GB
1929	-	1957	8th Coy	1987	73rd/2nd Sol GB
1930	-	1958	1st W/W Coy	1988	73rd/2nd Sol GB
1931	-	1959	8th Coy	1989	73rd/2nd Sol GB
1932	-	1960	1st W/W Coy	1990	73rd/2nd Sol GB
1933	-	1961	1st W/W Coy	1991	73rd/2nd Sol GB
1934	46th Coy	1962	12th Coy	1992	73rd/2nd Sol GB
1935	46th Coy	1963	1st Coy	1993	3rdS/C/1stS/C GB
1936	46th Coy	1964	78th Coy	1994	3rdS/C/1stS/C GB
1937	1stA Coy	1965	78th Coy	1995	73rd/2nd Sol GB
1938	46th Coy	1966	78th Coy	1996	73rd/2nd Sol GB
1939	65th Coy	1967	66th Coy	1997	73rd/2nd Sol GB
1940	29th Coy	1968	48th Coy	1998	73rd/2nd Sol GB
1941	N/A	1969	57th Coy	1999	73rd/2nd Sol GB
1942	N/A	1970	57th Coy	2000	51st/35th GB
1943	60th Coy	1971	57th & 78th Coys. Tie	2001	51st/35th GB
1944	55th Coy	1972	57th Coy	2002	51st/35th GB
1945	55th Coy	1973	57th Coy		
		1974	57th Coy		

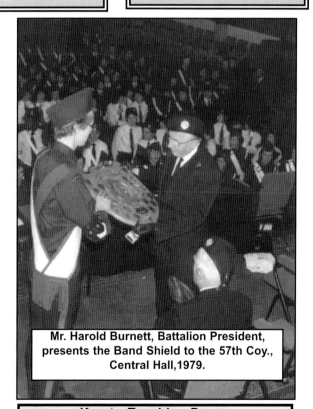

Mr. Harold Burnett, Battalion President, presents the Band Shield to the 57th Coy., Central Hall, 1979.

Key to Trophies Pages

W/W =	Walsall Wood
S/C =	Sutton Coldfield
Sol =	Solihull
W/O =	Water Orton
N/A =	Not Awarded or No Competition
- (Blank) =	No data available

Football Cup Competition

1923	22nd Coy	1963	48th Coy
1924	1st Coy	1964	25th Coy
1925	7th Coy	1965	36th Coy
1926	-	1966	19th Coy
1927	4thA Coy	1967	57th Coy
1928	10th Coy	1968	6th Coy
1929	-	1969	7th Coy
1930		1970	7th Coy
1931	27th Coy	1971	55th/16th Coy
1932	25th Coy	1972	38th Coy
1933	25th Coy	1973	85th Coy
1934	25th Coy	1974	19th Coy
1935	25th Coy	1975	19th Coy
1936	15th Coy	1976	1st A Coy
1937	25th Coy	1977	70th Coy
1938	15th Coy	1978	6th Coy
1939	11th Coy	1979	6th Coy
1940	28th Coy	1980	92nd Coy
1941	N/A	1981	57th Coy
1942	N/A	1982	66th Coy
1943	1stA Coy	1983	
1944	55th Coy	1984	66th Coy
1945	55th Coy	1985	34th Coy
1946	1stA Coy	1986	34th Coy
1947	1stA Coy	1987	34th Coy
1948	4th Coy	1988	66th Coy
1949	78th Coy	1989	11th Coy
1950	1stA Coy	1990	11th Coy
1951	46th Coy	1991	4th S/C Coy
1952	69th Coy	1992	4th S/C Coy
1953	1st W/W Coy	1993	39th Coy
1954	79th Coy	1994	29th Coy
1955	1st W/W Coy	1995	6th Coy
1956	1st W/W Coy	1996	88th Coy
1957	1st W/W Coy	1997	11th/1stA Coys
1958	1st Coy	1998	29th Coy
1959	1st W/W Coy	1999	29th Coy
1960	33rd Coy		
1961	1st W/W Coy		
1962	29th Coy		

Football League Div. 1
Football Shield.

Presented by Capt. T. O. Bowen

1912	1st Coy	1967	57th Coy
1913	4th Coy	1968	62nd Coy
1914	4th Coy	1969	7th Coy
1915	1st Coy	1970	89th Coy
1916	1st Coy	1971	6th Coy
1917	N/A	1972	6th Coy
1918	N/A	1973	85th Coy
1919	7th Coy	1974	85th Coy
1920	7th Coy	1975	19th Coy
1921	7th Coy	1976	1st A Coy
1922	7th Coy	1977	6th Coy
1923	12th Coy	1978	6th Coy
1924	6th Coy	1979	6th Coy
1925	1st Coy	1980	92nd Coy
1926	-	1981	66th Coy
1927	10th Coy	1982	66th Coy
1928	10th Coy	1983	57th Coy
1929	-	1984	66th Coy
1930	12th Coy	1985	34th Coy
1931	27th Coy	1986	34th Coy
1932	25th Coy	1987	66th Coy
1933	25th Coy	1988	66th Coy
1934	25th Coy	1989	29th Coy
1935	25th Coy	1990	
1936	25th Coy	1991	43rd Coy
1937	15th Coy	1992	39th & 4th S/C C's
1938	15th Coy	1993	39th Coy
1939	11th Coy	1994	6th Coy
1940	N/A	1995	6th Coy
1941	N/A	1996	6th Coy
1942	N/A	1997	29th Coy
1943	1stA Coy	1998	29th & 11th Coys
1944	55th Coy	1999	29th Coy
1945	1stA Coy		
1946	37th Coy		
1947	1stA Coy		

1948	4th Coy
1949	1stA Coy
1950	29th Coy
New Shield.	
Presented by Rotary Club,	
June 1951	
1951	46th Coy
1952	46th Coy
1953	14th Coy
1954	1st W/W Coy
1955	1st W/W Coy
1956	1st W/W Coy
1957	1st W/W Coy
1958	1st W/W Coy
1959	1st W/W Coy
1960	59th Coy
1961	1st W/W Coy
1962	6th Coy
1963	6th Coy
1964	48th Coy
1965	36th Coy
1966	10th Coy

Football Cup Under 14

1971	54th Coy
1972	6th Coy
1973	39th Coy
1974	1stA Coy
1975	19th Coy
1976	54th Coy
1977	6th Coy
1978	6th Coy
1979	66th Coy
1980	61st Coy
1981	94th Coy
1982	85th Coy
1983	66th Coy
1984	11th Coy
1985	6th Coy
1986	88th Coy
1987	88th Coy
1988	88th Coy
1989	6th Coy
1990	83rd Coy
1991	11th Coy
1992	4th S/C Coy
1993	6th Coy
1994	4th S/C Coy
1995	6th Coy
1996	29th Coy
1997	29th Coy
1998	29th Coy
1999	29th Coy
2000	
2001	

Football Shield Junior Section

Northern League		Southern League	
1970	1st S/C Coy	1970	1st Solihull Coy.
1971	11th Coy	1971	55th/16th
1972	1st S/C Coy	1972	58th Coy
1973	1st S/C Coy	1973	66th Coy
1974	78th Coy	**Southern League a.m.**	
1975	57th Coy	1974	66th Coy
1976	85th Coy	**Southern League p.m.**	
1977	85th Coy	1974	72nd Coy
1978	57th Coy	**Southern League**	
1979	89th Coy	1975	66th Coy
1980	89th Coy	1976	66th Coy
1981	57th, 89th Coys. Tie	1977	66th Coy
1982	85th Coy	1978	67th Coy
1983		1979	67th Coy
1984	85th Coy	1980	34th Coy
1985		1981	34th Coy
1986	75th Coy	1982	1st Sol Coy
1987	75th Coy	1983	
1988	4th S/C Coy	1984	
1989	1st W/O Coy	1985	43rd Coy
1990	11th Coy	1986	34th Coy
1991	11th Coy	1987	32nd Coy
1992	1st W/O Coy	1988	83rd Coy
1993	1st W/O Coy	1989	83rd Coy
1994	43rd Coy	1990	88th Coy
1995	70th Coy	1991	6th Coy
1996	70th Coy	1992	6th Coy
1997	4th S/CCoy	1993	88th Coy
1998	70th Coy	1994	67th Coy
1999	39th Coy	1995	67th Coy
2000	7 a Side -	1996	49th Coy
2001		1997	67th Coy
		1998	67th Coy
		1999	6th Coy
		2000	7 a Side-
		2001	

Five a Side Football Cup Seniors

1970	66th Coy
1971	91st Coy
1972	85th Coy
1973	85th Coy
1974	85th Coy
1975	62nd Coy
1976	62nd Coy
1977	2nd S/C Coy
1978	72nd Coy
1979	86th Coy
1980	92nd Coy
1981	43rd Coy
1982	4th S/C Coy
1983	66th Coy
1984	
1985	
1986	
1987	
1988	
1989	
1990	
1991	
1992	7th Coy
1993	
1994	7th Coy
1995	88th Coy
1996	7th Coy
1997	29th Coy
1998	11th Coy
1999	29th Coy
2000	61st Coy
2001	61st Coy
2002	29th Coy

1stA Football Cup Final Winners 28/4/1950 at Villa Park. Presented with the cup by Battalion President Ralph K. Brown. Beat 46th Coy 5 -1

Five a Side Football Cup Junior Section

1971	40th Coy	1987	67th Coy
1972	66th Coy	1988	4th S/C Coy
1973	66th Coy	1989	1st W/O Coy
1974	78th Coy	1990	11th Coy
1975	66th Coy	1991	11th Coy
1976	57th Coy	1992	88th Coy
1977	85th Coy	1993	70th Coy
1978	67th Coy	1994	43rd Coy
1979	85th Coy	1995	67th Coy
1980	89th Coy	1996	31st Coy
1981	89th Coy	1997	43rd Coy
1982	1st Sol Coy	1998	7th Coy
1983	4th S/C Coy	1999	61st Coy
1984	85th Coy	2000	61st Coy
1985	60th Coy	2001	85th Coy
1986	70th Coy		

Football Cup Junior Section

1971	55th/16th Coy	1987	75th Coy
1972	58th Coy	1988	4th S/C Coy
1973	66th Coy	1989	1st W/O Coy
1974	66th Coy	1990	11th Coy
1975	66th Coy	1991	1st W/O Coy
1976	57th Coy	1992	6th Coy
1977	66th Coy	1993	1st W/O Coy
1978	67th Coy	1994	67th Coy
1979	85th Coy	1995	67th Coy
1980	89th Coy	1996	4th S/CCoy
1981	34th Coy	1997	4th S/C Coy
1982	4th S/C Coy	1998	67th Coy
1983	4th S/C Coy	1999	39th Coy
1984	6th Coy	2000	7 a Side-
1985	32nd Coy	2001	
1986	34th Coy		

Cross Country Running

Junior	Inter	Senior
1946 21st & 33rd Coys	1971 40th Coy	1946 1stA Coy
1947 33rd Coy	1972 6th Coy	1947 1stA Coy
1948 26th Coy	1973 57th Coy	1948 33rd Coy
1949 1st A Coy	1974 57th Coy	1949 33rd Coy
1950 10th Coy	1975 85th Coy	1950 33rd Coy
1951 35th Coy	1976 35th Coy	1951 32nd Coy
1952 59th Coy	1977 57th Coy	1952 33rd Coy
1953 6th Coy	1978 2nd S/C Coy	1953 33rd Coy
1954 73rd Coy	1979 57th Coy	1954 29th Coy
1955 39th Coy	1980 57th Coy	1955 9th Coy
1956 29th Coy	1981 85th Coy	1956 29th Coy
1957 73rd Coy	1982 85th Coy	1957 29th Coy
1958 30th Coy	1983 6th Coy	1958 29th Coy
1959 33rd Coy	1984 6th Coy	1959 76th Coy
1960 6th Coy	1985 85th Coy	1960 78th Coy
1961 6th Coy	1986 40th Coy	1961 78th Coy
1962 88th Coy	1987 39th Coy	1962 78th Coy
1963 46th Coy	1988 6th Coy	1963 54th Coy
1964 30th Coy	1989 88th Coy	1964 36th Coy
1965 40th Coy	1990 73rd Coy	1965 3rd S/C Coy
1966 2nd S/C Coy	1991 6th Coy	1966 2nd S/C Coy
1967 6th Coy	1992 6th Coy	1967 43rd Coy
1968 1st W/W Coy	1993 88th Coy	1968 43rd Coy
1969 85th Coy	1994 88th Coy	1969 7th Coy
1970 57th Coy	1995 6th Coy	1970 6th Coy
1971 6th Coy	1996	1971 6th Coy
1972 85th Coy	1997 22nd Coy	1972 57th Coy
1973 85th Coy	1998 6th Coy	1973 3rd S/C Coy
1974 57th Coy	1999 29th Coy	1974 39th Coy
1975 57th Coy	2000 29th Coy	1975 57th Coy
1976 57th Coy	2001 4th S/C Coy	1976 57th Coy
1977 6th Coy	2002 7th Coy	1977 76th Coy
1978 57th Coy		1978 57th Coy
1979 51st Coy		1979 33rd Coy
1980 11th Coy		1980 1stA Coy
1981 6th Coy		1981 2nd S/C Coy
1982 78th, 88th Coys. Tie		1982 57th Coy
1983 11th Coy		1983 57th Coy
1984 6th Coy		1984 6th Coy
1985 6th Coy		1985 6th Coy
1986 6th Coy		1986 6th Coy
1987 6th Coy		1987 40th Coy
1988 6th Coy		1988 40th Coy
1989 4th S/C Coy		1989 88th Coy
1990 6th Coy		1990 43rd Coy
1991 11th Coy		1991 43rd Coy
1992 11th Coy		1992 43rd Coy
1993 80th Coy		1993 6th Coy
1994 6th Coy		1994 6th Coy
1995 88th Coy		1995 6th Coy
1996 80th Coy		1996 6th Coy
1997 4th S/C Coy		1997 6th Coy
1998 4th S/C Coy		1998 8th Coy
1999 4th S/C Coy		1999 72nd Coy
2000 7th Coy		2000 72nd Coy
2001 7th Coy		2001 4th S/C Coy
2002 33rd Coy		2002 4th S/C Coy

Cricket League

Shield Presented by County Alderman John Bowen J.P. 1924

1923 1st Coy. (No Shield)	
1924 10th Coy	
1925 4t, 18th Coys	
1926 -	
1927 10th, 33rd Coys	
1928 42nd Coy	
1929 12th Coy	
1930 37th Coy	
1931 18th Coy	
1932 -	
1933 -	
1934 25th Coy	
1935 33rd Coy	
1936 25th Coy	
1937 33rd Coy	
1938 10th Coy	
1939 33rd Coy	
1940 N/A	
1941 N/A	
1942 10th , 33rd Coys	
1943 33rd Coy	
1944 10th Coy	
1945 4th Coy	
1946 10th Coy	
1947 10th Coy	
1948 4th Coy	
1949 10th, 25th Coys	
1950 33rd Coy	

Cricket League (Weeknight)

1951 18th, 46th, 69th Coys	
1952 10thA, 23rd, 31st, 36th, 68th Coys	
1953 1st, 31st, 53rd Coys	
1954 36th, 54th,73rd Coys	
1955 66th Coy	
1956 10th, 46th, 73rd Coys	
1957 39th, 46th Coys	
1958 43rd, 46th, 71st, 76th Coys	
1959 2nd, 39th, 59th, 71st, 76th Coys	
1960 2nd, 23rd, 46th, 59th Coys	
1961 2nd, 23rd, 39t, 46th Coys	
1962 6th, 10th, 44th, 46th Coys	
1963 2nd, 25th,44th, 64th Coys	
1964 2nd, 10th, 31st, 52nd, 54th Coys	
1965 10th, 36th, 52nd, 71st Coys	
1966 10th, 52nd Coys	
1967 6th Coy	
1968 6th Coy	
1969 6th. 10th Coys	
1970 6th Coy	
1971 57th Coy	
1972 57th Coy	
1973 19th Coy	
1974 19th Coy	
1975 19th Coy	
1976 70th Coy	
1977 10th Coy	
1978 10th Coy	
1979 10th Coy	
1980 55th/16th Coy	
1981 1stA Coy	
1982 57th Coy	
1983 57th Coy	
1984 2nd S/C Coy	
1985 59th Coy	
1986 66th Coy	
1987 66th Coy	
1988 66th Coy	
1989 70th Coy	
1990 70th Coy	
1991 43rd Coy	
1992 39th Coy	
1993 39th Coy	
1994 39th Coy	
1995 1stA /39thCoys Joint Team	
N/A. No League after 1995	

33rd Coy. Joint Winners of the Cricket Shield 1927

Five a Side Football Under 14

1994 29th Coy	
1995 1st C/B Coy	
1996 29th Coy	
1997 57th Coy	
1998 61st Coy	
1999 29th Coy	
2000 4th S/C Coy	
2001 61st Coy	
2002	

Cricket Div. 1 Champs (Saturday League)

1951	46th Coy	1967	6th Coy
1952	46th Coy	1968	10th Coy
1953	1st.,10th, 33rd Coys	1969	62nd Coy
1954	1st Coy	1970	10th Coy
1955	39th Coy	1971	6th Coy
1956	46th Coy	1972	10th, 62nd Coys
1957	33rd Coy	1973	62nd Coy
1958	10th Coy	1974	62nd Coy
1959	39th Coy	1975	No League
1960	46th Coy	1976	No League
1961	6th, 46th Coys	1977	70th Coy
1962	6th Coy	1978	10th Coy
1963	6th Coy	1979	70th Coy
1964	6th Coy	1980	70th Coy
1965	62nd Coy	1981	70th Coy
1966	10th Coy	1982	N/A

Signalling Competition

The Morse Cup

Semaphore Shield/Cup

1949	51st Coy
1950	36th Coy
1951	16th Coy (Cup)
1952	16th Coy
1953	16th Coy
1954	16th Coy Called 'Cup'
1955	16th Coy
1956	48th Coy
1957	57th Coy
1958	48th Coy
1959	4th Coy
1960	87th Coy
1961	39th Coy
1962	39th Coy
1963	87th Coy
1964	55th/16th Coy
1965	55th/16th Coy
1966	55th/16th Coy
1967	78th Coy
1968	57th Coy
1969	N/A

Morse Cup

1949	22nd Coy
1950	29th Coy
1951	29th Coy
1952	36th Coy
1953	22nd Coy
1954	16th Coy
1955	39th Coy
1956	1st Coy
1957	39th Coy
1958	48th Coy
1959	52nd Coy
1960	39th Coy
1961	52nd Coy
1962	57th Coy
1963	39th Coy
1964	39th Coy
1965	66th Coy
1966	66th Coy
1967	66th Coy
1968	66th Coy
1969	66th Coy
1970	66th Coy

Called 'Communications Cup'

1971	Not competed for
1972	58th Coy
1973	-

Called Morse Cup again

1974	48th Coy
1975	48th Coy
1976	48th Coy
1977	No Competition

Scripture Knowledge/Christian Education

Seniors

Scripture Knowledge Prize (Seniors)

1956	6th Coy
1957	72nd Coy
1958	2nd S/C Coy
1959	15th Coy
1960	58th Coy
1961	87th Coy
1962	54th Coy
1963	40th Coy
1964	3rd S/C Coy
1965	3rd S/C Coy
1966	64th Coy
1967	1stA Coy
1968	73rd Coy
1969	3rd S/C Coy

Christian Education Prize (Seniors)

1970	58th Coy
1971	10th Coy
1972	93rd Coy

Juniors

Scripture Knowledge Prize (Juniors)

1956	2nd S/C Coy
1957	73rd Coy
1958	78th Coy
1959	78th Coy
1960	54th Coy
1961	3rd S/C Coy
1962	3rd S/C Coy
1963	54th Coy
1964	94th Coy
1965	78th Coy
1966	7th Coy
1967	31st Coy
1968	6th Coy
1969	33rd Coy

Christian Education Prize (Juniors)

1970	59th Coy
1971	93rd Coy
1972	59th Coy

Bible Knowledge Award Presented by R.H. Webb 1973

1974	58th Coy
1975	58th Coy
1976	3rd Coy
1977	3rd Coy
1978	3rd Coy
1979	6th Coy
1980	33rd Coy
1981	6th Coy
1982	6th Coy

Rev. David Woodfield Trophy

1997	4th S/C Coy
1998	4th S/C Coy
1999	4th S/C Coy
2000	4th S/C Coy
2001	N/A

Sports Cup

Sports Cup

1932	1st A Coy
1933	1st A Coy
1934	1stA Coy
1935	33rd Coy
1936	33rd Coy
1937	33rd Coy
1938	33rd Coy
1939	49th Coy
1940	39th Coy
1941	-
1942	1stA & 55th Coys
1943	1stA Coy
1944	55th Coy
1945	55th Coy
1946	1stA & 33rd
1947	33rd Coy
1948	33rd Coy
1949	33rd Coy
1950	33rd Coy
1951	1stA Coy
1952	36th Coy
1953	36th Coy
1954	79th Coy
1955	59th Coy
1956	1st A Coy
1957	73rd Coy
1958	9th Coy
1959	76th Coy
1960	6th Coy
1961	6th Coy
1962	6th Coy
1963	6th Coy
1964	6th Coy
1965	6th Coy
1966	57th Coy
1967	10th Coy
1968	10th Coy
1969	10th Coy
1970	10th Coy
1971	6th Coy
1972	1st A Coy
1973	6th Coy
1974	85th Coy

Sports Cup
1932 - 1974
Athletics Cup
1975 -

Athletics Cup

1975	78th Coy
1976	6th Coy
1977	6th Coy
1978	6th Coy
1979	6th Coy
1980	6th Coy
1981	66th Coy
1982	1st A Coy
1983	10th Coy
1984	6th Coy
1985	6th Coy
1986	6th Coy
1987	6th Coy
1988	66th Coy
1989	88th Coy
1990	43rd Coy
1991	29th Coy
1992	4th S/C Coy
1993	4th S/C Coy
1994	4th S/C Coy
1995	4th S/C Coy
1996	4th S/C Coy
1997	4th S/C Coy
1998	29th Coy
1999	4th S/C Coy
2000	4th S/C Coy
2001	29th Coy

Chris Upton Memorial Trophy
(Bible Drama)

1983	6th Coy
1984	73rd Coy
1985	73rd Coy
1986	4th S/C Coy
1987	73rd Coy
1988	73rd Coy
1989	22nd Coy
1990	73rd Coy
1991	22nd Coy
1992	22nd Coy
1993	4th S/C Coy
1994	22nd Coy
1995	4th S/C Coy
1996	22nd Coy
1997	4th S/C Coy
1998	22nd Coy
1999	22nd Coy
2000	73rd Coy
2001	22nd Coy
2002	22nd Coy

**'God the Builder' 22nd Coy.
Chris Upton Trophy winners 2001**

Chess

Junior Section		Company		Senior	
1977	55th/16th Coy	1977	55th/16th Coy	1977	54th Coy
1978	89th Coy	1978	89th Coy	1978	55th/16th Coy
1979	55th/16th Coy	1979	89th Coy	1979	55th/16th Coy
1980	85th Coy	1980	73rd Coy	1980	70th Coy
1981	46th Coy	1981	71st Coy	1981	56th Coy
1982	73rd Coy	1982	46th Coy	1982	70th Coy
1983	73rd Coy	1983	1st Sol Coy	1983	2nd S/C Coy
1984	66th Coy	1984	3rd Coy	1984	2nd S/C Coy
1985	73rd Coy	1985	70th Coy	1985	2nd S/C Coy
1986	2nd S/C Coy	1986		1986	
1987	34th Coy	1987	6th Coy	1987	73rd Coy
1988	73rd Coy	1988	73rd Coy	1988	73rd Coy
1989	85th Coy	1989	73rd Coy	1989	73rd Coy
1990	2nd S/C Coy	1990	85th Coy	1990	44th Coy
1991	40th Coy	1991	85th Coy	1991	73rd Coy
1992	49th Coy	1992	59th Coy	1992	73rd Coy
1993	22nd Coy	1993	85th Coy	1993	7th Coy
1994	49th Coy	1994	59th Coy	1994	73rd Coy
1995	49th Coy	1995	7th Coy	1995	59th Coy
1996	49th Coy	1996	49th Coy	1996	59th Coy
1997	49th Coy	1997	49th Coy	1997	59th Coy
1998	1st W/O	1998	49th Coy	1998	59th Coy
1999	1st W/O	1999	73rd Coy	1999	72nd & 59th
2000	1st W/O	2000	73rd Coy	2000	72nd Coy
2001	83rd Coy	2001	3rd S/C Coy	2001	73rd Coy
2002	31st Coy	2002	72nd Coy	2002	59th Coy

Drill - Squad/Basic/Recruit/Elementary

Squad Drill Certificate/ Challenge Cup
Presented by S. J. Pratt Esq., JP

1939	60th Coy (Cert.)
1940	42nd Coy (Cup)
1941	20th Coy
1942	N/A
1943	N/A
1944	62nd Coy
1945	53rd Coy.
1946	69th Coy
1947	22nd Coy
1948	72nd Coy
1949	11th Coy
1950	22nd Coy
1951	8th Coy
1952	8th Coy
1953	22nd Coy

Recruit Drill Cup

1954	4th Coy
1955	8th Coy
1956	8th Coy

Squad Drill Cup

1957	8th Coy
1958	4th Coy
1959	73rd Coy
1960	8th Coy
1961	44th Coy
1962	72nd Coy
1963	19th Coy
1964	94th Coy
1965	94th Coy
1966	78th Coy
1967	72nd Coy

Basic Drill Cup

1968	66th Coy
1969	57th Coy
1970	73rd Coy
1971	33rd Coy
1972	12th Coy
1973	57th Coy
1974	57th Coy
1975	29th Coy

Squad Drill Cup

1976	29th Coy
1977	45th Coy
1978	12th Coy
1979	N/A
1980	N/A
1981	
1982	29th Coy
1983	
1984	
1985	
1986	
1987	
1988	
1989	
1990	
1991	
1992	
1993	4th S/C Coy
1994	4th S/C Coy
1995	
1996	
1997	4th S/C Coy
1998	
1999	
2000	
2001	

The Elementary Drill Shield

Elementary Drill shield

1996	1stA Coy
1997	83rd Coy
1998	83rd Coy
1999	
2000	
2001	
2002	

Physical Drill Challenge Shield.
Presented by Major G.M. Marriott.
(Drill without arms)
PT Shield from 1924

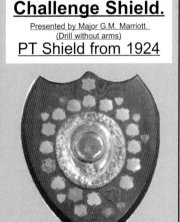

1920	8th Coy
1921	4th Coy
1922	4th Coy
	(PT Shield)
1924	4th Coy
1925	3rd Coy
1926	10th Coy
1927	10th Coy
1928	10th Coy
1929	-
1930	-
1931	-
1932	-
1933	-
1934	25th Coy
1935	25th Coy
1936	46th Coy
1937	9th Coy
1938	7th Coy
1939	20th Coy
1940	42nd Coy
1941	N/A
1942	N/A
1943	10th Coy
1944	10th Coy
1945	10th Coyy
1946	36th Coy
1947	10th Coy
1948	36th Coy
1949	36th Coy
1950	10th Coy
1951	36th Coy
1952	10th Coy
1953	10th Coy
1954	29th Coy
1955	29th Coy
1956	29th Coy
1957	10th Coy
1958	N/A.
1959	16th Coy
1960	16th Coy
1961	57th Coy
1962	6th Coy
1963	6th Coy
1964	6th Coy
1965	6th Coy
1966	57th Coy
1967	6th Coy
1968	95th Coy
1969	48th Coy
1970	89th Coy
1971	N/A
	Not awarded after 1970

Tug-of-War Cup

1950	29th Coy
1951	1st A Coy
1952	1st A Coy
1953	1st A Coy
1954	1st A Coy
1955	1st A Coy
1956	1st A Coy
1957	29th Coy
1958	29th Coy
1959	59th Coy
1960	55th Coy
1961	6th Coy
1962	6th Coy
1963	6th Coy
1964	1st A Coy
1965	55th/16th Coy
1966	6th Coy
1967	6th Coy
1968	6th Coy
1969	1st A Coy
1970	1st A Coy
1971	1st A Coy
1972	1st A Coy
1973	1st A Coy
1974	1st A Coy
1975	6th Coy
1976	1st A Coy
1977	6th Coy
1978	N/A
	No Competition after 1977

Note: The authors have endeavoured to make the Trophy Lists as accurate as possible. Generally, the trophies themselves have been used to obtain details. Where shields and engraving have been removed, written records have sometimes been both incomplete and contradictory. We apologise for any inaccuracy subsequently discovered.

Junior Section
Top of the Form Competition

1971	85th Coy
1972	35th Coy
1973	73rd Coy
1974	35th Coy
1975	4th S/C Coy.
1976	57th Coy
1977	73rd Coy
1978	35th Coy
1979	89th Coy
1980	67th Coy
1981	88th Coy
1982	4th S/C Coy
1983	4th S/C Coy
1984	60th Coy
1985	73rd Coy
1986	35th Coy
1987	29th Coy
1988	4th S/C. & 83rd Coys
1989	83rd Coy
1990	4th S/C Coy
1991	83rd Coy
1992	57th Coy
1993	4th S/C Coy
1994	61st Coy
1995	7th Coy
1996	4th S/C Coy
1997	4th S/C Coy
1998	7th Coy
1999	73rd Coy
2000	35th Coy
2001	2ndS/C & 72nd Coys
2002	80th Coy

Boy Reserves Efficiency Shield
Presented by Capt. H. Anderson.

1920	No 1 Section (1st B'ham Coy)
1921	No 1 Section (1st B'ham Coy)
1922	No 1 Section (1st B'ham Coy)
1923	1st Birmingham Section
1924	N/A

Seniors Ten Pin Bowling

1978	70th Coy
1979	70th Coy
1980	70th Coy
1981	73rd Coy

Life-Saving Cup

1951	N/A
1952	10th Coy
1953	N/A
1954	N/A

Senior General Knowledge Quiz

1979	1st Sol Coy
1980	73rd Coy

Table Tennis League Cup

Senior - Div. 1

Table Tennis League

1948	4th Coy
1949	26th Coy
1950	32nd Coy
1951	69th Coy
1952	69th Coy
1953	2nd Coy
1954	2nd Coy
1955	1st Coy
1956	10th Coy
1957	10th Coy
1958	10th Coy
1959	72nd Coy
1960	62nd Coy
1961	39th Coy
1962	23rd Coy

Table Tennis Cup (Division 1)

1963	2nd Coy
1964	88th Coy
1965	62nd Coy
1966	88th Coy
1967	10th Coy
1968	10th Coy

Table Tennis Cup Senior

1969	81st Coy
1970	57th Coy
1971	57th Coy
1972	10th Coy
1973	62nd Coy
1974	62nd Coy
1975	62nd Coy

Table Tennis Cup

1976	62nd Coy
1977	54th Coy
1978	57th Coy
1979	12th Coy
1980	12th Coy
1981	57th Coy
1982	57th Coy
1983	57th Coy
1984	85th Coy
1985	85th Coy
1986	66th Coy
1987	66th Coy
1988	29th Coy
1989	40th Coy
1990	44th Coy
1991	44th Coy
1992	29th Coy
1993	39th Coy
1994	39th Coy
1995	39th Coy
1996	29th Coy
1997	49th Coy
1998	49th Coy
1999	49th Coy
2000	72nd Coy
2001	N/A
League not run	

Junior

Table Tennis Cup Junior

1949	32nd Coy
1950	1st Coy
1951	24th Coy
1952	46th Coy
1953	24th Coy
1954	1st Coy
1955	39th Coy
1956	15th Coy
1957	10th Coy
1958	62nd Coy
1959	62nd Coy
1960	2nd Coy
1961	23rd Coy
1962	2nd Coy

Table Tennis Cup Junior

1969	10th Coy
1970	55th/16th Coy
1971	55th/16th Coy
1972	4th S/C Coy
1973	10th Coy
1974	10th Coy
1975	10th Coy

Table Tennis Cup Under 15s

1993	88th Coy
1994	88th Coy
1995	88th Coy
1996	49th Coy
1997	49th Coy
1998	49th Coy
1999	49th Coy
2000	2nd S/C Coy
2001	2nd S/C Coy

Table Tennis Individual

Junior		Senior		Officer	
1965	72nd Coy	1965	62nd Coy	1967	23rd Coy
1966	72nd Coy	1966	72nd Coy	1968	72nd Coy
1967	6th Coy	1967	78th Coy	1969	81st Coy
1968	6th Coy	1968	72nd Coy	1970	1st SolCoy
1969	81st Coy	1969	72nd Coy	1971	
1970	80th Coy	1970	10th Coy	1972	12th Coy
1971		1971		1973	78th Coy
1972	1stA Coy	1972	10th Coy	1974	22nd Coy
1973	62ndCoy	1973	1stA Coy	1975	78th Coy
1974	10th Coy	1974	89th Coy	1976	70th Coy
1975	12th Coy	1975	70th Coy	1977	53rd Coy
1976	96th Coy	1976	62nd Coy	1978	92nd Coy
1977	45th Coy	1977	54th Coy	1979	29th Coy
1978	66th Coy	1978	1stA Coy	1980	34th Coy
1979	58th Coy	1979	1stA Coy	1981	34th Coy
1980	58th Coy	1980	92nd Coy	1982	55/16th Coy
1981	3rd S/C Coy	1981	92nd Coy	1983	2nd S/C Coy
1982	57th Coy	1982	10th Coy	1984	55/16th Coy
1983	85th Coy	1983	35th Coy	1985	88th Coy
1984	66th Coy	1984	3rd S/CCoy	1986	2nd S/C Coy
1985	10th Coy	1985	66th Coy	1987	1st W/O Coy
1986	55/16th Coy	1986	66th Coy	1988	88th Coy
1987	66th Coy	1987	66th Coy	1989	18th Coy
1988	7th Coy	1988	29th Coy	1990	29th Coy
1989	40th Coy	1989	40th Coy	1991	72nd Coy
1990	44th Coy	1990	7th Coy	1992	72nd Coy
1991	66th Coy	1991	44th Coy	1993	2nd S/C Coy
1992	6th Coy	1992	40th Coy	1994	29th Coy
1993	2nd S/C Coy	1993	73rd Coy	1995	72nd Coy
1994	88tth Coy	1994	39th Coy	1996	72nd Coy
1995	88th Coy	1995	88th Coy	1997	2nd S/C Coy
1996	49th Coy	1996	88th Coy	1998	2nd S/C Coy
1997	49th Coy	1997	88th Coy	1999	2nd S/C Coy
1998	49th Coy	1998	45th Coy	2000	2nd S/C Coy
1999	39th Coy	1999	49th Coy	2001	45th Coy
2000	45th Coy	2000	39th Coy	2002	2nd S/C Coy
2001	45th Coy	2001	73rd Coy		

J. C. Kay Challenge Cup for Swimming.

Presented by B'ham & Dist Sec. Schools Joint Sports Assn.

1930	14th & 28th Coys	1966	78th Coy
1931	22nd Coy	1967	10th Coy
1932	3rd Coy	1968	78th Coy
1933	46th Coy	1969	6th Coy
1934	46th Coy	1970	6th Coy
1935	46th Coy	1971	6th Coy
1936	64th Coy	1972	78th Coy
1937	18th Coy	1973	78th Coy
1938	18th Coy	1974	78th Coy
1939	18th Coy	1975	6th Coy
1940	N/A	1976	6th Coy
1941	N/A	1977	6th Coy
1942	N/A	1978	6th Coy
1943	N/A	1979	6th Coy
1944	55th Coy	1980	6th Coy
1945	55th Coy	1981	6th Coy
1946	36th Coy	1982	6th Coy
1947	36th Coy	1983	6th Coy
1948	36th Coy	1984	59th Coy
1949	36th Coy	1985	59th Coy
1950	36th Coy	1986	6th Coy
1951	36th Coy	1987	59th Coy
1952	2nd Coy	1988	59th Coy
1953	1st Coy	1989	6th Coy
1954	1st Coy	1990	59th Coy
1955	1st & 33rd Coys	1991	59th Coy
1956	1st Coy	1992	4th S/C Coy
1957	6th Coy	1993	4th S/C Coy
1958	6th Coy	1994	4th S/C Coy
1959	12th Coy	1995	59th Coy
1960	6th Coy	1996	4th S/C Coy
1961	10th Coy	1997	4th S/C Coy
1962	6th Coy	1998	8th Coy
1963	10th Coy	1999	59th Coy
1964	10th Coy	2000	59th Coy
1965	48th Coy	2001	7th Coy

Intermediate Team Race Swimming Shield

Presented by R. H. Webb Batt. Sec & Training Officer

1967	78th Coy	1983	6th Coy
1968	78th Coy	1984	6th Coy
1969	6th Coy	1985	6th Coy
1970	78th Coy	1986	6th Coy
1971	78th Coy	1987	-
1972	6th Coy	1988	6th Coy
1973	-	1989	-
1974	6th Coy	1990	1st W/O Coy
1975	78th Coy	1991	59th Coy
1976	78th Coy	1992	6th Coy
1977	78th Coy	1993	59th Coy
1978	78th Coy	1994	4th S/C Coy
1979	6th Coy	1995	59th Coy
1980	70th Coy	1996	59th Coy
1981	-	1997	8th Coy
1982	-	1998	8th Coy
		1999	4th S/C Coy
		2000	59thCoy
		2001	N/A

Swimming Shields

Presented by Major D. G. Barnsley

1912	4th Coy		
1913			
1914	4th Coy		
1915	N/A	1961	44th Coy
1916	N/A	1962	6th Coy
1917	N/A	1963	10th Coy
1918	9th Coy	1964	10th Coy
1919	9th Coy	1965	48th Coy
1920	7th Coy		
1921	7th Coy		
1922	1st Coy		
1923	10th Coy		
1924	10th Coy		

Team Race Swimming Challenge Shield

1997	59th Coy
1998	59th Coy
1999	59th Coy

Statistics... *'For those who like them'*
(Phrase used by Reg Webb in Battalion Annual Reports 1964 - 76)

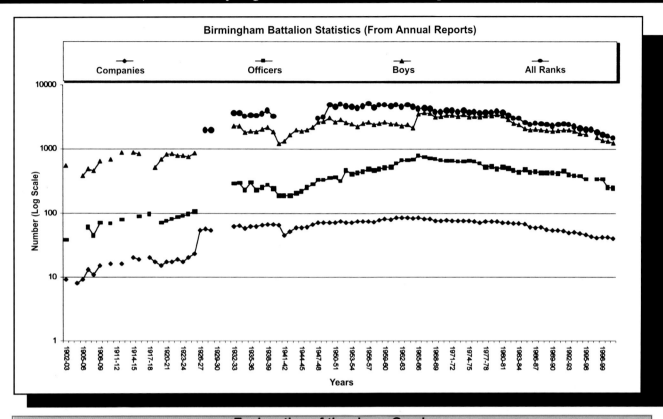

Birmingham Battalion Statistics (From Annual Reports)

Explanation of the above Graph:
It uses a Log/Normal Scale to show numbers of seven variables over 100 years 1902 - 2002.
The vertical axis showing numbers is the Log scale. There are in effect four scales.
In section 1, the lower, a scale of one interval represents 1 unit (1-10), In section 2 the same interval represents 10
units (10 - 100), In section 3 the interval represents 100 units (100 - 1000)
and In section 4 one interval represents 1000 units (1000 - 10,000).
The horizontal axis showing dates is the Normal scale. Each year is marked but the labels only show every three years.

Comments:

Companies (diamond)
A rather erratic growth is shown, for the first few years the Battalion was struggling to keep the number above ten. The number was increasing when in 1926 it shoots up. Data is missing in the late 1920s, but progress is steady. The fall in the Second World War can be clearly seen with the post war recovery reaching a peak in the 1960s. Company numbers didn t quite reach the magic one hundred. Although the numbers decline, the decline is far from being either sudden or dramatic.

Officers (square)
A slow start with a gradual increase until the Great War. Only after the war and union with the BLB did the numbers rise above one hundred. The numbers took a dip in World War Two, but post-war shows a steadily rising number. The peak is in 1966 due to the addition of former Life-Boy Leaders, now counted as officers. Until the mid-1990s there was a steady fall-off in line with reduced boy numbers. The late 1990s shows a steeper fall.

Boys (triangle) NB. Pre. 1966 excluding Life Boys
By 1914 numbers are nearing the one thousand mark, companies being quite large. Less companies in the Great War meant fewer boys but recovery to pre war levels had been reached by the early 1920s. The dip of the Second World War can be seen but with recovery by the late 1940s. Between 1950 and 1965 there is little or no loss. After 1966 the increase is due to Life Boy numbers being added. Numbers remained steady between 1966 - 1980 but reduced again in the early 1980s. Although remaining steady in the late 1980s the 1990s shows a continuing decline.

All Ranks (circle)
Numbers peaked at the time of the Battalion Jubilee in 1952 reaching five thousand members. Numbers declined in the early 1960s but then remained steady until about 1980. The decline of the mid 1980s was briefly stemmed in the 1990s with the Anchor Boys being included in the figures. There has been a steady decline in numbers since the mid 1990s.

Averages throughout the decades 1900s - 2000s

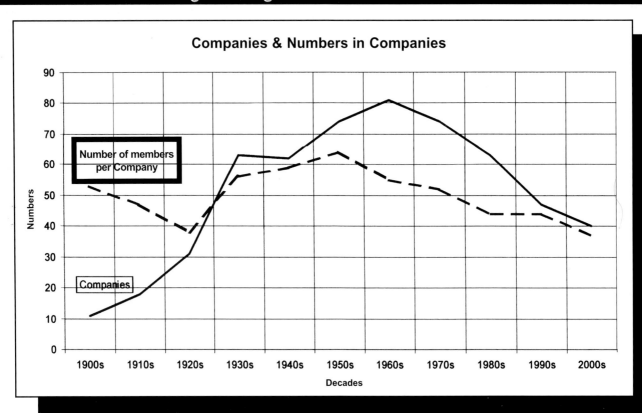

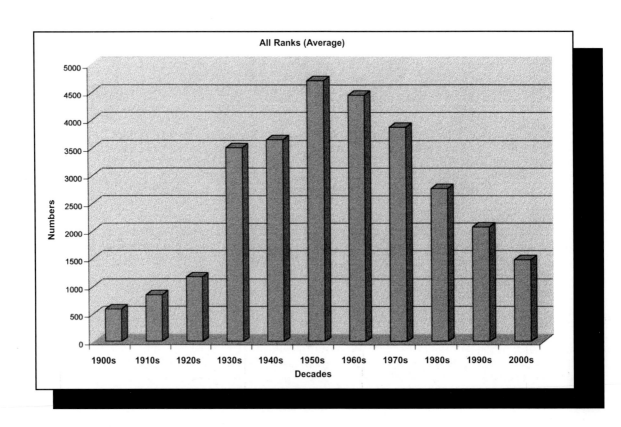